Schriften zur Restrukturierung

Institut für Interdisziplinäre Restrukturierung (iir) e. V.

Edited by

Dipl.-Kfm. Arndt Geiwitz
Dr. Frank Kebekus
Dr. Thomas C. Knecht
Prof. Dr. Christoph G. Paulus, LL. M.

Volume 9

Charlotte Julie Rault

The Legal Framework of Sovereign Debt Management

Nomos

The Deutsche Nationalbibliothek lists this publication in the Deutsche Nationalbibliografie; detailed bibliographic data are available on the Internet at http://dnb.d-nb.de

a.t.: Berlin, HU, Diss., 2015 and Université Paris 1 Panthéon-Sorbonne, Diss., 2015

ISBN 978-3-8487-4207-3 (Print)
978-3-8452-8476-7 (ePDF)

British Library Cataloguing-in-Publication Data
A catalogue record for this book is available from the British Library.

ISBN 978-3-8487-4207-3 (Print)
978-3-8452-8476-7 (ePDF)

Library of Congress Cataloging-in-Publication Data
Rault, Charlotte Julie
The Legal Framework of Sovereign Debt Management
Charlotte Julie Rault
278 p.
Includes bibliographic references and index.

ISBN 978-3-8487-4207-3 (Print)
978-3-8452-8476-7 (ePDF)

1st Edition 2017

À ma famille

Preface

Ce travail de recherche, issu d'une cotutelle de thèse entre l'Université Paris 1 Panthéon-Sorbonne et Humboldt Universität zu Berlin, a été soutenu publiquement en français le 23 novembre 2015 à Paris. La présente version est une traduction.

Mes remerciements et ma profonde gratitude s'adressent en premier lieu à mes directeurs de thèse, les Professeurs Jean-Marc Sorel et Christoph G. Paulus, pour avoir accepté de diriger cette thèse, pour leur écoute et leurs conseils constructifs et bienveillants.

Mes remerciements vont aussi aux membres des laboratoires de recherche qui m'ont si bien accueillie, tant du côté français avec l'Institut de Recherche en Droit International et Européen de la Sorbonne que du côté allemand au Lehrstuhl für Bürgerliches Recht, Zivilprozess- und Insolvenzrecht sowie Römisches Recht et à l'Institut für Interdisziplinäre Restrukturierung. Merci également aux chercheurs du Centre d'études et de recherche en droit international et relations internationales de l'Académie de Droit international de La Haye.

Cette thèse a fait l'objet d'un soutien financier du Centre interdisciplinaire d'études et de recherches sur l'Allemagne, de l'Université franco-allemande (UFA) et de la FAZIT-Stiftung. Je les remercie de leur confiance.

Outre ces différentes immersions dans le monde académique franco-allemand, j'ai eu la chance de nourrir ma réflexion lors d'un passage au sein de la Direction des affaires juridiques de la Banque européenne d'investissement.

Merci aux doctorants, jeunes docteurs et docteurs qui m'ont encouragée et soutenue dans cette recherche.

Mes remerciements s'adressent enfin à ma famille et à mes amis. Merci tout particulièrement à ma mère pour toutes les heures de relecture, à Camille pour le soutien absolu et indéfectible et à Hilger sans qui tout ça ne serait pas devenu le bonheur.

Berlin, Avril 2017 *Charlotte Rault*

Table of Contents

Abbreviations

AfDB	African Development Bank
AFD	Agence française de développement
AFT	Agence France Trésor
BIS	Bank for International Settlements
CAC	Collective Action Clause
CDO	Collateralized Debt Obligation
CDS	Credit Default Swap
CJEU	Court of Justice of the European Union
EBRD	European Bank for Reconstruction and Development
ECB	European Central Bank
EFSF	European Financial Stability Facility
EFSM	European Financial Stabilisation Mechanism
EIB	European Investment Bank
ESM	European Stability Mechanism
FSAP	Financial Sector Assessment Program
GIZ	Deutsche Gesellschaft für Internationale Zusammenarbeit
HIPC	Heavily Indebted Poor Countries (Initiative)
IBRD	International Bank for Reconstruction and Development
ICJ	International Court of Justice
ICMA	International Capital Market Association
ICSDI	International Centre for Settlement of Investment Disputes
IDA	International Development Association
IFC	International Finance Corporation
IFF	Institute of International Finance
IMF	International Monetary Fund
INTOSAI	International Organisation of Supreme Audit Institutions
ISDA	International Swaps and Derivatives Association
ISLA	International Securities Lending Association
ITLOS	International Tribunal for the Law of the Sea

LMA	Loan Market Association
KfW	Kreditanstalt für Wiederaufbau Entwicklungsbank
MDRI	Multilateral Debt Relief Initiative
OECD	Organisation for Economic Co-operation and Development
OMT	Outright Monetary Transactions
OTC	Over the counter
ROSC	Reports on the Observance of Standards and Codes
SDRM	Sovereign Debt Restructuring Mechanism
TFEU	Treaty on the Functioning of the European Union
UN	United Nations
UNCITRAL	United Nations Commission on International Trade Law
UNCTAD	United Nations Conference on Trade and Development
WTO	World Trade Organization

Introduction

The notion of sovereignty relates to the national and international supreme power of a State. In German, the term *Souveränität* contains both notions, whereas *Staatsgewalt* concerns a State's ability to wield power and *Herrschaft* refers to the power superiority of an entity. These variations on the notion of sovereignty can also be found in the French legal doctrine[1]. However, even if a State has a legal prerogative, the concrete use of such prerogative is not guaranteed[2]. Accordingly, the expression "sovereign debt" can be considered as an oxymoron. Debts relate to a constraint whereas sovereignty places the State in a superior level of obligation[3].

Debt is usually defined as an obligation that an individual or entity – a debtor – has towards another individual or entity – a creditor. When a

---

1 Raymond Carré de Malberg, Contribution à la théorie générale de l'État, réimpr. CNRS 1962 (Sirey. 1920), p. 79: « *Dans son sens originaire,* [le mot souveraineté] *désigne le caractère suprême de la puissance étatique. Dans une seconde acceptation, il désigne l'ensemble des pouvoirs compris dans la puissance d'État, et il est par suite synonyme de cette dernière. Enfin, il sert à caractériser la position qu'occupe dans l'État le titulaire suprême de la puissance étatique et ici la souveraineté est identifiée avec la puissance de l'organe.* ».

2 Michel Troper, *L'Europe politique et le concept de souveraineté, in* L'Europe en voie de Constitution. Pour un bilan critique des travaux de la Convention (Olivier Beaud, et al. eds., 2004): « *Si par conséquent les décisions imputées à un État sur le plan interne ou international sont formellement prises par ses propres organes, d'un strict point de vue juridique, il doit être considéré comme souverain, même si ces décisions ont été adoptées sous la pression. Inversement, une entité n'est pas souveraine, même si ses organes, comme ceux d'une grande société multinationale disposent d'une énorme puissance économique ou politique.* ».

3 Raphaële Rivier, Droit international public (PUF. 2012), pp. 1-2: « *Par 'souverains', on entend que les États n'ont pas, en droit, de supérieurs. Attribut consubstantiel à la qualité étatique, la souveraineté internationale* […] *qualifie les pouvoirs étatiques et exclut que leur exercice soit conditionné par un pouvoir équivalent ou supérieur.* […] *Le résultat le plus immédiat d'une telle conception négative de la souveraineté est qu'aucun élément du droit (une norme, une institution, une situation juridique, etc.) ne peut être imposé à un État donné sans que celui-ci ait consenti à ses effets.* ».

State undertakes a loan that will later be reimbursed to a creditor[4], it becomes a debtor of a public debt or sovereign debt. The financing is accomplished through national and international creditors that may be either public or private[5]. However, the State remains a particular borrower because its debt covers multiple situations[6]. A number of financial engagements, such as guarantees[7] or debts of municipal or local administrations[8], increase its debt. The State, local administrations and State-own companies[9] all borrow to finance their activities.

Loans have historically been employed as a technique of public financing[10]. Without being constant[11], loans have largely constituted the main

---

4 Louis Trotabas, Précis de science et législation financières (Petits précis Dalloz ed., Dalloz. 1953), p. 356: « *Les divers emprunts émis par l'État, que ce soit d'ailleurs pour des fins monétaires, de trésorerie, ou pour des fins financières, c'est-à-dire budgétaires, constituent ce que l'on appelle la dette publique.* ».

5 Dominique Carreau, *Le rééchelonnement de la dette extérieure des États*, 112 Journal du Droit International (1985).

6 It is important to distinguish debt from deficit. Deficit is understood as the negative difference between money spent and money owned. If the money owned exceeds the money spent, it is a surplus. Debt is the cumulative result of deficits and surpluses over several years. Debt service refers to the payments of borrowed amounts in principal and interest.

7 A guarantee is a collateral agreement to answer for the debt and cover the risks taken by a lender. At an international level, the Multilateral Investment Guarantee Agency, a member of the World Bank Group, promotes foreign investment by granting guarantees.

8 La gestion de la dette publique locale. (2011), 210p.; see also Franck Marmoz, *Les emprunts "toxiques" souscrits par les collectivités territoriales : quelle réponse juridique ?*, n° 120 Revue française de Finances Publiques (2012).

9 As defined in Commission Directive 80/723/EEC of 25 June 1980 on the transparency of financial relations between Member States and public undertakings.

10 Charles Gide, Cours d'économie politique § Vol. 1 (1923), p. 516: « *Les États, comme les particuliers, vivent normalement de leurs revenues. Mais, moins sages que les particuliers, il leur arrive souvent de dépenser plus que leurs revenus : alors ils empruntent, et il n'en est pas un seul, du moins parmi ceux qualifiés de civilisés, qui n'ait aujourd'hui sa dette publique, petite ou grande.* ».

11 See the historical study of Jean Andreau, et al., La dette publique dans l'histoire § VIII (Les journées du Centre de recherches historiques ed., Comité pour l'histoire économique et financière. 2006). They underline at page 473: « *Des cités grecques de l'Antiquité jusqu'à aujourd'hui, le recours des autorités politiques à l'emprunt, volontaire ou forcé, pour financer certaines dépenses exceptionnelles, ou pour disposer d'avances de trésorerie, a une très longue histoire, d'au moins deux millénaires et demi, avec, il est vrai, de longs temps morts.* ».

source of financing of public expenditures[12]. Historical moments characterised with a balanced budget were sporadic[13]. Theories regarding the appeal of indebtedness to States are plentiful. In political science, indebtedness is not seen as a negative concept. In fact, it can even be recommended as it allows the raising of money whilst avoiding unpopular increase in taxes[14]. State indebtedness has the reputation of being an easy and fast way to obtain resources. In the middle of the 18th century, a French economist claimed that a State could not be weakened by its debts because its interests were paid "*from the left hand to the right hand*". Debt would always be neutral and painless as it consists of a transfer from one side to another of what is taken from people[15]. For economic science, the debate is divided between those who consider lending as an expensive resource and proscribe it[16], and those who consider it as positive when it finances productive equipment[17].

---

12 « *La paix trouve notre économie privée d'une grande partie de ses moyens de production, nos finances écrasées d'une dette publique colossale, nos budgets condamnés pour longtemps à supporter les dépenses énormes de la reconstruction.* », Charles de Gaulle, Mémoires de guerre, 1959, p. 234.

13 François Colly, *Les emprunts de l'État et la loi organique du 1er août 2001 relative aux lois de finances*, *in* Études en l'honneur de Loïc Philip (2005).

14 Loans are taken out by citizens, as in the case of war bonds subscribed by national lenders or other countries' institutions and governments. In France, domestic borrowing has been largely used since the time of monarchy, with the notable exception of the reign of Napoleon I who considered borrowing both immoral and fatal because it imposes in advance for future generations, it sacrifices what humans hold most, the welfare of their children and imperceptibly undermines the public structure and condemns a generation to receive curses from those who follow. See the original version in French in the Preamble of the Decree of 29 December 1810 concerning the tobacco monopoly.

15 This theorem is attributed to the French economist Jean-Francois Melon (1675-1738).

16 The eviction effect refers to financing the budget deficit by national savings. The snowball effect refers to the situation where public debt increases automatically due to an interest rate higher than the growth rate.

17 Jérôme Sgard, *La faillite souveraine en économie : l'économie politique des défauts souverains*, *in* Insolvabilité des États et dettes souveraines (Mathias Audit ed. 2011).

Legal science and public finances[18], as shown in international treaties[19], refer purposefully to "*government debt*". This concept designates the obligations resulting from financial engagements established by a State and its territorial and organic entities[20]. Political and economic sciences prefer the term "*sovereign debt*"[21]. Its use is generalised in media and academic texts[22]. In international legal doctrine, State debt has been defined by the International Law Commission in Article 33 of the Vienna Convention on Succession of States in Respect of State Property, Archives and Debts as:

> "any financial obligation of a predecessor State arising in conformity with international law towards another State, an international organization or any other subject of international law"[23].

However, this definition excludes part of the phenomenon, as it does not consider State indebtedness owed to a private creditor[24].

---

18 Michel Bouvier, *La dette publique*, 123 Revue française de finances publiques (2013), p. 3 and foll.; Christian Eckert, *Le contrôle de la dette publique par le Parlement : un enjeu politique devenu majeur*, 123 Revue française de Finances Publiques (2013).

19 For instance, the Maastricht criteria set out in the Treaty on European Union refer to "*government debt*" by mentioning excessive government deficit as follows: "*The Commission shall monitor the development of the budgetary situation and of the stock of government debt in the Member States with a view to identifying gross errors. In particular it shall examine compliance with budgetary discipline [...]*".

20 Public borrowers whose commitments constitute State's debt are either public organisations or debts guaranteed by the State or by its entities. Other borrowers are considered private borrowers.

21 Régis Bismuth, *Dette de l'État (droit)*, *in* Dictionnaire Encyclopédique de l'État (François Hervouët, et al. eds., 2014).

22 Benjamin Lemoine, *Les « dealers » de la dette souveraine*, 4 Sociétés contemporaines (2013): « *Ironie de l'histoire, le terme de dette souveraine s'est imposé dans le débat public et dans les travaux académiques au moment précis où les marchés de l'argent privé ont repris d'importants pouvoirs dans la définition des politiques économiques, et que les États ont vu leurs capacités d'action sur l'économie et la monnaie circonscrites ainsi que leurs périmètres comptables surveillés et limités.* ».

23 United Nations, *Vienna Convention on Succession of States in Respect of State Property, Archives and Debts*, Vienna, 8 April 1983.

24 ILC Report of the Commission to the General Assembly on the work of its thirty-third session, (1981), pp. 79-80: "*the definition of State debt should be limited to financial obligations arising at the* international level, *that is to say, between subjects of international law. Debts owed by a State to private creditors [...] fell outside the scope of the present draft. Although protected, such debts were not the subject of the law of succession of States*".

Therefore, it is important to distinguish external – or international – debt from internal – or domestic – debt. This distinction is based on the applicable law of the concerned jurisdiction and the currency in which it is drawn up. External debt refers to the total amount of debts denominated in a foreign currency when the applicable law is either the creditor's country or international law. Internal debt, which is denominated in local currency, is issued inside the national legal framework and submitted to domestic law without taking into account creditors' nationality. This first distinction can be completed by another subsystem based on the quality of the lender or creditor. External public debt is the one contracted to a State or an international intergovernmental organisation, whereas private external debt is related to commercial banks or international financial markets[25].

In this dissertation, we will use the term "*sovereign debt*" in a pluralistic assertion to take into account specific situations existing for each period and State. This term implies also, beyond the complexity of the legal framework, difficulties concerning the articulation of law and singular realities. The understanding of this indebtedness is as complex as the multiplicity of levels composing the financial and institutional architecture of every State. Sovereign debt is the product of entities that follow distinct financial logics[26]. By extension, public accounting is as divided as institutional entities are. It cannot be consolidated similarly to private account because there is no authority able to arbitrate such consolidation[27].

Considering sovereign debts management from the perspective of a legal framework consists of defining its limits and analysing national, European or international institutions. Our starting point is based on the hypothesis that there is a legal framework for sovereign debt. It implies that indebtedness is a result of a sovereign decision process delimited by legal constraints. *Ex ante*, at the level of indebtedness, this framework responds to a phenomenon moderately controlled by the State. *Ex post*, the situation

25 Dominique Carreau & Malcolm N. Shaw, La dette extérieure / The External Debt § Vol. 17 (Académie de droit international de La Haye ed., Martinus Nijhoff Publishers. 1995), pp. 4-6.

26 Robert Hertzog, *À la recherche d'une théorie du système financier public complexe*, *in* Études en l'honneur de Loïc Philip (2005). *« Un système financier peut être composé d'entités multiples et rester néanmoins lisible dès lors que ces entités suivent des principes financiers similaires et qu'elles sont soumises à un même pouvoir de régulation. »*. This is not the case here.

27 This is why national economic accounting highlights overall tables for all economic agents' activities, including public entities.

differs. In case of excessive indebtedness, creditors can act against 'bad payer' States to recover their money regardless of the limits usually applicable due to sovereign immunity. Indebtedness' level constitutes the problem as Adam Smith emphasised it:

> "the progress of the enormous debts which at present oppress, and will in the long-run probably ruin, all the great nations of Europe, has been pretty uniform"[28].

Indebtedness evolves until achieving a decisive phase called a "crisis". This moment corresponds to an abrupt perturbation of economic stability. Etymologically, the word crisis relates to the conception of judgment[29]. For some jurists, crises are in the core of international law as an epistemological element[30]. The present dissertation is connected to this context. The sovereign debt crisis has pushed researchers to renew the study, to return to past analyses in order to bring new approaches to contemporary issues. The current events in Argentina and Greece opened new paths of reflexion in a European and international legal framework.

This dissertation aims at analysing the evolution of the legal framework of sovereign debt management. Its purpose is to gather legal measures taken by each stakeholder in order to understand their normative choices. The actual scenario of sovereign indebtedness necessarily leads to an irreversible disruption of legal rules and structures that currently support global economy. Due to the current uncertainty, it is imperative to analyse the treatment of crises, the proposals of reform, the search of system's regulation improvement and the role of multilateral institutions in the management of sovereign debt. Such analysis is framed in an international legal environment characterised by multiple conceptions and methods. This dissertation attempts such an analysis, in particular via the contrast between French and German conceptions of sovereign debt. Such contrast

---

28 Adam Smith, An Inquiry into the Nature and Causes of the Wealth of Nations (1776). Book V, Chapter III, pp. 173 and foll.

29 The word comes from the Greek *krinein* meaning "*decide, separate, judge*".

30 See Michael Reisman & Andrew Willard, International Incidents: The Law that Counts in World Politics (Princeton University Press. 2014), originally published in 1988. Hilary Charlesworth, *Le droit international, une discipline de la crise*, *in* Sexe, genre et droit international (Hilary Charlesworth ed. 2013).

is interesting to understand the commonly perceived 'apprehension' of European responses to the current crisis[31].

In historical perspective, sovereign defaults are not isolated incidents. The current situation echoes the past. Yet, no international institutional mechanism exists to manage sovereign debt (1.). Ambitious legal proposals considering a specific framework in case of sovereign default have failed so far. This study examines the proper categorisation of sovereign debt management in international law while recognizing the competing importance of its financial and economic consequences on a State (2.).

1. The persistence of sovereign defaults

International conventions require State consent. In the particular case of sovereign financing, the situation is more complex due to the fact that a State is a particular borrower. This is especially the case in terms of applicable law. Technically, a State can be considered as infinitely solvent thanks to its ability to issue money (1.1.). However, the history of the global financial system is filled with instances of sovereign defaults. Sovereign indebtedness has repeatedly been characterised by failures for as long as loaning practices have existed (1.2.). Despite this reality, there is no general institutional mechanism and crisis resolution is determined on a case-by-case basis by applying *ad hoc* measures (1.3.).

1.1. The insolvency of sovereign borrowers

Some economic theory considers that a State is always a solvent borrower. As a sovereign entity, it can raise taxes as much as required to repay its debts. Several other examples support this theory: raising money by selling natural resources, cutting costs by increasing debt service, borrowing to repay older debts and even controlling money supply[32]. Government

31 In particular, the critical positivist approach favoured by contemporary French doctrine is decidedly more descriptive than normative. It deploys a system of analysis and an explanation of law, whereas the German approach tends to advocate solutions to remediate to defects identified.

32 State's existence would be eternal and its potential of taxation infinite. Borrowing would influence the State to reduce its future consumption in order to be able to

debt is sometimes presented as a source of wealth creation[33]. From this point of view, the issuance of sovereign debt is considered as an asset. It undoubtedly constitutes an opportunity for the private creditors[34]. But this is an economic fiction that reinforces the false belief in the infallibility of States' finances[35]. As illustrated in the succession of sovereign defaults over the last 200 years, this myth of infallibility has now disappeared among international finance community[36].

---

repay. A moderate growth rate and prudent expenses would provide its way out of debt. State's wealth control would regulate money supply. The inability to repay may only be related to securities in foreign currency.

33 Some jurists follow this economic analysis' position: Carlo Santulli, *L'Euro : analyse juridique de la "crise de la dette"*, 115 Revue générale de droit international public (2011).

34 Yeva S. Nersisyan & Wray L. Randall, *Un excès de dette publique handicape-t-il réellement la croissance?*, 116 Revue de l'OFCE (2011): « *Si l'on comprend que les émissions obligataires sont une opération volontaire par un gouvernement souverain, et que les titres ne sont rien d'autre que des comptes différents auprès de la même banque centrale utilisés par le même gouvernement, il devient non pertinent pour des questions de solvabilité et de taux d'intérêt de savoir s'il y a des acheteurs pour les obligations d'État et si les obligations sont détenues par des entités nationales ou étrangères.* ». But this reasoning applies *ceteris paribus* and only as part of an issuance in national currency. However, jurists cannot limit their analysis to such *ceteris paribus* criteria.

35 In the 1970s, the CEO of Citicorp, Walter Wriston claimed that: "*Countries do not go bust. The infrastructure does not go away, the productivity of the people does not go away, the natural resources do not go away. And so their assets always exceed their liabilities, which is the technical reason for bankruptcy*". However, "*the sentiment did not originate with Wriston in 1982. It was already part of the conventional wisdom in 1977, echoed by highly respected officials such as Federal Reserve Governor Henry Wallich. More importantly, the comment calls attention to the fundamental distinction between lending to national governments and lending to private corporations. This distinction, which is not intuitively obvious, has much to do with why sovereign workouts cannot be carried out under the domestic bankruptcy-insolvency laws used for corporate workouts*". See Lex Rieffel, Restructuring Sovereign Debt: The Case for Ad Hoc Machinery (Brookings Institution Press. 2003), Appendix A "Countries do not go bankrupt", pp. 289-294.

36 Margaret Atwood, Comptes et légendes : La dette et la face cachée de la richesse (Boréal. 2009): « *La perception d'une insolvabilité peut créer de l'insolvabilité, car elle conduit à des niveaux d'intérêt insoutenables. En fin de compte, la soutenabilité dépend des croyances, et une crise de la dette, qu'elle soit privée ou publique, n'est rien d'autre qu'un revirement des croyances.* ».

What are the implications of bankruptcy, failure or State indebtedness[37]? The fact that a State is a particular borrower does not protect creditors. On the contrary, economic history is replete with illustrations of States defaulting on their commitments in many forms[38]. Far from being limited to the suspension of payment of interests or capital, debt has been periodically depreciated by currency manipulation or even repudiation[39]. The situations are so diverse that the legal doctrine compiled an inventory. The non-payment of financial obligations is a sovereign default. The refusal to pay is similar to the non-recognition of debt. The inability to settle an expired claim refers to a case of bankruptcy[40]. For this dissertation, the concept of default refers to the general situation in which a State imposes losses on its private and public creditors.

However, a State does not file for bankruptcy like a private company. Public borrowers, that is to say sovereign entities linked to the State, have specific legal characteristics. Unlike an insolvency plan for a private company, creditors cannot replace governments by court order. Similarly, increase of taxes and reduction of public services are limited tools[41]. These features emphasise the singular dimension of sovereign debt. It is closely

---

37 Adam Smith wrote about it: "*Almost all states, however, ancient as well as modern, when reduced to this necessity have, upon some occasions, played this very juggling trick*". He called for an organised insolvency: "*When it becomes necessary for a state to declare itself bankrupt, in the same manner as when it becomes necessary for an individual to do so, a fair, open, and avowed bankruptcy is always the measure which is both least dishonourable to the debtor and least hurtful to the creditor*". Smith, An Inquiry into the Nature and Causes of the Wealth of Nations. 1776.

38 Carmen M. Reinhart & Kenneth S. Rogoff, This Time is Different. Eight Centuries of Financial Folly (Princeton University Press. 2009).

39 States have the power to suspend payments or to repudiate their debt. It is a characteristic of the "sovereign risk" taken into account by the markets. See Jochen Andritzky, Sovereign Default Risk Valuation: Implications of Debt Crises and Bond Restructurings (Springer. 2006), pp. 15-60.

40 It is important to differentiate between simple default, non-payment, moratorium or repudiation since debt restructuring depends on the initial situation. See Odette Lienau, *The longer-term consequences of sovereign debt restructuring*, *in* Sovereign Debt Management (Lee Buchheit & Rosa Lastra eds., 2014); Michael Waibel, *La faillite souveraine en droit – Un État peut-il faire faillite?*, *in* Insolvabilité des États et dettes souveraines (Mathias Audit ed. 2011).

41 Peter B. Kenen, *The International Financial Architecture: Old Issues and New Initiatives*, 5 International Finance (2002): "*An insolvent country is one that cannot mobilize the revenues required to service its debt without imposing great pain on*

linked to political philosophy. Indeed, direct beneficiaries of today's loans will vote in the next election, while potential payers are perhaps not born yet[42].

1.2. The timelessness of modified debt crisis

Debt crises seem as old as sovereign debt itself. For historians, the first known default dates from the 4th century BC. Ten of the thirteen Greek municipalities of the Attic Maritime Association were unable to honour their debts to the Delos Temple[43]. In the early modern period, monarchies were so often defaulting in the repayment of their loans that the practice of default was institutionalised. The debt maturity was calculated after estimating the monarch's lifetime[44]. A historical analysis of economic situation demonstrates that some States default regularly, such as France and Germany. In fact, they defaulted as many time as the most recent cases in Latin America[45]. International financial crises are not rare and isolated events in time. There are conventional common denominators to any financial crisis in every historical case, mainly a deterioration of macroeconomic indicators, a panic of investors, and speculation.

The loan structure has evolved. Historically, the richest States assumed the role of lenders in bilateral relations through the conclusion of financial agreements. These international treaties constitute an assistance for specific development projects or more general financing, especially in war

its citizens, jeopardizing the survival of its government and impairing the social and political stability of the country itself'.

42 Lee C. Buchheit & G. Mitu Gulati, *Responsible Sovereign Lending and Borrowing*, 73 Law and Contemporary Problems (2010). On this issue of intergenerational accounting in relation to the German population, see Ralf Möller, Generationengerechtigkeit im Steuerrecht: die generationengerechte Fortentwicklung des Steuerrechts unter besonderer Berücksichtigung der prognostizierten demographischen Entwicklung (Kova. 2005), 412p.

43 Federico Sturzenegger & Jeromin Zettelmeyer, Debt Defaults and Lessons from a Decade of Crises (The MIT Press. 2007), pp. 3-29.

44 Waibel, La faillite souveraine en droit – Un État peut-il faire faillite? 2011.

45 Carmen M. Reinhart & Kenneth S. Rogoff, *Serial Default and the "Paradox" of Rich-to-Poor Capital Flows*, 94 American Economic Review (2004); J. Bradford Delong, et al., *Financial Crises in the 1890s and the 1990s: Must History Repeat?*, Brookings Papers on Economic Activity (1999).

times[46]. Since the end of World War II, international financial institutions and development banks have taken most precedence over such bilateral loans[47].

To finance quicker and cheaper, States have turned to private operators. In the 1980s, more than a half of sovereign debt originated from commercial banks[48]. These lenders had at their disposal a considerable reserve of foreign currency from the oil shocks of 1973 and 1979. These banks formed banking syndicates and provided large-scale loans to States[49] until facing sovereign defaults[50]. Commercial banks freed themselves from the burden of these loan agreements with the assistance of the International Monetary Fund and the World Bank. They securitised their loan agreements and resold them as bonds, called "*Brady bonds*", to the financial markets. This technique of financial engineering met a great success amongst private investors and subsequently marked the beginning of a widespread use of financial markets by developing countries. Since 1990, bonds issued by States on financial markets are increasing. They are now the most common form of State financing[51].

Issuing bonds may allow for a faster financing and diversifies the financial sources to decrease dependency *vis-à-vis* the banking sector and public funding. Yet this phenomenon has led to the proliferation of State creditors. Traditional creditors and new investors form a heterogeneous mix of commercial and investment banks, insurance companies and hedge funds.

Debt instruments have also changed through the use of new products: securities for classic bonds, swaps and options, warrants and credit derivatives have exploded both for direct financing, for refinancing and hedging.

---

46 See examples of the Middle Ages and the Modern time in David Graeber, Debt: The First 5000 Years (Melville House. 2011), pp. 223-345.

47 See Chapter 1.

48 Daniel McGovern, *Different Market Windows on Sovereign Debt: Private-sector Credit from the 1980s to the present, in* Sovereign Debt: Origins, Crisis and Restructuring (Vinod K. Aggarwal & Brigitte Granville eds., 2003), pp. 67-91.

49 See Chapter 2.

50 Between 1980 and 1983, the Latin American States were no longer able to repay their bank loans and successively defaulted: Bolivia and Nicaragua in 1980, Honduras in 1981, Argentina, Cuba, Ecuador, the Dominican Republic, Mexico, Panama and Venezuela in 1982, Brazil, Chile, Costa Rica, Peru and Uruguay in 1983. See Sturzenegger & Zettelmeyer, Debt Defaults and Lessons from a Decade of Crises. 2007, pp. 7-8.

51 See Chapter 3.

This evolution gives an explanation of today's sovereign default that is mainly characterised by situations where States are subjected to the hazards of finance. Price volatility, credit availability and sensitivity to market operators may directly influence the shape and structure of sovereign debt. The current crises have an international impact due to the financialisation of States debt techniques. Subsequently, we could consider whether sovereign debt crises are endemic due to the absence of debts limitations. In any case, it is essential to consider whether States can prevent or mitigate the effects of such crises[52].

1.3. The absence of institutional mechanisms

There is a lack of comprehensive legal framework in case of sovereign default. The search for solutions to non-repayment of contractual debts has always existed.

Historically, the State has endorsed claims of creditors in the form of a diplomatic protection[53]. Such governmental intervention transposes the debt problem from a domestic and private level to an interstate level[54]. This transposition was accompanied by negotiations between States. These negotiations gradually gave rise to the establishment of basic institutional mechanisms to collect and allocate the amounts due to creditors[55].

---

52 See Chapter 4.

53 John Fischer Williams, International Law and International Financial Obligations Arising from Contracts § 2 (Bibliotheca Visseriana. 1924), pp. 10-11, in particular the 1848 circular of Lord Palmerston.

54 See the dispute between France and Russia concerning the repudiation of the tsarist empire's debt by the Bolsheviks in January 1918: Patrick Julliard & Brigitte Stern, Les emprunts russes : aspects juridiques, 16 (Pedone. 2002); Sébastien Touzé, *L'affaire des emprunts russes devant la Cour européenne des droits de l'homme*, 15 Revue trimestrielle des droits de l'homme (2003); Julien Boucher, *Le juge administratif et la combinaison des conventions internationales – Conseil d'État, assemblée, 23 décembre 2011, M. Eduardo José Kandyrine de Brito Paiva, n° 303678*, 28 Revue française de droit administratif (2012).

55 For a discussion on the institutional control mechanisms established by the European powers, including the sovereign debts of Greece, Egypt, Tunisia, Turkey and the Ottoman Empire, see André Andréadès, *Les contrôles financiers internationaux*, *in* Recueil des cours de l'Académie de droit international de La Haye (1924).

By ensuring a similar treatment to debt holders, diplomatic protection also aimed at ensuring a balance of power between European States.

Interference in the activities of debtor countries in the name of debt collection[56] has led to armed intervention. In 1902, the United Kingdom, Germany and Italy blocked Venezuelan ports to pressure Venezuela to abide by its financial obligations[57]. The international community condemned such method of debt recovery[58]. During the Second International Peace Conference at The Hague in 1907, the Drago-Porter Convention "*respecting the Limitation of the Employment of Force for the Recovery of Contract Debts*"[59] was signed. Such beginning of the internationalisation of sovereign debt settlement was ambiguous. While prohibiting the use of force for the first time, this Convention is imperfect. Its first article prohibits the use of force in the first paragraph. However, the second paragraph legitimates armed interventions in the event of refusal of an offer of arbitration or refusal to comply with an arbitration award[60].

Since the 1980s, there are key moments in the debate concerning debt structure. Until the early 1990s, restructuring billions of dollars from commercial bank credits constituted a major issue to avoid disrupting their balance sheets. The goal was to restructure private loans while managing a debt relief from multilateral and bilateral creditors. Since 2000, the issue of restructuring sovereign bond titles has focused upon the management of sovereign debt[61]. Techniques for collective debt treatment have been developed in the context of the Paris Club[62] and the London Club, which respectively include the bilateral creditors and lending commercial banks. In

56 Karl Strupp, *L'intervention en matière financière*, (1925), see especially p. 78.

57 James Brown Scott, "The Venezuelan Preferential Case between Germany, Great Britain, Italy and Venezuela et al." (1916), New York, Carnegie Endowment for International Peace.

58 Luis Maria Drago, *The State Loans in Their Relation to International Policy*, 1 American Journal of International Law (1907).

59 Convention respecting the Limitation of the Employment of Force for the Recovery of Contract Debts (done 18 October 1907, entered into force 26 January 1910) (1908) 2 AJIL Supp 81 (Drago-Porter Convention).

60 See Chapter 1.

61 Lee C. Buchheit, *A Quarter Century of Sovereign Debt Management: An Overview*, Vol. 35 Georgetown Journal of International Law (2004).

62 Composed of twenty permanent members (Australia, Austria, Belgium, Canada, Denmark, Finland, France, Germany, Ireland, Israel, Italy, Japan, Norway, Netherlands, United Kingdom, United States of America, Russia, Spain, Sweden and Switzerland), this informal group also includes *ad hoc* participants (for instance

late 2001, the IMF even launched a proposal to implement a sovereign debt restructuring mechanism, the Krueger Proposal, which was later abandoned in 2003.

In an international context, the IMF and private mechanisms define their respective rules in order to regulate private aspects. The purpose of this is to avoid any debacle. The creation of the G20 in November 2008 represents a strong indicator of States' will to address the crisis in a coordinated way. Within the European Union, a legal framework was formed gradually. It began in 1978 with the idea of a European monetary fund. The ambition was to develop a crisis management mechanism. Left out, the debate about the creation of a European monetary fund is experiencing renewed interest due to the Greek crisis. The current target is to provide a sustainable response to the current legal lack.

2. *The place of international law in sovereign debt management*

In the absence of an international legal status and a standardised legal framework for sovereign debt, the legal possibilities that may be provided for optimal international debt management are studied (2.1.). The failures of previous initiatives (2.2.) are not an impediment for a renewed analysis of the subject (2.3.).

2.1. The search of a legal framework

Nowadays, there is an international economy of debt that can neither meet a particular legal regime nor an established body for sovereign debt management. Sovereign-debt related contracts, primarily private law contracts, are internationalised due to their circulation between financial market participants[63]. International markets have such an impact on transactions that

---

Argentina, Brazil, Mexico, Morocco, Portugal) and observers invited to attend the negotiations (including representatives of international financial institutions and of sovereign debtors).

63 Prosper Weil, *Problèmes relatifs aux contrats passés entre un État et un particulier*, *in* Recueil des cours de l'Académie de droit international de La Haye (1969), p. 188: « *L'internationalisation ne signifie ni que le contrat devienne l'équivalent d'un traité international ni que les règles du droit international interétatique soient transposables purement et simplement au domaine des contrats. Le contrat*

they cannot exclusively be considered as purely internal or domestic[64]. The goal of a legal framework is at the junction of contracting sovereign debt and internationalisation. The current lack of international legal framework mainly arises from an absence of specific legal status for sovereign debt.

The current financial crisis reveals the quest for solutions started in the 1980s, but this time from the political perspective of developed countries. Sovereign debt does not consist of a single loan agreement. In a crisis, many contracts between the sovereign debtor in difficulty and its creditors cannot be resolved. To finance its needs, a State may use multilateral debt financed by various stakeholders, such as private investors, multilateral institutions, other governments, and commercial banks. To the extent that these creditors are public or private, there are several ways to manage sovereign debt. The joint efforts of national authorities, central banks, the IMF and the active involvement of the private sector demonstrate interdependence in international relations.

Financialisation and internationalisation of sovereign debt have complicated the situation in terms of applicable law to debt products. Thus, when a State is committed to another State or an international institution like the World Bank, international public law is the applicable law of the signed loan agreement. On the other hand, private law is the applicable law for syndicated loan contracts[65] and bond issuance contracts. Therefore, the legal structure of sovereign debt, eminently public, is almost exclusively dominated by private law.

As revealed in 2008, the international financial supervision is incomplete. The current crisis situation highlights the complexity of financial

---

internationalisé n'est pas assimilable à un traité, il est simplement un acte international d'un type nouveau. Le droit international qui lui est applicable ne sera pas exactement le même qui celui qui régit les rapports entre États, et notamment les traités internationaux ; rien n'interdit de penser, en effet, que des principes empruntés au droit international général, tels que pacta sunt servanda *ou* rebus sic stantibus, *ou bien le principe du respect des droits acquis, ou bien celui de l'enrichissement sans cause, puissent recevoir un contenu concret spécifique en matière contractuelle.* ».

64 Francisco Orrego Vicuña, *Of Contracts and Treaties in the Global Market*, 8 Max Planck Yearbook of United Nations Law (2004).

65 A syndicated loan agreement is a banking operation corresponding to the provision of a borrowed sum of money made by two or more lenders acting in cooperation.

products traded in different markets and the proliferation of stakeholders. Moreover, the recent financial turmoil affects developing countries, but also developed countries. Indeed, the issue of sovereign debt management arises particularly in Japan, in the United States of America and within the European Union. Cooperation between States is necessary, especially when there is no institutional harmonisation.

As no general mechanism manages private flows, the existing answers are essentially constituted of temporarily relieves in case of repayment difficulties. International law is presented as marginal *vis-à-vis* sovereign debt management. No international agreement establishes standardised rules to deal with sovereign debt and the observation stays the same:

> "no rule of international law dealing with debt between States has ever been formulated"[66].

In case of default, the solution is an *ad hoc* mechanism.

2.2. The unsuccessful concrete proposals

The debate regarding the implementation of a sovereign debt mechanism in the international financial architecture has divided the international community since the mid-1970s. The attempts of the IMF to establish a global mechanism have failed in early 2000. The Krueger Proposal was based on a new reality of sovereign debt. Commercial banks were previously the main creditors. Sharing clauses were contractually included. They required commercial banks to negotiate together in case of restructuring. Litigations against States increased due to the spread of bonds and the securitisation. The IMF consequently proposed an organised solution.

The failure to implement this IMF solution raises the question of the necessity of such framework. Opponents claimed that if over-indebted States benefited from such framework, creditors would not be able to recover any money. A solution applicable to States raises irreducible problems to creditors. Which of the following shall be privileged: the benefits of the

66 John Fischer Williams K.C, *Le droit international et les obligations financières internationales qui naissent d'un contrat*, *in* Recueil des cours de l'Académie de droit international de La Haye (1923), pp. 298-302: « *aucune règle de droit international […] n'a jamais été formulée s'occupant spécialement de la question des dettes entre États* ».

contractors or the functioning of the international financial system? We consider that implementing a sovereign debt mechanism is only one part of sovereign debt management. Preventing over-indebtedness and implementing an effective management of public finance are fundamental.

Without clear initiatives, the legal framework of sovereign financing still operates under the interactions between private economic operators. The purpose of this study is to analyse the different methods of sovereign financing. Once identified, it becomes possible to evaluate sovereign debt management.

Recent financial turmoil caused different reactions by international financial institutions, governments and private entities. Their collective aim has been to control the short-term situation and its effects, while simultaneously constructing a long-term legal framework for sovereign debt management. Located at the intersection of different branches of law, sovereign debt management is at the heart of international economic law, mixing public and private, national and European laws[67].

2.3. Determination of the field of study

Nowadays, the topic of sovereign debt is widely discussed. However, an overall perspective is often lacking. In this study, we will differentiate *ex post* situations of default from measures applicable *ex ante*. Our goal is to present a broad legal view to justify the demonstration. This choice implies that we will focus on our demonstration, i.e. a plea for State's intervention towards more regulation. We will consider external debt in a global perspective for efficiency purposes. The advantage of such method is that it provides a broad vision.

We will analyse sovereign financing by considering multiple debt situations and providing examples. This global approach will take into account, when appropriate, economic distinction between developing countries and

67 Jean-Marc Sorel, *Le droit international au début du XXIe siècle : un salutaire chaos permanent mêlant humanisme et réalisme*, *in* Regards d'une génération sur le Droit International (Emmanuelle Jouannet, et al. eds., 2008): « *Il faut se saisir des croisements entre droit interne et droit international, de leur comparaison, de la rencontre entre droits nationaux et droit international privé, pour comprendre ce qu'est le droit international aujourd'hui, et ce que sont le droit interne et ses évolutions.* ».

developed countries. The normative continuity of debt is intrinsically linked to historical and political variables. Political players, changing ideologies and shifted public and private structures influence those variables. In this study, we will not mention all categories of debt but present examples. Moreover, we will not focus on the treatment of sovereign debt litigation. We will restrict the analysis to a part of the jurisprudence related to sovereign debt enforcement. Besides, the purpose of this dissertation is not to evaluate the reforms that have been or may be adopted in banking or financial matters. When some of these reforms interact with the legal framework of sovereign debt management, we will discuss them.

This dissertation analyses the existing tools and recommends additional measures. It does not provide an answer to sovereign debt crisis, but rather develops a position in favour of strengthening current methods. We will use the European sovereign debt crisis and the Greek restructuring to examine legal causes that led to the crisis. This examination will help us to determine principles that may provide a legal framework for sovereign debt management. The purpose is not to solve debt problem through laws, but to see how law is closely related to debt management and how the development of rules is correlated to the changing of indebtedness situations.

Knowing that law *a priori* allows a possibility of action, the objective of the first part is to analyse the legal instruments used by States. The second part utilises such an approach for the purpose of complementing the existing legal framework. This will be accomplished by specific proposals intended to address and strengthen the current regulatory framework. Chronology is not always respected as the central argumentation is the *instrumentum* of debt.

At a time when economic discourse dominates politics, considering a legal framework for sovereign debt management may seem secondary. Jurists are often less taken into account than economists. Moreover, the actual treatment of debts is highly political and economic, while also raising important legal questions. Subsequently, international law is shrunk to:

> "a manual for a better life instead of an ideal construction; a skillful technique instead of a pure science, an art of imbrication instead of a set of commands without future"[68] (translation by the author).

68 Jean-Marc Sorel, Id. « *une manière d'aider à vivre plus qu'une construction idéale, une technique adroite plus qu'une science pure, un art de l'imbrication plus qu'un ensemble de commandements sans lendemains* ».

It is particularly the case when considering sovereign debt, where rules are shelved and where international law seems disconnected to debt processing mechanisms.

This paradox is strengthened by the apparent impossibility to elaborate a normative framework proposal. Debt "players" even refuse to recognise applicable rules. They develop *sui generis* legal measures that ignore traditional categories of international law. These measures are combined with effective legal effects. Subsequently, they are consolidated and binding not because of their legality, but because their omission would be detrimental. Such debt management rules constitute a prelude to an international debt law.

This study illustrates the vicissitudes of international law and the dispute over its standards. Without looking for a new system, we take into account that law is confronted with economic problems, that international relations are dominated by economic phenomena[69]. The international community structures are transformed by the proliferation of tools and operators. It is in this ensemble that international law has its place, sometimes appearing spontaneously[70]. Ultimately, there is not a unified or codified law, but only general or common principles.

In this dissertation, we argue that sovereign debt management leads to greater State intervention. We consider that a significant portion of the current framing wrongly support the idea of the legal framework for sovereign debt management by dragging all players to immobility. Therefore, no reforms were implemented in the past. The United Nations is now addressing the question[71]. Thus, sovereign debt management is more than ever political. We are far from the emergence of a new theory of

---

69 René-Jean Dupuy, La communauté internationale entre le mythe et l'histoire (Economica. 1986), pp. 29-33.

70 Pascale Deumier, Le droit spontané (Économica. 2002), pp. 10-15.

71 On 11 September 2015, the General Assembly of the United Nations adopted a resolution on principles to guide sovereign debt restructuring processes. With 136 votes in favour, 6 against and 41 abstentions, it reflects the geo-political pattern in the United Nations. Developing countries are in favour of financial measures to increase stability and fairness, while developed countries may choose to block such measures, arguing that the United Nations is not the place to discuss it. See UNCTAD, United Nations General Assembly adopts basic principles on sovereign debt restructuring (11 September 2015).

sovereignty that would provide an apolitical treatment of sovereign indebtedness[72].

Beyond legal gaps, this analysis addresses the existence of current legal instruments while considering the development of a hypothetical international legal framework to be utilised in the event of sovereign default. This dissertation will focus on the international legal framework for sovereign debt management in general, inherently located at the intersection of private interests (Part I) and public administration (Part II).

72 Odette Lienau, Rethinking Sovereign Debt: Debt and Reputation in the Twentieth Century (Harvard University Press. 2014), 344p.

PART I. SOVEREIGN DEBT – BETWEEN PUBLIC INTEREST AND PRIVATE INSTRUMENTS

This first part focuses on the study of the phenomenon of sovereign financing not as an isolated event, but as the result of a set of mechanisms and instruments derived from contractual relationships between economic operators. Questions arise from this tangle of public interests and private instruments, for instance what is the law applicable to sovereign debt and what is the place of the State in this financing.

While responding to purely factual questions such as "How is debt contracted? Why? To whom?" we will focus on the analysis of legal methods used to structure debt. Here, there is no hierarchical model dominated by State. When borrowing, the State is no longer in a position of supremacy and becomes economically subjected to its creditors. We identify a networked system[73] of coexisting public interests crystallised in private instruments (Title I). Sovereign indebtedness and default are essentially privatised (Title II).

As a whole, the State and the public sector gather multilateral debt and official bilateral debt (Chapter 1), debt to commercial banks (Chapter 2) and debt constituted by bonds and other securities (Chapter 3), as outlined in the IMF guide on external debt statistics[74]. This structure, mostly quantitative and oriented to the private sector, is a risk factor in case of economic and financial crisis (Chapter 4).

---

73 Francois Ost & Michel van de Kerchove, De la pyramide au réseau ? Pour une théorie dialectique du droit, Facultés universitaires Saint-Louis, 2002, pp. 13-22.

74 External Debt Statistics: Guide for Compilers and Users, 2003, updated in 2013.

Title I. CONTRACTUALISATION OF DEBT SUPPORTS

There is a broad agreement on the fact that international treaties are the basis of interstate relations. Those treaties are governed by international public law. Yet in terms of financing, their use is sporadic[75]. Apart from the case of bilateral investment treaties[76], international public law is only occasionally used in the fields of finance and development. The majority of debt instruments – or debt supports – are contracts governed by international private law.

This observation leads us to the following question: what is left to State intervention regarding sovereign debt management? In fact, this intervention is limited, both at the stage of contractual negotiations and choice of applicable law. In practise, each contract refers to an applicable law, which is usually not the debtor domestic law. While reviewing the contractual provisions imposed by market discipline, we analyse the rules that control renegotiations in case of default. We conclude that there is nowadays a generalisation of standard contracts. This practice suggests that market discipline is ruling the field of sovereign debt contracts.

Historically, international treaties and commercial contracts were developed jointly. Sovereign financing methods cannot be artificially distinguished between a first prolific period of international financial treaties and a second period characterised by private contracts. However, there is a

75 Sporadic but not inexistent as demonstrated by current practices. China recently offered bilateral sovereign lending to Greece.

76 Bilateral investment treaties have increased in the last twenty years to ensure a protection and a fair and equitable treatment to investors of a State on the territory of another State. We do not include bilateral investment treaties in the first part of this dissertation related to the analysis of sovereign debt instruments. However, we will mention them in the second part by analysing sovereign debt litigation. See also Ellie Norton, *International Investment Arbitration and the European Debt Crisis*, Vol. 13 Chicago Journal of International Law, 2012; W. Mark C. Weidemaier, *Contracting for State Intervention: The Origins of Sovereign Debt Arbitration*, 73 Law and Contemporary Problems, 2010; Esther Kentin, *Economic Crisis and Investment Arbitration: The Argentine Cases*, *in* Les aspects nouveaux du droit des investissements internationaux / New Aspects of International Investment Law, Philippe Kahn & Thomas W. Wälde, 2004.

rarefaction of financial treaties (Chapter 1). This phenomenon is offset by a general use of private contracts (Chapter 2).

CHAPTER 1. Decline of International Financial Agreements

This first chapter focuses on public external debt as part of sovereign financing conducted with international law subjects. Initially, financial agreements between States were concluded during armed conflicts. However, these agreements are not representative of sovereign lending activity. We will consider cases in which a sovereign debtor negotiates with other States or international institutions. Their agreements are governed by international law.

Far from presenting a complete panorama of the diversity of international financial relations, we rather determine how States can act as creditors. Based on this information, we apprehend how international public law is used and which *instrumentum* is privileged to conclude international agreements. We conclude that the rarefaction of these agreements marginalises the use of international law in the financial field. International law remains the law applicable to financial agreements signed by States (1.). Moreover, some loan agreements granted by international financial institutions are also governed by international law (2.). Nevertheless, there is a gradual integration of private law in this field.

1. Financial cooperation and debt policy

Financial agreements were historically widespread until the end of World War II as part of military conflicts or wars results. Now, they are primarily used to finance public development aid (1.1.). While these constant and former financial relations are made between States, a consensus on an international treaty instrument regulating this type of international public debt may emerge. Meanwhile, no legal instrument emerged (1.2.).

1.1. International relations and interstate financial agreements

International agreements[77], by creating legal obligations between States, formalise the concurrence of wills between parties as subjects of international law. Similarly to any other treaty, the validity of international financial agreements depends on the respect of international law (1.1.1.). These requirements, normally containing long and complex procedures, are not the only factors explaining the marginalisation of these typical agreements that illustrate the role of State as international lender (1.1.2.).

1.1.1. Sovereign financial obligations and international law

The financial obligations of a State can arise from a treaty, conflict or action causing damages[78]. The origin of financial agreements governed by international law can be found in military practices. In case of armed conflict, the allied powers agreed on granting credits among them. This practice is evidenced by several agreements concluded in the 19th century. If

---

77 International agreements between States can take different forms and names, as Article 2, paragraph (1)(a) of the Vienna Convention on the Law of Treaties of 23 May 1969 confirmed and as the ICJ reaffirmed: "*'treaty' means an international agreement concluded between States in written form and governed by international law; whether embodied in a single instrument or in two or more related instruments and whatever its particular designation*" (Maritime Delimitation and Territorial Questions between Qatar and Bahrain, Jurisdiction and Admissibility, Judgment, I.C.J. Reports 1994, p.112). Thus the names agreement, convention, statement, memorandum of understanding, treaty, etc. can be used. The ICJ considers that "*terminology is not a determinant factor as to the character of an international agreement or understanding*" (South West Africa Cases (Ethiopia v. South Africa; Liberia v. South Africa), Preliminary Objections, Judgment of 21 December 1962: I.C.J. Reports 1962, p. 319).

78 Litigation can lead to an international recognition of State's debt, particularly in the case of compensation set by the International Court of Justice. For example, see the judgment of 19 June 2012 fixing a compensation owed by the Democratic Republic of the Congo to the Republic of Guinea (Ahmadou Sadio Diallo (Republic of Guinea v. Democratic Republic of the Congo), Compensation, Judgment, I.C.J. Reports 2012, p. 324). These tort obligations, although essential to the theory and practice of international law, have only secondary importance in relation to the financing of States and will not be analysed. Philippe Weckel, *Chronique de jurisprudence internationale*, 3, Revue générale de droit international public, 2012.

we look back even further in time, we can see that since the Napoleonic wars, the losing powers are commonly forced to compensate the winners in the form of war reparations. Article 7 of the Treaty of Frankfurt signed at the end of the Franco-Prussian war on 10 May 1871 illustrates this compensation[79]. The escalation of war reparations found its end in Europe at the Yalta conference in 1945. Still, the settlement of debts of the First and Second World Wars deeply marked international law.

At the end of the First World War, two types of debt were renegotiated: the German reparations[80] and the inter-allied debts. The German reparations were integrated in an international institutional framework that indicates the emergence of legal principles. The nature of these war debts is far from a contractual logic, as recalled in sections 231 and 232 of the Treaty of Versailles of 1919[81]. Section 233 instituted a commission of reparations aiming at setting the amount owed and the terms of settlement[82]. These amounts were paid to the Bank for International Settle-

79 Article 7: „*Die Zahlung von 500 Millionen soll erfolgen innerhalb der dreißig Tage, welche der Wiederherstellung der Autorität der Französischen Regierung in der Stadt Paris folgen werden. Eine Milliarde soll im Laufe des Jahres und eine halbe Milliarde am 1. Mai 1872. bezahlt werden. Die letzten drei Milliarden bleiben zahlbar am 2. März 1874, so wie es durch den Präliminar-Friedensvertrag vereinbart worden ist. Vom 2. März des laufenden Jahres an werden die Zinsen dieser drei Milliarden Franks jedes Jahr am 3. März mit 5 Prozent für das Jahr bezahlt werden*".

80 For more details, see Germain Calmette, Recueil de documents sur l'histoire de la question des réparations (1919-1921) (Alfred Costes. 1935). Richard Castillon, Les réparations allemandes : deux expériences – 1919-1932; 1945-1952, PUF, 1953, 200p.

81 Article 231: „*Die alliierten und assoziierten Regierungen erklären und Deutschland erkennt an, daß Deutschland und seine Verbündeten als Urheber aller Verluste und aller Schäden verantwortlich sind, welche die alliierten und assoziierten Regierungen und ihre Angehörigen infolge des ihnen durch den Angriff Deutschlands und seiner Verbündeten aufgezwungenen Krieges erlitten haben*". Article 232: „*Die alliierten und assoziierten Regierungen verlangen indessen und Deutschland übernimmt die Verpflichtung, daß alle Schäden wieder gutgemacht werden, die der Zivilbevölkerung jeder der alliierten und assoziierten Regierungen und ihrem Eigentum während der Zeit, da diese Macht sich im Kriegszustand mit Deutschland befand, durch den erwähnten Angriff zu Lande, zur See und aus der Luft zugefügt sind (...)*".

82 It was not until October 2010 that Germany finished to reimburse the amount imposed by the allies: Eric Chol & Romaric Godin, *L'Allemagne a remboursé ses dernières dettes datant de la 1ère Guerre mondiale*, La Tribune. See also Zur Au-

ments, established in 1930 specifically to handle these reparations[83]. After the Dawes Plan (1924-1929) and the Young Plan (1930-1932), the Weimar Republic was affected by hyperinflation. Therefore, a new agreement was concluded in 1932 in Lausanne to cancel ninety percent of the original amount of reparation[84]. We can deduce from these German reparations the existence of a concrete debt relief.

The inter-allied debts, entered into as part of a military alliance, consisted of the commitments made by the United States' Allies to finance the war against Germany[85]. While it was expected to be amicably settled, France and the United Kingdom questioned the legal nature of the agreement and actual repayment obligations[86]. These commitments had both a commercial and political characters as they were used to finance equipments. As such, these were bonds subscribed by individuals but were also part of a military alliance. Because of its limited capacity for repayment, France alleged that it would only be able to transfer the amounts that it would receive under the Treaty of Versailles[87]. However, the United States had not ratified the Treaty of Versailles. On behalf of the principle *pacta*

---

flösung der Bundeswertpapierverwaltung: Ein Rückblick auf die Schuldenverwaltung in Deutschland von 1820 bis 2006, pp. 91-99 (2006).

83 Benvenuto Griziotti, *La Banque des Règlements Internationaux*, IV Recueil des cours de l'Académie de droit international de La Haye, 1932.

84 Hans Ronde, Von Versailles bis Lausanne : der Verlauf der Reparationsverhandlungen nach dem ersten Weltkrieg, Kohlhammer, 1950, pp. 161-207.

85 Called *First Liberty Bonds*, these bonds were supervised by the US Treasury. Harry Gideonse, War Debts, Chicago, The University of Chicago Press, 1933, pp. 3-9, quoting Professor Taussig from Harvard University: "*The form of loan was chosen because it was the easiest and quickest way to get the thing done. Doubtless in the rush and pressure of the crisis no deliberate choice was made. It was all a matter of getting things done*".

86 For a thorough study of inter-allied debts, see Denise Artaud, La question des dettes interalliées et la reconstruction de l'Europe (1917-1929), Librairie Honoré Champion, 1978, 999p.

87 Roger Picard & Paul Hugon, Le problème des dettes inter-alliées – nécessité d'une révision, Librairie Plon, 1934, pp. 77-89 et pp. 154-162: « *Plus encore, la France posa deux questions éthique : comment les États-Unis pouvaient-ils se prévaloir de leurs droits alors que leurs citoyens se trouvèrent enrichis suite aux profits commerciaux réalisés grâce à la guerre tandis que la France avait essuyé de considérables pertes et ne disposait donc pas des ressources nécessaires pour s'acquitter de ses dettes? et comment ceux-ci pouvaient-ils s'attendre à ce que des crédits consentis dans une optique destructive et non constructive puissent effectivement être remboursés?* ».

sunt servanda, the compensation proposed by France was rejected. Finally, the payment was settled by bilateral negotiations. These negotiations resulted in the Mellon-Baldwin Agreement for the United Kingdom in June 1923 and the Mellon-Berenger Agreement for France in April 1926. These two agreements included a debt reduction[88]. Apart from this debt reduction, it is important to mention that before the end of the repayments, a moratorium suspended all payments due to the global economic situation following the 1929 stock market crash[89]. Thus, the settlement of inter-allied debts, similarly to the German reparations, included a debt reduction.

The legal treatment of reparations and war debts arose again at the end of the Second World War. This time, the right to compensation left a greater emphasis on the need to cooperate. Indeed, the establishment of the Marshall Plan in Europe initiates an economic cooperation. The Yalta Agreement signed in February 1945 granted a secondary focus on reparations, peace being the initial objective[90]. These objectives were discussed at the Potsdam Conference in July 1945. On this occasion, the concept of responsibility of the National Socialist government was placed outside of international law but recognised on the basis of the concept of *Gesunde Volksempfinden*[91]. The German territory was divided into four zones intended as direct charge for repairs. Yet, the search for new ways to manage war reparations led indirectly to the Cold War.

---

88 It is interesting to note that this agreement does not contain a covenant linking the reimbursement of French debts to the amounts received for the German reparations, but a clause offering the possibility to postpone repayment obligations in case of default of Germany. See statement of President Herbert Hoover: "*The definite settlement of the amounts to be paid in complete discharge of this debt is a cause for mutual satisfaction, removing as it does a question that has occasioned much controversy and debate*". "Statement on France's Ratification of the Mellon-Berenger Agreement for Settling Its War Debt", July 28, 1929. See online The American Presidency Project, Gerhard Peters and John T. Woolley.

89 Paris Club, Deuxième rapport annuel, 1932, pp. 21-25.

90 Article V.1. of the Protocol of Proceedings of the Yalta Conference: "*Germany must pay in kind of the losses caused by her to the Allied nations in the course of the war. Reparations are to be received in the first instance by those countries which have borne the main burden of the war, have suffered the heaviest losses and have organised victory over the enemy*".

91 See Angelika Kleinz, Individuum und Gemeinschaft in der juristischen Germanistik. Die Geschworenengerichte und das ‚gesunde Volksempfinden', Universitätsverlag C. Winter. 2001, 257p.

If these treaties on war reparations are now part of history, there is nevertheless a remnant of the end of conflict agreements in the Resolution 687 dated 3 April 1991 adopted by the Security Council. This resolution concerns the invasion of Kuwait by Iraq. As recognised in paragraph 16, Iraq is liable under international law for the "*unlawful invasion and occupation of Kuwait*"[92]. Moreover, the Eritrea-Ethiopia Claims Commission acknowledged on 17 August 2009 the responsibility of both States, deciding that a monetary compensation should be allocated to each one[93]. In such cases, international law has the relevant expertise to deal with such debt.

While armed conflicts represent the first cause of inter-state financial arrangements, it does not represent the role of State as lender in international financing. This is an important distinction that should be acknowledged during debt negotiations. In discussing a comprehensive overview of the diversity of international relations and agreements, we rather illustrate the role of State as lender to better understand in which context international public law is used in international financing agreements.

When a State signed a loan agreement with another State to be financed, the *instrumentum* is subjected to international public law and governed by the Vienna Convention of 1969 on the Law of Treaties. Its conclusion focuses on both the exercise and attributes of sovereignty, as the State is free to enter into a financial commitment. The State negotiates the terms, particularly the terms on loan currency and repayment. To that end, it is conventionally agreed that the national legislation, especially regarding exchange control, does not affect liabilities subjected to international

---

92 See resolution S/RES/687 (1991): "*16. Reaffirms that Iraq, without prejudice to the debts and obligations of Iraq arising prior to 2 August 1990, which will be addressed through the normal mechanisms, is liable under international law for any direct loss, damage, including environmental damage and the depletion of natural resources, or injury to foreign Governments, nationals and corporations, as a result of Iraq's unlawful invasion and occupation of Kuwait*".

93 Eritrea Ethiopia Claims Commission, Final award, Ethiopia's Damages Claims between the Federal Democratic Republic of Ethiopia and the State of Eritrea, The Hague, 17 August 2009. See Pierre D'Argent, *La Commission des réclamations Erythrée/Ethiopie : suite et fin*, 55 Annuaire français de droit international, 2009. See also, by the same author *Les réparations de guerre en droit international public – La responsabilité internationale des états à l'épreuve de la guerre*, Bruylant, 2002, 904p.

law[94]. Indeed, the State cannot use its legislative power to avoid its obligations under international law[95].

To ensure the validity of the agreement, international public law related to substantive and procedural principles is applied. In terms of procedural principles, international law and domestic law are jointly applied at the stage of conclusion and adoption. The State freely applies its domestic law, that is to say, it submits the treaty to the constitutional procedure effectively in force. For instance in France, after defining the negotiating mandate of its representatives, the signed text must be ratified by the executive power before entering into effect. International relations have changed the practice to shorten these formalities. Indeed, those so-called "long procedures" do not meet requirements in economic and financial areas. They are too slow. Therefore, shorter procedures are more generally applied, inspired by the executive agreements coming from the United States[96]. In all cases, the instrument is registered and published in accordance with Article 102 of the UN Charter.

In terms of substantive principles, the State incurs international responsibility if it does not comply with the obligations stipulated under Article 26 of the Vienna Convention. Article 26 enshrines the principle of respect of the rule *pacta sunt servanda*[97]. The breach of this commitment is usually taken into account in a classic clause that provides legal bases to further negotiations. Such clause usually specifies the use of diplomatic negotiations between States or the application of international law in case of discrepancy on the interpretation or application of the agreement. For instance:

---

94 "*From the standpoint of International Law and of the Court which is its organ, municipal laws are merely facts which express the will and constitute the activities of States, in the same manner as do legal decisions or administrative measures*" (Permanent Court of International Justice, 25 May 1926, Case concerning certain German Interests in Polish Upper Silesia (The Merits), Serie A, Judgment No. 7, p. 19).

95 Hugo J. Hahn, *Public foreign debts and international law*, 33 Law and state : a biannual coll. of recent German contributions to these fields (1986). However, it is important to mention that those executive agreements can be easily overturned.

96 Patrick Daillier, et al., Droit international public, 8ème édition, L.G.D.J., 2009, pp. 157-160.

97 Article 26. Pacta Sunt Servanda: "*Every treaty in force is binding upon the parties to it and must be performed by them in good faith*".

> "The competent authorities of the Contracting Parties concerned shall endeavour to resolve by negotiation any dispute relating to the interpretation or application of this Agreement."[98] (translation by the author).

Any dispute arising from these treaties shall be resolved in accordance with the dispute resolution procedures in international law:

> "The Contracting Parties agree that any dispute that arises in regard to the interpretation or execution of this Treaty that would not be resolved by direct negotiation shall be submitted to the procedures of international law."[99] (translation by the author).

Under these international agreements, one State is committed to provide a loan to another State through a credit institution. The debtor is responsible for the full repayment. These international financial agreements are often not concluded independently. They are part of a general framework negotiated between States[100]. These financial agreements constitute a sort of bilateral economic order, establishing an economic diplomacy based on the conclusion of financial agreements. For this reason, we refer to "political debt" to designate sovereign external debt.

1.1.2. Economic diplomacy through financial agreements

Financial agreements are a part of an economic diplomacy. Indeed, those financing can be used for investments, public aid, or various development projects. The background of these agreements is often characterised by political strategies. Diplomatic manoeuvres using financial agreements are at the heart of lender State's international action. Through those agreements,

---

98 Original version in French: « *Toute difficulté relative à l'interprétation ou à l'application du présent Accord sera réglée d'un commun accord entre les deux gouvernements.* » Accord entre la République française et la République populaire fédérative de Yougoslavie sur le règlement des créances financières françaises, 2 août 1958.

99 Original version in French: « *Les Hautes Parties contractantes conviennent que tout différend au sujet de l'interprétation ou de l'application du présent Traité qu'Elles ne seraient pas parvenues à résoudre par des négociations directes sera réglé suivant les procédures prévues par le droit international.* » Traité de coopération entre la République française et la République du Niger, 24 avril 1961.

100 Dominique Carreau & Patrick Julliard, Droit international économique, 5ème édition, Dalloz, 2013, pp. 1-57.

it seeks to ensure its political influence and encourages trade relations. These financial agreements are part of a logic focused on strengthening alliances between States. Such agreements are still present in modern negotiations[101]. For example, French bilateral negotiations frequently take place in the context of a general cooperation agreement, followed by financial and sectorial agreements[102]. Traditionally, these agreements offer an appeal privilege or directly assign missions to French companies[103].

These direct States' lending actions are concluded in terms of public development aid. They enable developing countries to finance either importations, implementations of projects or economic development programmes. Recent examples of agreements signed between Germany and partners worldwide illustrate this phenomenon[104]. For researchers, these bilateral loans are difficult to identify because their political dimension is particularly pronounced and their publication is rare. While sources of financing diversify, economic diplomacy does not lose its importance[105].

---

101 See the financial agreement between the Government of the French Republic and the Government of the Republic of Tajikistan signed in Dushanbe 8 August 2008, JORF n°0257 du 4 November 2008, p. 16759, text n° 27.

102 Laurence Badel, *Pour une histoire de la diplomatie économique de la France*, 2, Vingtième Siècle. Revue d'histoire (2006). See Laurence Badel, Diplomatie et grands contrats. L'État français et les marchés extérieurs au XXe siècle, Publications de la Sorbonne, 2010, 512p.

103 This explains the participation of 57 prospective founding members in the Asian Infrastructure Investment Bank: Claude Meyer, *Le succès éclatant, mais ambigu, de la Banque asiatique d'investissement pour les infrastructures*, Le Monde, 2015.

104 See for instance the financial cooperation agreement between the Government of the Federal Republic of Germany and the Government of the Republic of India, signed in New Delhi, 21 May 2008; the financial cooperation agreement between the Government of the Federal Republic of Germany and the Government of the Republic of Indonesia, signed in Jakarta, 3 May 2007; the financial cooperation agreement between the Government of the Federal Republic of Germany and the Government of the Republic of Uganda, signed in Kampala, 7 February 2008; and the financial cooperation agreement between the Government of the Federal Republic of Germany and the Government of the Republic of Rwanda, signed in Kigali, 14 October 2008.

105 Paris Club, Rapport annuel d'activité, (2013): « *[...] le prêt bilatéral officiel demeure un élément clé du paysage financier international. La nécessité d'une coordination entre souverains est donc plus importante aujourd'hui qu'elle ne l'a jamais été. Il est de la plus haute importance pour tous les acteurs souverains, créanciers comme débiteurs, de favoriser un dialogue ouvert et inclusif sur les questions de la dette, qui est le fondement de la prévention des crises de la dette*

State's action is diversified across financial projects. If interstate cooperation is still reflected in the form of agreements, development aid is often increasingly delegated to agencies or national government agencies whose mandate is at the heart of the strategy chosen by the State. When the United States is financially committed to assist a country, it is the United States Agency for International Development[106] that is responsible for putting in place the conditions for cooperation. In the United Kingdom, the Department for International Development[107], directly dependent on the government, is responsible for overseeing the development mission through the work of two agencies. In Germany, the joint action of the *Deutsche Gesellschaft für Internationale Zusammenarbeit* (GIZ) and the *Kreditanstalt für Wiederaufbau Entwicklungsbank* (KfW) allows a financial cooperation to developing countries on a bilateral basis. In France, the French Development Agency (AFD) is the financial institution of cooperation. The European Union also has its own bank: the European Investment Bank. Far from acting only bilaterally, these development agencies cooperate in joint projects. For example, the mutual recognition initiative developed in 2010 between the EIB, KfW and AFD facilitates collective funding. These agencies constitute a multilateralisation of development aid[108].

Under these conditions, instead of going through an international agreement followed by several treaties and private contracts, State agencies work directly with the final contracting party of the borrower States. Consequently, this delegation of power has a direct impact on the applicable law to loan agreements. These agreements are not concluded exclusively between subjects of international law. They are governed by domestic law[109]. In general, States use public entities to borrow. The political risk is

---

et de leur restructuration ordonnée, contribuant ainsi à une plus grande stabilité financière internationale. ».

106 United States Agency for International Development: see *U.S. Overseas Loans and Grants: Obligations and Loan Authorizations*, 1 July 1945 – 30 Sept. 2011.

107 See list of cases on the website of the Department for International Development.

108 Jun Inoue, *Internationally Shared Goals and National Governments: a Case Study of France and Financing for Development*, 38 Hitotsubashi Journal of Law and Politics (2010).

109 In the AFD model agreement for States loans available online, the applicable law is the French law. An arbitration clause submits disputes to the Arbitration Rules of the International Chamber of Commerce. Similarly, GIZ choses the application of German law.

substituted by the commercial risk. In that case, we consider that a private debt is created[110]. Private law is progressively governing agreements applicable to subjects of international law.

Apart from development aid, bilateral funding is also fundamental in times of crisis. Thus, the US Economic Support Fund uses economic assistance to convey the goals and strategies of the United States in countries considered to be of particular importance to foreign policy. The main beneficiaries of recent years are Afghanistan, Iraq, South Sudan, Egypt, Colombia and Jordan. Funding decisions are made by the State Department and the programmes are generally largely implemented by USAID[111].

From this overview of sovereign financial obligations governed by international law, it is possible to conclude that this activity is a useful tool for States. It may however be quantitatively small compared to other mechanisms that we will study later on in this dissertation.

We are now approaching a new aspect of the use of international public law. Parallel to the development of these financial agreements, did States implement a legal framework to manage potential risk?

1.2. The termination of bilateral financial agreements

States lending activity has not led to the implementation of mechanism to settle disputes arising from the breach of sovereign financial obligations (1.2.1.). Through international law, it is possible to terminate an international commitment, but the absence of applicable international rules complexifies such termination (1.2.2.). This negative answer augurs a similar situation concerning relations between the State and its private creditors.

---

110 Jean-Luc Herrenschmidt, *Présentation des euro-crédits*, *in* Les euro-crédits. Un instrument du système bancaire pour le financement international (Jean-Bernard Blaise, et al. eds., 1981), pp. 52-53.

111 State, Foreign Operations Appropriations: A Guide to Component Accounts, 2014, p. 10.

1.2.1. The absence of an international conventional framework

International law regarding States' sovereign indebtedness indicates that the State, as a creditor, is strongly committed to the principle *pacta sunt servanda*. This principle is the basis of international relations. It is correlated to the absence of higher jurisdiction. Any dispute related to international financial agreements is governed by international public law. However, due to the nature of diplomatic relations, this right is rarely used in practice for financial matters. In the absence of international mechanism, diplomacy is preferred. Arguments based on international public law have in such cases only known little success when presented in front of a judge.

In the nineteenth century, the losses on foreign securities increased. Consequently, investors seek for protection of their property rights under the guise of diplomatic protection. In response to these demands, in 1848, the British foreign minister Lord Palmerston wrote a circular in which he requested investors to face their responsibilities. He argued that investors had to take into account the risks as well as the benefits that may emerge from their operations[112]. This is the first known doctrine of diplomatic protection. It stated that the sovereign action is executed at the discretion of the British government. Diplomatic protection was by no means an obligation[113]. The intervention was based on internal considerations of the public interest[114]; indeed, in the event of non-repayment of debts to British individuals, the negative impact on the balance of payments would affect the interests of the nation and justify an intervention.

Repeatedly confirmed[115], this doctrine was also valid in France. The French Foreign Minister, Stephen Pichon, included the notion of good

112 See Strupp, L'intervention en matière financière, 1925.

113 "*It is for the British Government entirely a question of discretion and by no means a question of international rights, whether they should or should not make this matte the subject of diplomatic negotiation. And the decision of that question of discretion turns entirely on British and domestic considerations*".

114 "*The British Government has considered that the losses of imprudent men who have placed mistaken confidence in the good faith of foreign governments would prove a salutary warning to others, and would prevent any foreign loans being raised in Great Britain, except by governments of known good faith and ascertained solvency*".

115 In the United Kingdom by Lord Granville in 1871 and by Lord Salisbury in 1880: K.C, Le droit international et les obligations financières internationales qui naissent d'un contrat, 1923, p. 10-11. In the United States in 1885, see Karl Strupp, *L'intervention en matière financière*, see id.,1925.

faith to the Lord Palmerston' doctrine. Pichon explained that the use of diplomatic protection should depend on the behaviour of both contractual parties. The French government considered speculation or discriminatory treatment to determine bad faith. In case of discriminatory treatment or refusal to accept financial claims, the State's liability derived from the violation of international law[116].

Various diplomatic arrangements were realised in the form of international agreements concluded between States representing private creditors and the sovereign debtor. These arrangements established entities that interfered in internal affairs[117]. For instance, in the Ottoman Empire, European foreign powers instituted a commission of Ottoman debt. This commission had the power to manage the revenue of certain sectors of the Turkish economy[118]. In Greece, an international commission representing six European powers was established, including the United Kingdom, France and Italy[119]. This Commission was responsible for representing foreign debt holders. It received revenues from salt, oil and tobacco and managed public services. These historical examples demonstrate how European powers were interfering in the internal affairs of the sovereign debtors. In other cases, notably Tunisia in 1870, Egypt and Morocco in 1882, the establishment of protectorates resulted in the loss of political independence[120].

During the Congress of Berlin in 1878, the European powers discussed an elementary institutional mechanism to collect and allocate amounts owed by debtors. This was the beginning of concerted actions between

116 Christina Holmgren, La renégociation multilatérale des dettes : le Club de Paris au regard du droit international, Bruylant, 1998, pp. 17-21.

117 See for a discussion about countries where an institutional control mechanism was set up by European powers: Andréadès, Les contrôles financiers internationaux, 1924.

118 For the Ottoman Empire and the issue of colonisation through loans, see Murat Birdal, The political economy of Ottoman public debt: insolvency and European financial control in the late nineteenth century, Tauris Academic Studies, 2010, 256p.

119 Michael Waibel, *Echoes of History: The International Financial Commission in Greece, in* A Debt Restructuring Mechanism for Sovereigns. Do we need a legal procedure?, Christoph G. Paulus, 2014.

120 Kris James Mitchener & Marc D. Weidenmier, *Supersanctions and sovereign debt repayment*, 29, Journal of International Money and Finance, 2010.

creditor States, both institutionally and diplomatically. They sought to avoid any discrimination *vis-à-vis* their national debt holders.

In some cases, the non-repayment of loans led to the use of force. In the nineteenth century, European powers reacted to a set of conflicts (civil wars, territorial disputes, claims) via a military response[121]. In December 1902, the gunboat diplomacy culminated with the joint military intervention of the United Kingdom, Italy and Germany in Venezuela.

This intervention was formally criticised with regard to the concept of sovereignty. The Argentine Minister of Foreign Affairs, Luis Maria Drago, strongly condemned this intervention in a letter dated 29 December 1902[122]. Fearing a repetition of the Monroe Doctrine[123], he condemned this attack, considering it a violation of international law that intended to cover debts by force. He emphasised that military interventions were based on the strength of the debtor, since the belligerents were attacking the weak debtors while avoiding attack on Russia or Portugal[124].

Based on international law, the Argentine minister called for the establishment of international rules, procedures and alternative measures[125]. According to him, the sovereignty of the sovereign debtor forbids execution by force or territorial occupation. Without challenging the international courts or diplomatic protection, he urged that the sovereign debtor could determine the terms of its debts repayment according to its own interest.

---

121 Michael Tomz, Reputation and International Cooperation: Sovereign Debt Across Three Centuries, Princeton University Press, 2007, 328p.

122 For the complete text, see Strupp, L'intervention en matière financière, 1925, in particular pp. 53-94.

123 James Monroe, Seventh Annual Message, 2 December 1823: "*The occasion has been judged proper for asserting, as a principle in which the rights and interests of the United States are involved, that the American continents, by the free and independent condition which they have assumed and maintain, are henceforth not to be considered as subjects for future colonization by any European powers. [...] We owe it, therefore, to candor and to the amicable relations existing between the United States and those powers to declare that we should consider any attempt on their part to extend their system to any portion of this hemisphere as dangerous to our peace and safety*".

124 William H. Wynne, State Insolvency and Foreign Bondholders, Vol. II, p. 376.

125 Luis Maria Drago, *Les emprunts d'État et leurs rapports avec la politique internationale*, Revue générale de droit international public, 1907.

His doctrine gave rise to an international debate on the legitimacy of the use of force in the recovery of public debts[126]. It was discussed in 1902 during the Second Inter-American Conference[127]. Negotiations between Venezuela and the United States led to an arbitral sentence of the Permanent Court of Arbitration in The Hague. The Court granted preferential treatment to national creditors from Germany, the United Kingdom and Italy[128]. The problem of sovereign debt settlement had never been subjected to an international judicial decision before. Such an arbitral sentence may serve as a precedent in international law.

Accordingly, in 1906, the Third Pan-American Conference held in Rio de Janeiro focused on the issue of debt recovery. It was again discussed in 1907 at the Second Peace Conference at The Hague, following the proposition of the Latin American countries that participated for the first time[129]. The US representative General Porter submitted a project of a convention limiting the employment of force for recovery of contract debts. This so-called Drago-Porter Convention was signed in The Hague[130]. The first paragraph of its article 1 prohibits the use of force. However, the second paragraph authorises armed intervention in the event of refusal of an offer of arbitration or refusal to comply with an arbitration sentence[131]. The Convention is silent on several points: the legalisation of armed intervention in the event of the refusal of an offer of arbitration or

126 On 5 December 1905, US President Theodore Roosevelt confirms the thesis of the Argentine Minister. He warned European powers that no military action would be tolerated in America.

127 The Treaty of Arbitration for Pecuniary Claims was signed during this conference.

128 Permanent Court of Arbitration, Preferential treatment of claims of blockading powers against Venezuela – Germany, Great Britain and Italy v. Venezuela, Award of the Tribunal, The Hague, 22 February 1904. For a review of the sentence, see André Mallarmé, *L'arbitrage vénézuélien devant la Cour de la Haye (1903-1904)*, Revue générale de droit international public, 1906.

129 With the exception of Mexico.

130 The Convention respecting the limitation of the employment of force for recovery of contract debts of 18 October 1907 is the so-called Drago-Porter Convention, which entered into force in 26 January 1910.

131 "*The Contracting Powers agree not to have recourse to armed force for the recovery of contract debts claimed from the Government of one country by the Government of another country as being due to its nationals. This undertaking is, however, not applicable when the debtor State refuses or neglects to reply to an offer of arbitration, or, after accepting the offer, prevents any compromise from being agreed on, or, after the arbitration, fails to submit to the award*".

compliance with the arbitral sentence, the formerly submission of the arbitration to the sovereign debtor's national legal system[132]. Nevertheless, the Convention helped to internationalise discussions on debt settlement. Creditors States and debtors States discussed the terms of an international convention. 31 States ratified this convention[133]. Even if international law was not used to resolve financial disputes, this convention still constitutes the beginning of a formal internationalisation of settlement for sovereign debt. Arbitration became mandatory to replace any unilateral sovereign decision.

After the Drago-Porter Convention, the UN Charter prohibited the use of military force against a State in 1945. However, in case of insolvency that could threat international peace and security, the exception provisions of Chapter VII may justify an intervention of the United Nations[134].

As we noted, the only proposal of conventional framework dates from the early twentieth century. It was in the context of an armed dispute involving the settlement of debts. Through diplomatic protection, States engaged in a military intervention were strongly criticised by the international community. Diplomatic protection led to the internationalisation of private litigation.

1.2.2. The challenge of international financial treaties

As part of these international financial commitments, the use of diplomacy is preferred to the judicial practice. Indeed, the judicial practice is mainly used for debt instruments subjected to the application of private law. We

---

132 Out of the seven articles of the Convention, only the first one establishes a substantial principle.

133 Wolfgang Benedek, "Drago-Porter Convention (1907)", *Oxford Public International Law*, Max Planck Encyclopaedia of Public International Law, 2007.

134 Mathias Forteau, *Le défaut souverain en droit international public : les instruments de droit international public pour remédier à l'insolvabilité des États, in* Insolvabilité des États et dettes souveraines, Mathias Audit, 2011. After Iraq's occupation in 2003, the Security Council "*calls upon the international financial institutions to assist the people of Iraq in the reconstruction and development of their economy and to facilitate assistance by the broader donor community, and welcomes the readiness of creditors, including those of the Paris Club, to seek a solution to Iraq's sovereign debt problems*" (paragraph 15 of Resolution 1483 (2003) adopted by the UN Security Council on 22 May 2003).

therefore observe that international law is being limited to the establishment of agreements and to the resolution of conventional financial issues.

Even if the use of armed force is prohibited, no State can be forced to choose a dispute resolution system[135]. In principle, the use of diplomacy is privileged to handle a disagreement within the framework of international financial commitments. This method circumvents litigation. In general, most of the cases in this area are settled in a political negotiation[136].

Indeed, there is no international judicial practice on international financial treaty violations, not only because dispute resolution mechanisms are extrajudicial, but also because of the limited number of existing instruments. International jurisprudence on debt securities is related to the application of private law. For instance, the judgment of the Permanent Court of International Justice in 1929 regarding Serbian and Brazilian loans[137] concerns a contractual debt problem. The dispute does not involve directly international public law[138]. Similarly, the judgment of the International Court of Justice in 1957 regarding certain Norwegian loans relates to bonds issued by the Norwegian government and two banks, some of which were purchased by France[139].

Recourse to arguments based on international law is limited. The practice of sovereign financing through financial agreements is sparse. Therefore, the use of international law is restricted to a reduced number of in-

---

135 "*It is well established in international law that no State can, without its consent, be compelled to submit its disputes with other States either to mediation or to arbitration, or to any other kind of pacific settlement*" (Status of Eastern Carelia, P.C.I.J., Series B, No. 5).

136 Jean Combacau & Serge Sur, Droit international public, 10e éd., Montchrétien, 2012, pp. 562-569.

137 Case concerning the payment of various Serbian loans issued in France – Case concerning the payment in gold of the Brazilian Federal loans issued in France, Judgment No. 14/15, 1929, P.C.I.J., Series A/B, No. 20/21.

138 "*The Controversy submitted to the Court in the present case, on the contrary, solely relates to the existence and extent of certain obligations which the Serbian State is alleged to have assumed in respect of the holders of certain loans. It therefore is exclusively concerned with relations between the borrowing State and private persons, that is to Say, relations which are, in themselves, within the domain of municipal law*".

139 Case of certain Norwegian loans (France v. Norway), Judgment of 6 July 1957, Vol II. See Denis Lévy, *L'arrêt de la Cour Internationale de Justice dans l'affaire relative à certains emprunts norvégiens (France c. Norvège)*, 3, Annuaire français de droit international, 1957.

struments. Thus, even if error, fraud, corruption and coercion of the State's representatives are recognised in international law, they have not thrived on the termination of financial agreements. Other principles of international law, *ad impossibilitatem nemo tenetur*, *rebus sic stantibus* and *force majeure* may be used. However, under Article 62 of the Vienna Convention on the Law of Treaties relating to fundamental change of circumstances, the *rebus sic stantibus* clause provides only limited opportunities to avoid an international commitment; its application to debt suspensions or cancellations is restricted as the fundamental change of circumstances must be important.

Similarly, the notion of state of necessity has been invoked as a defence against claims directed to States in financial trouble. This practice began with the ICJ case concerning the Serbian loans[140] and is ongoing with several ICSID arbitrations[141]. This substantive defence is still unsatisfactory from the international public law side due to stringent application conditions. In fact, the State itself must not have contributed to the situation of necessity[142]. This requirement has limited the possibility of defaulted States to use this defence; a sovereign default is usually multi-causal and may include mistakes committed by the own government[143]. Furthermore, invoking the state of necessity has legal consequences that do not correspond to the objectives of a sovereign debt restructuring. Indeed, once the economic and financial situation is improved, the state of necessity disap-

---

140 This defence has also been used in the ICJ case concerning the Gabcikovo-Nagymaros project (Hungary/Slovakia), Judgment of 25 September 1997.

141 For a critique of the ICSID, see Stephan W. Schill, *International Investment Law and the Host State's Power to Handle Economic Crises*, 24, Journal of International Arbitration, 2007. Christina Binder, *Changed Circumstances in Investment Law: Interfaces between the Law of Treaties and the Law of State Responsibility with a Special Focus on the Argentine Crisis, in* International Investment Law for the 21st Century, Christina Binder, 2009. Michael Waibel, *Two Worlds of Necessity in ICSID Arbitration: CMS and LG&E*, 20 Leiden Journal of International Law, 2007.

142 Sarah Cassella, La nécessité en droit international: de l'état de nécessité aux situations de nécessité, Brill Academic Pub., 2011, pp. 27-82.

143 Armin von Bogdandy & Matthias Goldmann, *Sovereign Debt Restructurings as Exercises of International Public Authority: Towards a Decentralized Sovereign Insolvency Law, in* Sovereign Financing and International Law. The UNCTAD Principles on Responsible Sovereign Lending and Borrowing, Carlos Espósito, 2013.

pears. However, the success of any restructuring is based on a long-term programme.

Following a similar reasoning, the concept of odious debt can be relevant for the analysis. This concept was theorised in 1927 by a Russian professor of law who studied the Bolshevik repudiation of the tsarist debts[144]. By definition, three cumulative criteria were gathered to characterise an odious debt: the lack of consent of the debtor country's population, the lack of benefit of the debt for this population, and the fact that the creditor knew or should have been aware of these two conditions and of the odious nature of the debt[145]. Until now, no court formally recognised the notion[146]. However, this concept was debated during the Jubilee Debt Campaign in 2000 for the debt cancellation of developing countries[147] and after the fall of Saddam Hussein's regime in Iraq in 2003. Since then, legal strategies used to repudiate financial obligations increasingly refer to odious debt. More recently, Ecuador is an emblematic example if the development of this concept[148]. In July 2007, a public debt audit commission was created to evaluate the debts contracted between 1976 and 2006[149]. In 2008, the Ecuadorian President Rafael Correa announced that Ecuador would not reimburse some of the audited bonds as they are considered part of an odious debt.

Thus, international law does provide tools to challenge financial agreements. Diplomacy or extra-judicial solutions are preferred. This decline of international law is also present in the decrease of financial agreements in favour of a multilateralisation of sovereign financing.

---

144 « *Si un pouvoir despotique contracte une dette non pas pour les besoins et dans les intérêts de l'État, mais pour fortifier son régime despotique, pour réprimer la population qui le combat, etc., cette dette est odieuse pour la population de l'État entier* », see *Alexander Nahum SACK, Les effets des transformations des États sur leurs dettes publiques et autres obligations financières*, Recueil Sirey, 1927.

145 Sabine Michalowski, Unconstitutional Regimes and the Validity of Sovereign Debt: A Legal Perspective, Ashgate, 2007, 240p. Paulus, ZfaöRV 2008, 291 ff.

146 The Concept of Odious Debt: Some Considerations, 2008; Christiana Ochoa, *From Odious Debt to Odious Finance: Avoiding the Externalities of a Functional Odious Debt Doctrine*, 19, 1 Harvard International Law Journal, 2008.

147 Ann Pettifor, The coming First World debt crisis, Palgrave, 2006.

148 Adam Feibelman, *Ecuador's sovereign default: a Pyrrhic victory for odious debt?*, 25, Journal of International Banking Law and Regulation, 2010.

149 See the website of Comisión para la auditoría integral del crédito público (CA-IC): auditoriadeuda.org.ec.

2. Multilateral financial cooperation

International and regional institutions operate in almost all areas related to States activities. The development of international financial institutions leads to a multilateralisation of sovereign development policy by ensuring a transfer of financial resources. In this regard, the International Bank for Reconstruction and Development (IBRD), the International Development Association (IDA) and the International Monetary Fund (IMF) provide a wide range of financial assistance. Beyond their financing activities, these institutions have expanded their skills to specialise in sovereign debt management (2.1.). Development banks provide regionally a similar assistance via instruments used on the financial market (2.2.).

2.1. Multilateralisation of public financing

As previously analysed, international financial institutions provide a part of the sovereign financing through legal instruments governed by international law. They can provide a range of possibilities depending on the sovereign needs (2.1.1.). The financial agreements concluded depend on conditionality. We will highlight to what extend conditionality is the core notion of those financial operations (2.1.2.).

2.1.1. Sovereign financing by the World Bank and the International Monetary Fund

The purpose of the Bretton Woods institutions established in 1944 was to reorganise the international economic disorder due to the 1929 crisis and the Second World War. By stimulating the international capital flow, the IBRD and the IMF would, thanks to their complementary action[150], assist States that are facing cyclical or structural difficulties.

---

150 In both institutions' common areas, a concordat signed in 1989 that defines the scope of cooperation and joint actions framework are regularly revisited. See Enhancing Collaboration: Joint Management Action Plan (JMAP), 2007.

With nearly 10,000 treaties signed since its creation, the World Bank is considered the preferred operator to finance development projects[151]. On the one hand, the IBRD loans are intended for middle-income and solvent poor countries. On the other hand, the poorest countries benefit from favourable conditions via the IDA. Established in 1960, this institution grants loans and donations[152]. In practice, the World Bank staff is active both on IBRD and IDA projects.

The IBRD is an intergovernmental institution created by an international treaty. This development bank is structured like a corporation. Member States subscribes its shares. The released capital mainly manages its administrative activity, while its operational missions are financed from the financial markets. Indeed, the IBRD raises capital for its lending operations. The IBRD also plays an important intermediary role when capital markets are closed to developing countries; it issues bonds on the financial markets of developed countries to lend the money to developing countries.

The main activities of IBRD consist of granting loans to either a Member State of the Bank or a public or private entity established in the territory of a Member State. In this case, loans are systematically guaranteed by the State[153]. The IBRD *instrumentum* consists of two separate agreements: the general conditions for loans and the negotiated loan agreement.

---

151 The World Bank Group refers to all five international institutions that compose it: the International Bank for Reconstruction and Development, the International Development Association, the International Finance Corporation, the Multilateral Guarantee Investment Agency and the International Centre for Settlement of investment Disputes.

152 Article 1 of IDA Articles of Agreement: "*The purposes of the Association are to promote economic development, increase productivity and thus raise standards of living in the less-developed areas of the world included within the Association's membership, in particular* by providing finance to meet their important developmental requirements on terms which are more flexible and bear less heavily on the balance of payments than those of conventional loans, *thereby furthering the developmental objectives of the International Bank for Reconstruction and Development and supplementing its activities*" (we emphasise).

153 IBRD Articles of Agreement, Article III, Section 4: "*The Bank may guarantee, participate in, or make loans to any member or any political sub-division thereof and any business, industrial, and agricultural enterprise in the territories of a member, subject to the following conditions: (i) When the member in whose territories the project is located is not itself the borrower,* the member or the central bank or some comparable agency of the member which is acceptable to the Bank, fully guarantees the repayment of the principal and the payment of interest and other charges on the loan" (we emphasise). In case of loans to private entities that

According to Section 8.01 of the general conditions for loans[154], although these provisions do not refer to international law[155], loans concluded with States are international treaties governed by international law[156]. When a loan agreement is concluded with a non-sovereign borrower, it is also governed by international law due to the interdependence between the agreement and the sovereign guarantor[157]. These agreements are then registered within the United Nations Secretariat in accordance with Article 102 of the Charter.

These agreements can refer to loans, project agreements, endorsements or additional provisions[158]. They are concluded for specific investments, debt reduction, structural adjustment, financial supports, technical assistance, or reconstruction in case of emergency situations. These agreements include operations based on currencies, markets, and interest rates. The World Bank has always sought to expand its range of financing instruments. The World Bank has a real expertise and started to use swaps currency in the 1980s[159].

As for the IMF, it declined after the end of the Bretton Woods system in 1971. Its conditionality was strongly criticised. The current financial crisis

---

are not guaranteed by the States, the International Finance Corporation carried them out.

154 IBRD, General Conditions for Loans, 12 March 2012: Section 8.01. Enforceability "*The rights and obligations of the Bank and the Loan Parties under the Legal Agreements shall be valid and enforceable in accordance with their terms notwithstanding the law of any state or political subdivision thereof to the contrary*".

155 See the comparison with the EBRD: John W. Head, *Evolution of the governing law for loan agreements of the World Bank and other multilateral development banks*, Vol. 90, American journal of international law, 1996.

156 Aron Broches, *International Legal Aspects of the Operations of the World Bank*, 98, Recueil des cours de l'Académie de droit international de La Haye (1959); Why Treaties Matter? (2006).

157 The State remains the principal debtor. It is in fact a co-joint debtor and not a mere guarantor. Georges R. Delaume, *Issues of Applicable Law in the Context of the World Bank's Operations*, *in* The Transnational Law of International Commercial Transactions, Norbert Horn & Clive M. Schmitthoff, 1982.

158 Lester Nurick, *Certain Aspects of the Law and Practice of the International Bank for Reconstruction and Development*, *in* The Effectiveness of International Decisions, Stephen Myron Schwebel, 1971.

159 In its annual report of January 1987, the World Bank indicates how swaps had enabled it to reduce its debt cost from 6.60 % to 5.77 % on a total of $ 49 billion during the second half of 1986.

seems to offer it a new opportunity. The Fund has worked to become an expert in crisis management through its almost universal presence and its statutory objectives[160]. Since 2008, the Fund provided over USD 325 billion to fifty members[161], including Member States of the European Union[162]. Beyond a role of monetary guard, the purpose of the Fund is to facilitate the equilibrium of the sovereign balance of payments[163]. It grants financing to States, mostly in the form of currency purchases. Indeed, the Fund does not work like a conventional bank. A part of the Fund's capital is assigned to each member[164]. This distribution defines the number of votes attributed and the amount available. A State can access its quota depending on its participation[165]. Unlike IBRD loans, IMF financing is not for projects but aims at redressing the balance of payments. Therefore, such assistance can be requested for the reimbursement of international payments, including for sovereign debt[166].

IMF recommendations on economic policy shall legally be observed. A State shall imply those conditions to be granted a financing. After receiving the State's intent letter, the IMF provides the payments. Some financial products are specially designed for States, whether for their balance of payments or other particular requests[167].

---

160 188 countries are members of the IMF. Its objectives are "*to facilitate the expansion and balanced growth of international trade, and to contribute thereby to the promotion and maintenance of high levels of employment and real income and to the development of the productive resources of all members as primary objectives of economic policy*" (Article I (ii) of the Articles of Agreement of the International Monetary Fund).

161 IMF, "Lending by the IMF: the changing nature of lending", available on the IMF website.

162 Régis Bismuth, *L'assistance financière du FMI aux États membres de la zone euro : de l'inconcevable au conventionnel*, 4, Revue des affaires européennes, 2012.

163 IMF Articles of Agreement, Article I(v): "*To give confidence to members by making the general resources of the Fund temporarily available to them under adequate safeguards, thus providing them with opportunity to correct maladjustments in their balance of payments without resorting to measures destructive of national or international prosperity*".

164 The fourteenth general review of quotas in December 2010 has doubled the total of IMF quotas, increased to 476.8 billion SDRs.

165 Jean-Marc Sorel, *Sur quelques aspects juridiques de la conditionnalité du FMI et leurs conséquences*, 7, European Journal of International Law, 1996.

166 View data on the use of IMF credit (debt outstanding and disbursed, current US$) on the World Bank website.

167 See the IMF crisis loans policy on its website.

Unlike the IBRD, the IMF's resources are derived entirely from public sources[168]. Additional to State assessments and the exceptional sale of part of its gold stock[169], the Fund uses different borrowing mechanisms: Extended Fund Facility, Standing Borrowing Arrangements and Bilateral Borrowing. It can also issue bonds that can exclusively be subscribed by States[170]. Thus, States are always lenders; they contribute bilaterally, in the form of multilateral borrowing arrangements, or by purchasing bonds. This public origin is based on the objective of developing a better multilateral cooperation to eradicate poverty[171]. However, all these financing agreements are insufficient to finance States.

2.1.2. The objective of a sovereign debt management

International financial institutions are specialised in sovereign debt management. They do more than providing credits as they analyse public finances to find balancing mechanisms. They have sought to encourage the establishment of international standards of accounting and auditing.

While financial agreements are based on political and diplomatic strategies, multilateral funding responds directly to economic requirements. Disbursement conditions are the core of international public finance. They are derived from the role assigned to these international financial institutions in their Articles of Agreements. These disbursement conditions changed a lot due to various institutional reforms resulting from failures to eradicate poverty.

Article IV of the IMF Articles of Agreement ensures financial stability by stabilising the balance of payments. To accomplish this, the Fund applies a conditionality that imposes a financial management to the States. In case of crisis prevention, all sovereign debts are analysed. Thus, for least developed countries, balance of payments problems and development aid

168 Joseph Gold, *Borrowing by the International Monetary Fund from Nonofficial Lenders*, 20, The International Lawyer, 1986.

169 In September 2009, the Board of Directors approved the sale of 403 tonnes of gold. In December 2010, 222 tonnes were sold to official buyers. The product supports programs and special funding of the IMF.

170 In July 2009, the IMF Executive Board approved a legal framework for the issuance of bonds exclusively to the public sector.

171 Coopération pour le développement 2013 : Mettre fin à la pauvreté, 2013.

are linked[172]. All IMF and World Bank loans apply a conditionality that the State undertakes to perform. It can be a reduction in public spending and external borrowing, as well as inflation control and increase in bank supervision. Critics led both institutions to review their conditions and reform their lending policies[173].

Sovereign indebtedness is one of the areas of expertise of the Bretton Woods institutions. The World Bank has paid particular attention to sovereign over borrowing, while the IMF has a role of safeguard. Both institutions no longer have the monopoly on sovereign economic issues, partially due to political reasons[174]. However, the involvement of new public and private stakeholders that redeployed their activities in the field of sovereign debt management also explains the end of the Bretton Woods institutions' supremacy[175].

The IBRD is an execution institution that provides non-financial services and plays an expert role in the field of sovereign debt management. Debt of developing countries is one of its key themes. It focuses on this since the 1960s. While observing the increase of debt indicators, it concluded in the mid-1960s that the problems came from borrowing and reckless lending[176]. In 1985, it brought to light the unfortunate external borrowing resources[177]. The IBRD also participated jointly with the IMF in the Baker Plan in 1985, followed by the Brady Plan in 1989[178].

The World Bank' analysis of indebtedness and over-indebtedness led to the establishment of debt reduction programmes[179]. The overall assessment of financial stability supports the World Bank actions, assisted in this

---

172 James M. Boughton & Domenico Lombardi, Finance, Development, and the IMF, Oxford University Press, 2009, pp. 113-222.

173 John W. Head, Losing the global development war: a contemporary critique of the IMF, the World Bank, and the WTO, Martinus Nijhoff, 2008, 344p.

174 There are plenty of critics of the World Bank programs, see in particular the NGO "Bretton Woods Project".

175 Jean-Marc Sorel, *L'évolution des institutions financières internationales : entre redéploiement et fragilité, une restructuration systémique en chantier*, Annuaire Français de Droit International, 2006.

176 World Bank and IDA annual report 1964-1965, pp. 57-63.

177 World Bank annual report 1985, pp. 85-118.

178 Manuel Monteagudo, *The Debt Problem: The Baker Plan (1985) And The Brady Initiative (1989) – History, Experience, Practice And Prospects*, *in* La dette extérieure / The external debt (Martinus Nijhoff Publishers ed. 1995). See infra Chapter 2.

179 See infra Chapter 2.

task by the IMF. Thus, since 1999, an evaluation programme focuses on the strength of the financial sectors of member countries and the effectiveness of their regulation to identify strengths and weaknesses and propose recommendations. Additionally, the IMF and the IBRD, using their seniority and expertise, informally impose themselves as regional banks coordinators and operators of sovereign financing.

2.2. Regionalisation of sovereign financing

As we previously analysed, sovereign financing from agreements governed by international law declined. Private law contracts signed with State agencies are preferred (2.2.1.). Multilateral financing is moving towards regionalisation with private law contracts signed directly with the counterparts (2.2.2.).

2.2.1. Multiplication of public operators

The sovereign financing public network has become denser with the inclusion of regional banks as new operators.

Since the creation of the Bretton Woods institutions, the landscape of financial institutions has changed significantly with the establishment of regional development banks. Examples are the Inter-American Development Bank (IADB) established in 1959, the African Development Bank (AfDB) in 1964, the Asian Development Bank (ADB) in 1966 and the European Bank for Reconstruction and Development (EBRD) in 1991. The success of regional development banks is explained by the preference given to informalism as compared to formalism. Moreover, flexible financing mechanisms and loans are adapted to the international economic situation.

Loan agreements used by these banks usually follow the same structure. First, the project and the lenders relationship are described, followed by disbursement, fees, and repayment provisions. Then, clauses set out the measures taken in the event of breach of contract. The agreement also specifies the modalities of a change of circumstances. Finally, applicable law and dispute resolution clauses are inserted. The law applicable to the operations between these regional banks and sovereign borrowers is governed by international law. For example, the law applicable to loan operations between States and the AfDB is international law, in accordance to terms and conditions[180].

However, the domestic law of the sovereign borrower may be favoured. It depends on the entity negotiating the loan agreement. Thus regionalised financing takes place under a new dimension in the European Union; one witnesses not only a Europeanisation of projects but also a Europeanisation of development aid that result in joint financial commitments[181]. For instance, the European Investment Bank (EIB) operates in the EU and outside the EU, in particular under the framework of the Cotonou Agreement for the African, Caribbean and Pacific countries. This is accomplished on the basis of an explicit mandate from the EU Council for other countries. According to its Statutes, the EIB has the option of requesting a State guarantee[182]. These guarantees, which assist in the financing of transactions, are subjected to the same national laws than the main instrument of the loan.

Under their statutes, development banks cannot finance a full project. They are therefore working together. In the field of international financing, joint financing is occasional because it requires only one contract signed between several lenders. Moreover, each bank has its own characteristics in terms of credit risk, public procurement, anti-corruption standards, or environmental and social standards. Thus, parallel financing is

---

180 General Conditions Applicable to the African Development Bank Loan Agreements and Guarantee Agreements (Sovereign Entities), Section 10.05: "*The Law to be applied to the Loan Agreement and to the Guarantee Agreement shall be public international law, the sources of which shall be taken for these purposes to include: (a) any relevant treaty obligations that are binding reciprocally on the parties to these agreements; (b) the provisions of any international conventions and treaties (whether or not binding directly as such on the parties) generally recognized as having codified or ripened into binding rules of customary law applicable to states and to international financial institutions, as appropriate; (c) international custom, as evidence of a practice accepted as law; and (d) general principles of law applicable to multilateral economic development activities*".

181 Charlotte Bué, *La politique de développement de l'Union européenne : réformes et européanisation*, 53, Critique internationale, 2011.

182 Article 16.3 of EIB Statutes: "*When granting a loan to an undertaking or to a body other than a Member State, the Bank shall make the loan conditional either on a guarantee from the Member State in whose territory the investment will be carried out or on other adequate guarantees, or on the financial strength of the debtor*".

more frequent as it counts as many contracts as banks. Common terms are defined and each bank keeps its contractual specificities.

The development of co-financing leads to the application of private law into multilateral lending agreements previously subjected exclusively to international public law[183]. This choice of applicable law favoured by banks reflects the diversity of contracts, fora and borrowers. Above all, the source of financing rationalises the applicable law.

2.2.2. Entry of financial markets in international public finance

International financial institutions that borrow on the financial markets provide public financing. The result is the predominance of private law contracts. This transition is abrupt between multilateral public lenders signing international agreements and regionalisation working closely with financial markets.

The market's impact is so important that, to ensure an optimal refinancing, loan conditions are modified according to market conditions. This impact was highlighted by the financial crisis in 2008[184]. Sovereign bonds issued by developed countries have long been considered as a safe investment by international financial institutions. They used to buy those bonds to protect their resources from loss of value or imposed cut-offs. The financial crisis forces them to reconsider their investment policies.

International financial institutions benefit from a status under international law that allows privileged treatments. For instance, the IBRD requires in its general conditions the inclusion of a negative pledge, but there is no *pari passu*[185] considering that it has a preferred creditor status. In practice, this means that in case of difficulty to reimburse, the sovereign borrower ensures payments to international financial institutions, such as the IBRD, but commercial banks do not receive the same treatment.

This observation of the multilateral public financing leads us to the conclusion that only a small part of the overall sovereign financing is con-

---

183 Co-Financing Transactions between Multilateral Institutions and International Banks, 1992.

184 Rutsel Silvestre J. Martha, *International Organizations as Sovereign Bondholders: An Unexplored Dimension of the Sovereign Debt Crisis*, 10, Manchester Journal of International Economic Law, 2013.

185 For the definition of these terms, see infra Chapter 2.

cerned. The impact of the international financial institutions is more qualitative than quantitative. A more general questioning on sovereign debt management is needed to ensure its financial viability.

A new Bretton Woods is desired to solve the latest crisis. At its time, the Bretton Woods conference resulted from a remarkable concentration of power around a transnational expert consensus in wartime[186]. Such a situation is difficult to reproduce. Bretton Woods constitutes a symbol of a long negotiation process. This process was dominated by an American leadership and by the ideas of the economist Harry Dexter White[187]. At that time, the creation of a new international financial system followed a process: first a crisis of legitimacy, then a grey area of transition, later a constituent phase and finally an implementation period. Therefore, the conference was the result of a post-war system that may no longer be adequate or proper.

The objective today is not to rebuild an economic order after the collapse of the world economy in the 1930s. In a decentralised world, it is now time to find a way to reconcile multilateral global economy with aspirations for greater national autonomy.

*

This chapter assumes that the State is financed from other legal entities under the application of international public law. Nevertheless, this initial presentation is quickly overtaken by the complexity of financing. States also delegate their lending activities to agencies that use private law in their financing agreements. Following the same logic, we questioned the implementation of a technique of external public debt settlement. Yet, international law application provides no legal solution.

From this brief overview on international public finance, we identify that the legal framework is evolving.

---

186 Eric Helleiner, *A Bretton Woods moment? The 2007-2008 crisis and the future of global finance*, 86, International Affairs, 2010.

187 White was interested in the creditor States' needs, while Keynes focused on debtors States. See Rosa M. Lastra, *The Role of the International Monetary Fund, in* Sovereign Debt Management (Rosa M. Lastra & Lee Buchheit eds., 2014).

CHAPTER 2. Generalisation of Private Contracts through Banking Intermediation

Commercial banks represented in the late 1970s the primary sovereign financing source due to the creation of the Eurocurrency market. This market benefited from the recycling of petrodollars after the oil crises of 1973 and 1979. Between 1970 and 1989, more than a half of credits came from commercial banks[188], while financing from international financial institutions decreased to only one fifth of all sovereign debt[189]. With the development of the activity of commercial banks in the Eurocurrency market, an international private monetary and financial system has emerged[190]. Sovereign indebtedness was privatised at two levels: the lending commercial banks were now private operators (1.) and debt instruments were contracts subjected to private law (2.).

1. Banking intermediation in sovereign financing

The privatisation of sovereign debts support is characterised by rules imposed by private creditors in opposition to the privileges of sovereign status (1.1.) This bank intermediation is central for sovereign indebtedness (1.2.).

1.1. Private creditors versus sovereignty

The debt to private creditors has historically been a matter of monarchs in an environment characterised by war, colonial financing, public debt and

188 McGovern, Different Market Windows on Sovereign Debt: Private-sector Credit from the 1980s to the present, 2003, pp. 69-91.

189 In 1977, the proportion of sovereign debt was divided as follows: 23 % from other States, 21 % from international financial institutions, 51 % from banks and financial markets and 5 % from suppliers and other sources private. In early 1970, suppliers like General Electric, Siemens and Mitsubishi provided medium-term loans to public enterprises or public infrastructure projects. See figures published on the World Bank website.

190 Luis Jorge Garay Salamanca, *The 1980s Crisis in Syndicated Bank Lending to Sovereigns and the Sequence of Mechanisms to Fix it, in* Overcoming Developing Country Debt Crises (Barry Herman, et al. eds., 2010).

decline of empires (1.1.1.). We will focus on historical sovereign debt operations to consider current issues through a special hindsight on the particularities of sovereign borrowers (1.1.2.).

1.1.1. Historical intervention of private creditors

The history of sovereign debt has historically been a matter of monarchs[191]. From King Solomon of Israel in the ninth century BC to Queen Elizabeth I in the sixteenth century, monarchs concluded financial transactions. They were representing the State[192] and often considered as the defaulters[193]. Consequently, the maturity of a debt was calculated based on the estimated life of the monarch. Creditors took insurance with jewellery, part of tax revenue or even land appropriation[194]. Yet the contractual commitments of sovereign monarchs were replaced by suspension of interests' payment, currency depreciation or diversion of securities.

The nature of monarchs' loans evolved in the nineteenth century with the reduction of monarchical power and the growing importance of parliaments. The term public debt helped to distinguish the debt contracted by the State from the notion of sovereign debt, the latter being neither contin-

---

191 See the distinction between public debt and royal debt: Philippe Hamon, *Les dettes du roi de France (fin du Moyen-Âge – XVIe siècle) : une dette "publique"?*, *in* La dette publique dans l'histoire (Jean Andreau, et al. eds., 2006).

192 K.C, Le droit international et les obligations financières internationales qui naissent d'un contrat, 1923, pp. 298-302.

193 « *[Le Roi] ne payoit ni les financiers ni les négocians desquels il avait emprunté des sommes considérables; il leur accordoit des surséances, ou des sauf-conduits contre leurs créanciers, autre désordre qui dérangeoit et troubloit encore extrêmement le commerce, dans lequel on ne voyait presque plus d'argent. Le crédit qui supplée à l'argent comptant était entièrement évanoui. Le discrédit était universel, le commerce anéanti, la consommation affoiblie de moitié, la culture des terres négligées; les ouvriers passoient à l'étranger.* » Nicolas Dutot, Réflexions politiques sur les finances et le commerce, Paris, 1738, cited by Jean-Marie Thiveaud, *Crises et cycles, visions de l'histoire, du temps et de l'argent : Essai de généalogie d'un modèle épistémologique*, 26, Revue d'économie financière (1993), pp. 391-416.

194 Gaston Jèze, *La garantie des emprunts publics d'État*, *in* Recueil des cours de l'Académie de droit international de La Haye (1925), pp. 155-156.

uous nor sustainable nor transferable[195]. Public debt was intended as a contract with a collective interest purpose. It was marked by a legal nature involving States' responsibility facing default with creditors[196].

State creditors were often wealthy owners who lent at their own risk to monarchs. They were fundamental intermediaries in the collection of savings and the financing of the economy. The first modern banks emerged in Italian cities at the beginning of the Renaissance. They were not only financing merchants' international trade activities, but also State's activities[197]. The most famous bank is the Medici Bank created in 1397 in Florence by Giovanni de Medici associated with the banker Vieri Di Cambio. This bank granted loans to several European powers[198]. Other Italian banks such as Bardi Bank and Peruzzi Bank flourished in the fourteenth century. They went bankrupt towards the end of the same century when Edward III of England defaulted as a result of the Hundred Years War against France[199].

Examples of bankruptcy resulting from non-repayment of sovereign debt are numerous. Throughout the reign of Philip II of Spain, from 1556 to 1598, the monarch was permanently in war. He borrowed to finance ships and soldiers by issuing bonds from major bankers. After suspending the payment of his debts four times, some of its creditors went bankrupt[200]. Another illustration of the close relationship between debt

---

195 The distinction was quickly made: "*the public credit is national, not personal, so it depends upon no thing or person, no man or body of men, but upon the government, that is, the queen and parliament*" according to Daniel Defoe, An Essay Upon Public Credit: Being an Enquiry how the Publick Credit Comes to Depend Upon the Change of the Ministry, Or the Dissolutions of Parliaments, and Whether it Does So Or No? § 54 (W. Baynes, Paternoster-Row, J.S. Jordan. 1710), pp. 22-23.

196 K.C, Le droit international et les obligations financières internationales qui naissent d'un contrat, 1923, pp. 5 and foll.

197 François Crouzet, A history of the European Economy, 1000-2000 (University of Virginia Press. 2001), pp. 38-50.

198 Raymond de Roover, The Rise and Decline of the Medici Bank, 1397-1494 (Harvard University Press. 1963), pp. 194-224.

199 Richard Scott Carnell, et al., The Law of Banking and Financial Institutions (Aspen. 2009), pp. 739-771.

200 The Fugger family was a German family of bankers that went bankrupt in 1607 after the succession of defaults of the King of Spain. See Mauricio Drelichman & Hans-Joachim Voth, *Lending to the borrower from Hell: Debt and Default in the Age of Philip II*, 121, The Economic Journal (2011). Anne Dubet, *Les rois d'Es-*

and imperial wars is the reign of the Bourbons between 1760 and 1810. The Spanish State had risen up relentlessly heavy taxes in its Latin American colonies, particularly in Mexico, to finance his empire and face incessant wars[201].

Beyond the financial aspect, the political dimension of the allocation of private funds is invariably present in the history of sovereign debt. For example, in 1898 the US government was developing strategies for granting loans to governments through private banks[202]. This dollars diplomacy was decisive between 1904 and 1929. It was associated with the emergence of investment bank. Issues related to the interests of private banks over public goals arose, especially when private entities were appointed in the governments' list of borrowers to ensure control of public finances[203].

1.1.2. Sovereign debtors through economic prism

Since sovereign debt has always been characterised by the involvement of private creditors, the peculiarity of this kind of debt is not new. However sovereign immunity and economic consequences have changed. When debts are incurred in the form of a loan agreement governed by the debtor domestic law, creditors are subjected to the sovereign debtor's legislation. The State may unilaterally revoke internal monetary laws, manipulate national currency, divert affected guarantee or reduce debt service[204].

The State is a particular debtor due to this sovereign power. Its sovereignty is reflected in its monetary, legislative and regulatory power. The State can freely proscribe rules of applicable law in its territory by its

---

pagne et leurs créanciers. Une collaboration conflictuelle, in La dette publique dans l'histoire (Jean Andreau, et al. eds., 2006).

201 Carlos Marichal, Bankruptcy of Empire: Mexican Silver and the Wars between Spain, Britain and France, 1760-1810 (Cambridge University Press. 2007), pp. 48-80.

202 Emily S. Rosenberg, Financial Missionaries to the World: The Politics and Culture of Dollar Diplomacy, 1900–1930 (Gilbert M. Joseph & Emily S. Rosenberg eds. 2004), pp. 219-261.

203 Faisal Z. Ahmed, et al., *Lawsuits and Empire: on the Enforcement of Sovereign Debt in Latin America*, 73 Law and Contemporary Problems (2010).

204 For a complete overview on the different means used, see Edwin Borchard, State Insolvency and Foreign Bondholders: General Principles § 1 (Yale University Press. 1951), pp. 123-142.

courts. A notorious example of the eighteenth century illustrates the use of this legislative and regulatory power. The French Revolution is indeed partially due to the catastrophic finances of Louis XVI. The Constituent Assembly proclaimed in June 1789 its formal commitment to reimburse debt. This commitment was recalled in the Constitutions of 1791 and 1793[205]. However, such promise was short-lived and the bankruptcy law of *deux tiers du 8 nivôse an VI* recognised a right to default to the French State[206].

International law recognises monetary power as a sovereign prerogative[207]. Therefore, any State is theoretically free to devalue its currency, change its rates, inject liquidity and thus influence the actual amount of its loans denominated in domestic currency. Such a change in the value of money can lead to substantial reduction of the debt burden. However, this monetary sovereignty has created obligations[208]. At the end of the Second World War, rules limiting State's monetary practices were adopted. They changed the concepts of currency and State power. More recently, the construction of the European Monetary System radically changed the sovereign intervention on debt. Article 127 of the Treaty on the Functioning of the European Union has in fact de-sovereignised currency. This article blocked State debt intervention by prohibiting modification of the euro

---

205 Title V, Article 2, § 1 of the French Constitution of 3 September 1791: "*Under no pretext may the funds necessary for the payment of the national debt and the civil list be refused or suspended*". Article 122 of the French Constitution of 24 June 1793: "*The constitution guarantees to all Frenchmen equality, liberty, security, property, the public debt, free exercise of religion, general instruction, public assistance, absolute liberty of the press, the right of petition, the right to hold popular assemblies, and the enjoyment of all the rights of man*".

206 Gaston Jèze, *Les défaillances d'État, in* Recueil des cours de l'Académie de droit international de La Haye (1935), pp. 387-388.

207 "*It is indeed a generally accepted principle that a State is entitled to regulate its own currency*" Case concerning the payment of various Serbian loans issued in France – Case concerning the payment in gold of the Brazilian Federal loans issued in France, Judgment No. 14/15, 1929, P.C.I.J., Series A/B, No. 20/21. *See also* Charter of Economic Rights and Duties of States, Resolution 3281 (XXIX) adopted by the General Assembly of the United Nations on 12 December 1974, Article 1: "*Every State has the sovereign and inalienable right to choose its economic system*".

208 Geneviève Bastid-Burdeau, *Les euro-crédits. L'apparition des contrôles étatiques, in* Les euro-crédits, un instrument du système bancaire pour le financement international (Jean-Bernard Blaise, et al. eds., 1981).

currency[209]. In addition, monetary sovereignty does not imply that a State holds sovereign authority over its debt when debt instruments are not governed by public law.

The generalisation of the use of private capital has changed the prerogatives of States immunity. Jurisdictional immunities are contractually taken into account. A distinction should be made between the State acting in its sovereign functions – *jure imperii* – or acting as a commercial entity – *jure gestionis*. Sovereign borrowers highlighted that such contract is an act of sovereignty, whereas creditors considered it part of an economic management policy. But many commitments were not honoured on the basis of this distinction, until the financing was considered an act of *jure gestionis*[210]. In 1976, the United States allowed civil proceedings against the State in case of an act *jure gestionis*. More recently, the United Nations Convention on States Jurisdictional Immunities and Their Property acknowledged on 2 December 2004 that immunity for acts *jure gestionis* is relative[211].

By inserting contractual terms, the State waives its jurisdictional immunity. Thus, such waiver is systematically inserted in sovereign debt contracts. For instance, the selected courts hearing disputes related to Eurocredits may be those of the borrower's country, the guarantor's country or the country whose law governs the agreement. In the first case, the courts

---

209 Mathias Audit, *La dette souveraine appelle-t-elle un statut juridique particulier?*, *in* Insolvabilité des États et dettes souveraines (Mathias Audit ed. 2011).

210 In the United States, general exceptions to State's sovereign immunity are presented in the Foreign Sovereign Immunity Act of 21 October 1976: "*(a) A foreign state shall not be immune from the Jurisdiction of courts of the United States or of the States in any case: (1) in which the foreign state has waived its immunity either explicitly or by implication, notwithstanding any withdrawal of the waiver which the foreign state may purport to effect except in accordance with the terms of the waiver; (2) in which the action is based upon a commercial activity carried on in the United States by the foreign state; or upon an act performed in the United States in connection with a commercial activity of the foreign state elsewhere; or upon an act outside the territory of the United States in connection with a commercial activity of the foreign state elsewhere and that act causes a direct effect in the United States*".

211 Article 7 Express consent to exercise of jurisdiction: "*1. A State cannot invoke immunity from jurisdiction in a proceeding before a court of another State with regard to a matter or case if it has expressly consented to the exercise of jurisdiction by the court with regard to the matter or case: (a) by international agreement; (b) in a written contract*".

are those from the place where the assets are located. In the last case, the courts can be located in other countries.

A waiver of enforcement, as stated in this example, usually completes this sovereign immunity clause:

> "The State irrevocably waives all immunity to which it may be or become entitled in relation to this agreement including immunity form jurisdiction, enforcement, prejudgment proceedings, injunctions and all other legal proceedings and relief, both in respect of itself and its assets, and consents to such proceedings and relief"[212].

This immunity from execution applies to all assets with a commercial purpose. Yet it is relieved when public powers are at stake, as they involve the protection of international law[213]. These contractual clauses remain limited because of the lack of a credible debt-restructuring plan. Current practice easily allows a contractor to sue a State. However, when it comes to seizing property, success is uncertain[214].

As we analysed it, private creditors, particularly commercial banks, have always been involved in the financing of sovereign debt. However, the financing has been characterised by an unprecedented development of international syndicated loans. European banks gathered in international banking syndicates established these international loans based on Eurocurrency.

1.2. Emergence of international syndicated loan markets

The widespread use of internationally syndicated loans has allowed commercial banks to finance sovereign debt (1.2.1.). However, sovereign defaults in Latin American States have brought the system into question due to the fear of systemic risk affecting all US banks (1.2.2.).

---

212 Robert R. Wood, International Loans, Bonds, Guarantees, Legal Opinions (Sweet & Maxwell 2 ed. 2007), pp. 141-142.

213 Rivier, Droit international public, 2012, pp. 262-270.

214 Jonathan Eaton & Mark Gersovitz, *Debt with Potential Repudiation: Theoretical and Empirical Analysis*, 48 The Review of Economic Studies (1981). "*Unless the governments of private creditors are willing to coerce debtor governments not repaying loans, there is no explicit mechanism deterring a government from repudiating its external debts*".

1.2.1. International syndicated loans financing sovereign debt

International syndicated loans were widely used in the domestic market[215] of the United States. Originated from Germany before the First World War[216], internationally syndicated loans[217] had widespread in the 1960s. So did the Eurocredits. Both have formed the main vehicle of sovereign financing in the 1970s and transformed the interactions between State, economy and markets in sovereign financing.

International syndication brings together two or more credit institutions located in different countries[218]. Syndicated loans contracts are not an invention of the Euromarkets but thrived due to its rise[219]. It is a banking technique used to satisfy State's multiple financial requirements. Loans can be used to finance a rebalancing of payments, to increase the reserves of the central bank or to support large exportations. During the 1970s, Eurocredits were international finance's main instrument.

The development of syndicated loans can be divided into several phases[220]. During the 1970s, sovereign borrowers mainly used Eurocredits. They have been internationalised to face an increasing demand of funding

---

215 Benjamin Lemoine, *Dette publique, débat confisqué. Pourquoi la France emprunte-t-elle sur les marchés ?*, La Vie des idées (2013).

216 Philipp R. Wood, The Law and Practice of International Finance (Sweet & Maxwell. 2008), p. 256.

217 Syndication refers to the situation in which several banks grant together a loan to a borrower based on common conditions under a single agreement. In practice, a leader negotiates the terms of the loan. An agent is appointed among those banks to manage the syndication. See Jean-Bernard Blaise & Philippe Fouchard, *La valeur juridique de la syndication, in* Les euro-crédits, un instrument du système bancaire pour le financement international (Jean-Bernard Blaise, et al. eds., 1981, pp. 155-241.

218 Steven A. Dennis & Donald J. Mullineaux, *Syndicated loans*, 9, Journal of Financial Intermediation (2000).

219 « *Les [...] crédits internationaux n'ont pas débuté avec la crise du pétrole de 1974, et la nécessité de recycler des montants importants d'excédents pétroliers. Mais la crise a considérablement accentué le rôle des banques sur le plan international.* » in Archives de la Banque de France, 1489200304-15, G. Aubanel, Directeur-adjoint de première classe, Direction Générale des Services Etrangers, « Le rôle des banques dans le recyclage des capitaux », 29 avril 1980, cited by Carlo Edoardo Altamura, *La banque dans la tourmente : les banques françaises, la Banque de France et le marché de l'euro-dollar*, 19, Histoire@Politique (2013).

220 The syndicated loan market: structure, development and implications, (2004).

to develop large economic projects[221]. Eurocredits provide an amount much higher than what a bank can generate. During this period, States and public companies financed their deficits without assistance or control of international financial institutions. Between 1971 and 1982, developing countries in Africa, Asia and especially Latin America were mainly financed through medium-term syndicated loans.

In parallel to the increase of international liquidity due to the surplus of petrodollars, the overall amount of debt exploded[222]. Loans offered by commercial banks provided an opportunity for diversification of funding sources. This diversification improved the position of sovereign borrowers *vis-à-vis* international financial institutions. It also facilitated the reduction of official lenders' power that imposed a conditionality considered too restrictive or inappropriate.

Given the lack of funding from international financial institutions or States for major economic projects, bank syndication was considered an appropriate technique. Indeed, syndication is mainly based on a practice that intends to disaggregate risks and consolidates the largest number of banks to grant loans or increase opportunities for complex operations[223]. Consequently, private banks had in a way supplanted multilateral institutions and governments[224]. Thus, public debt of developing countries relied on banks due to the insufficiency of official lenders. The political will to break up the conditionality imposed by international financial institutions also explains this dependence to banks.

Within such financial globalisation, the trend is to concentrate banks in parallel with the diversification of their activities. Two banking models structurally exist. On one side, there is the universal bank offering all financial services, from deposit to capital markets' operations, including insurance services. On the other, there are specialised banks: commercial and investment banks. In the former, banks are responsible for collecting savings and managing money deposits. In the later, they do not receive deposits and finance their activity via the financial markets. The latest are

221 Philippe Fouchard, *Financement et endettement internationaux : aspects juridiques*, Vol. 635 Journées de la Société de législation comparée (1986).

222 Kunifert Raffer, Debt Management for Development. Protection of the Poor and the Millennium Development Goals (Edward Elgar. 2010), pp. 7-8.

223 Herrenschmidt, Présentation des euro-crédits, 1981, pp. 46-47.

224 Emmanuelle Bouretz, Crédits syndiqués. Transfert et partage du risque entre banques (La Revue Banque. 2005), pp. 25-58.

dedicated to manage portfolios of large companies, investment on capital markets and financing transactions. The separation of these banking activities is still debated in the United States, even if the Glass-Steagall Act of 1933 ratified such separation[225]. Clinton's government repealed the text and allowed the use of deposits for markets investment[226]. In Europe, the United Kingdom and France are currently addressing separation of banking activities, while Germany partially retains the universal banking model[227].

The banking structure complicates the calculation and understanding of debt. We will now analyse the restructuring of the debt in the 1980s as it involved a large part of syndicated loans[228].

1.2.2. Collapse of US banks and fear of contagion

The default of Mexico in 1982 abruptly slowed the development of this debt technique, marking the end of the expansion of Eurobank loans. To save the banking system, the US government implemented successive programmes through securitisation.

In 1982, syndicated loans amounted nearly $ 46 billion dollars. In August of that year, Mexico suspended payments on its sovereign debt, fol-

---

225 Banking Act of 1933 (Pub.L. 73-66, 48 Stat. 162, Enacted June 16, 1933): "*SECTION 21 Receipt of deposits by securities companies and other non-banking institutions. It is made unlawful, after a period of one year: (1) For any person, corporation or other organization engaged in the issue, underwriting or selling of securities to receive deposits subject to check or to repayment upon presentation of a pass book or certificate. (2) For any person, corporation or organization, other than a financial institution or private banker subject to examination and regulation under State or Federal law, to receive deposits subject to check or to repayment upon presentation of a pass book or certificate, unless such person, corporation or organization shall submit to periodic examination by the Comptroller of the Currency or Federal reserve bank and shall make periodic reports of condition in the same manner and at the same time as is required of national banks*".

226 Dimitris N. Chorafas, Sovereign Debt Crisis: The New Normal and the Newly Poor (Palgrave Macmillan Studies in Banking and Financial Institutions ed., Palgrave Macmillan. 2011), pp. 41-58.

227 Laurence Scialom, Économie bancaire (La découverte 4e éd. ed. 2013), pp. 25-40. The recent enacted *Trennbankengesetzt* is changing the situation.

228 Rieffel, Restructuring Sovereign Debt: The Case for Ad Hoc Machinery, 2003, pp. 122 and foll.

lowed by Brazil, Argentina, Venezuela and the Philippines. Initially, a rescue plan was settled to assure Mexico's reimbursement during the summer 1982. Then, under the influence of the US government, commercial banks had to continue lending to indebted States with lower interest rates, while suspending the application of negative pledge and sharing clauses[229]. The objective was to prevent the break-up of the US banking system.

Consequently, US banks sought to preserve the facial value of loans to save time and constitute reserves. Therefore, the indebted States were forced to repay their loans in full. In parallel, the US government acted to ensure guarantees to indebted States through the Export-Import Bank of the United States. In 1983, the capital of the IMF increased to assist operators affected by the defaults. In October 1985, a programme for sustainable growth was set up at the initiative of the US Secretary of Treasury, James Baker[230]. It was based on a bank-oriented strategy to transform assets into loan swap.

In 1989, the Brady Plan was implemented to reduce debt. The objective was to save banks and the financial system. The financial techniques of the menu approach options derived from the Baker Plan, which had introduced in April 1987. Debt buy-back, debt-equity swaps and exit bonds helped to restructure the Mexican debt in the form of Brady Bonds. Between 1989 and 1995, the introduction of these Brady Bonds allowed banks to remove loans after the sovereign debt crises in Latin America.

Sovereign syndicated loans decreased during the 1980s. In 1985, they amounted $ 9 billion dollars. Since the 1990s, these loans have mainly been used for businesses and decreased to nearly $ 1.3 billion dollars in 2003. Nevertheless, this banking technology remains an indispensable tool for the financing of major projects and restructuring.

Commercial bank loans to governments generally exist in two forms: bank loans with a single credit institution or syndicated loans. Single credit institutions are used for small amounts with shorter terms, while syndicated loans involve a group of banks for higher amount. These syndicated loans were the dominant form of medium-term loans in the 1970s. This variety of banks allowed financing all kinds of projects. By granting these

229 Edgar Nassar Guier, *La position du Gouvernement américain en matière d'endettement des États : du plan Baker à l'initiative Brady*, *in* La dette extérieure / The external debt (Martinus Nijhoff Publishers ed. 1995).

230 Manuel Monteagudo, *The Debt Problem: The Baker Plan (1985) And The Brady Initiative (1989) – History, Experience, Practice And Prospects*, id.

loans to States, banks increased significantly their income while avoiding risks. This was partly based on the idea of the creditworthiness of borrowers[231].

2. *Privatisation of sovereign debt*

The international Eurocredits market has emerged from sovereign financing. This construction has led to the privatisation of sovereign debt holders (2.1.). Moreover, this market was developed in the margins of State's rules. We will analyse how States adopted a *laissez-faire* attitude towards rules and structures of bank syndication (2.2.).

2.1. Private law and sovereign debt

Commercial banks have established a special legal instrument to recycle petrodollar, taking into account the nature of the liquidity, borrowers' risks and characteristics of the international operation (2.1.1.). This instrument has been standardised by the banking industry (2.1.2.). Such standardisation integrated safeguard clauses (2.1.3.).

2.1.1. Contractual standardisation

The practice of Eurocredits has led to the establishment of a *sui generis* contractual scheme that leaves little room for negotiations. We consider that these contracts are similar to quasi-contracts due to the lack of negotiation.

Loan, contractual liability and legal obligations are particular to each domestic law. Therefore, no local instrument has matched bank requests. Since the late 1960s, law firms specialised in drafting eurocredit contracts have developed a contractual instrument following a similar *sui generis* framework. Indeed, the homogeneous community of professional bankers share the same interest: securing the market without competing against

---

231 Rieffel, Restructuring Sovereign Debt: The Case for Ad Hoc Machinery, 2003, pp. 107 and foll.

each other through the insertion of legal clauses. The legal engineering developed by the banking syndicate has standardised contracts.

Commercial banks ensure an intermediary function by receiving deposits in Eurocurrency. Eurobanks are around thirty active banking institutions from ten countries. However, about two hundred other banks participate. Therefore, syndications often gather the same leaders and the same agents, while the same law firms draft contracts. This is why we consider that there is a standardisation of the Eurocurrency market[232]. Indeed, the banking syndicate brings out some kind of *lex mercatoria* on debt matters and on bond issues. The parties may also decide to refer to that *lex mercatoria* as the applicable law[233].

This standardisation of practices is encouraged by the work of the Loan Market Association (LMA). The LMA, inspired by the practices of Anglo-American law, systematises and regularly publishes the best market practices in standard contracts[234]. The drafting tends to be similar. The contractual requirements are intended to protect banks as much as possible against sovereign borrowers' risks. The terms of these standard contracts reflect the problems of risk and hazard. Although contractual freedom is required, it is often restricted as negotiations are limited to financial conditions of the operation.

Although a financing operation is adapted to the situation and the risk involved, the flexibility to negotiate these quasi-contracts is limited. Indeed, banks are intermediaries between the Eurocurrency market – where they are refinanced – and end-borrowers. Therefore, loans reflect conditions imposed on them when they are refinanced. Subsequently, Eurocredits' conditions are indirectly set by the Eurocurrency market. Refinancing requirements are contractually stipulated and integrate a factor of instability.

Many features of these contracts display the absence of negotiation. Disbursement conditions can hardly be negotiated. They constitute the last

232 Standardisation refers to a practical and a repeated use of general and objective legal provisions which are not subordinated to the stipulations of each contract. See Blaise & Fouchard, La valeur juridique de la syndication, 1981, pp. 210 and foll.

233 Klaus Peter Berger, The creeping codification of the lex mercatoria (Kluwer Law International. 1999).

234 Marc Favéro, *La standardisation contractuelle, enjeu de pouvoir entre les parties et de compétition entre systèmes juridiques*, n° 3, Revue Trimestrielle de Droit Commercial (2003).

step before disbursement and banks use these conditions to verify that all due diligence and contractual obligations are respected. These warranties include powers of attorney, deeds of covenant, or registrations of business. Conflict of laws and validity of transactions are also covered in the legal opinion requested by the banking syndicate.

States are generally able to negotiate financial terms of credit when their solvency is not in doubt, depending on economic situation, liquidity and debt ratios. Following the Brady Plan, loans' contractual terms have evolved to include the actual default risk of sovereign borrowers. These clauses are intended to protect banks. Banks seek for general guarantees in granted loans. However, far from classic guarantees, States count a large number of clauses that intend to protect them without creating securities[235]. Representations and warranties, covenants, guarantee, and events of default are conventionally found in such contracts. In the case of a sovereign borrower, they are adapted to its characteristics and specific risks. They can be analysed in terms of a potential lawsuit or arbitration, especially in the context of negotiations between lender and borrower. When borrowers are States, negotiation can also depend on the law. International public law is rarely applied because banking operators consider it too vague and unpredictable. However, Brazil, Venezuela and Colombia often denied the application of English law on behalf of the Calvo Doctrine[236].

This standardisation of practices comes from different professional associations. For example, in the area of derivatives, the International Swaps and Derivatives Association (ISDA) brought together businesses and banks to analyse the contractual provisions privileged by each one of them. It promotes the election of English and American laws. It organises training sessions in various European capitals to ensure its implementation in the field. In response, the European Banking Federation competed with a European master agreement. This model contract developed in cooperation with the European Savings Bank Group and the European Association of Cooperative Banks competes with the ISLA model to:

235 Camille Jauffret-Spinosi & Claude Kelly, *La protection contractuelle*, *in* Les euro-crédits, un instrument du système bancaire pour le financement international (Jean-Bernard Blaise, et al. eds., 1981).

236 Philip R. Wood, *Essay: Sovereign Syndicated Bank Credits in the 1970s*, 73 Law and Contemporary Problems (2010).

> "consolidate into a single set of harmonised documents, various master agreements used within the euro zone and certain neighbouring countries, particularly for repurchase transactions and securities lending. At the same time, parties to the EMA are able to choose the applicable law, jurisdiction and contractual language and can take into account various specific national legal requirements"[237].

The objective is to be able to choose an applicable local law.

2.1.2. Managing sovereign risk

For banks, sovereign risk is defined as the probability that a State will refuse to comply with its financial obligations. It refers to a commercial risk, a monetary risk and a legal risk up to expropriation.

Sovereign risk can refer to legal, monetary and financial issues that creditors usually take into account when they finance. The first risk refers to State's currency intervention. The second comes from the issuance of new rules to modify the body of standards applied to loan contracts. The third problem is divided into interest rate risk and credit risk. Indeed, the bond value fluctuates based on interest rates. Some mechanisms allow investors to consider these fluctuations in order to ensure a profitability comparable to the new issued bonds. These sensitivity coefficients establish the portfolio risk objective and help select securities[238]. Credit risk is the default possibility of the bond issuer. To compensate it, a higher rate is applied depending on the risk level borne incurred by the investor. The spread indicates the risk level of investor's credit that is periodically reviewed by rating agencies[239].

In the case of syndication, commercial banks share common goals and a pecuniary advantage through a commission. This commission remunerates risk taken. Syndication is primarily based on the need to mitigate risk, the main risk being borrower's default. Contractually, each bank supports its

---

237 Banking Federation of the European Union, European Savings Bank Group, European Association of cooperative Banks, "Master Agreement for Financial Transactions – Explanatory Memorandum", 2004, available on EBF website.

238 Bertrand Jacquillat, et al., Marchés financiers : Gestion de portefeuille et des risques (5ème édition ed., Dunod. 2009).

239 These agencies use a rating scale in form of letters. The highest rating is AAA, and AA and A, etc. From BB, bonds are risky and may not be held by certain institutional investors.

obligations and hazards related to its part of loan[240]. When signing the contract, each bank is separately committed for the amount corresponding to its contribution, as shown in the following standard clause:

> "Each of the Lenders severally agrees, on the terms and conditions of this Agreement, to make loans to the Borrower at such Lender's office specified in Schedule [1] […] up to an aggregate amount not exceeding the amount of such Lender's Commitment".

The total Eurocredit consists of the addition of individual loans granted by each syndicated bank. Thus, there is not a single bond assembling several debtors. On the contrary, creditors join separate obligations towards a single debtor. A typical definition at the beginning of the contract specifies:

> "Contribution means, as to each of the Banks, the principal sum specified against its name at the end of this Agreement which such Bank is obliged to contribute, subject to the terms hereof, to the Loan Commitment under Clause [X] or, as the context requires, the portion of such principal sum advanced by a Bank and outstanding for the time being".

A proportional distribution of repayments is set up between the syndicated banks to dilute the risk. If at the time of reimbursement each bank manages its loan, the principle of proportionality then reappears due to the reinstallation of systemic risk and permeability between banks[241]. It is also contractually possible to further transfer commercial risk, as illustrated in this standard clause:

> "This Agreement shall be binding upon and shall inure to the borrower, the Banks, the Agent and their respective successors and assigns, except that the Borrower may not assign its rights or obligations hereunder without the prior consent of all the Banks.
> Each of the Banks shall have the right to sell to other financial institutions participations of any amount and any maturity in its loans hereunder. Each of the Banks may transfer all or any part of its rights and obligations under this Agreement to any branch or affiliate (provided that such transfer does not as of the time therefor result in any increased cost to the Borrower hereunder) and the Borrower agrees to execute any documentation necessary to effect any such transfer, but no Bank may otherwise assign its rights or obligations, hereunder unless the Borrower shall have first given to the Agent its written

240 Christian Puhr, *L'organisation bancaire des euro-crédits : la pratique de la syndication, la constitution du syndicat, in* Les euro-crédits. Un instrument du système bancaire pour le financement international (Jean-Bernard Blaise, et al. eds., 1981), pp. 107-114.

241 Blaise & Fouchard, La valeur juridique de la syndication, 1981, pp. 155-184.

consent to such assignment (which consent shall not be unreasonably withheld)".

The diversity of the applicable law and loan terms can cause changes in legal circumstances. In practice, the loan agreement organises both credit relations and banking syndication in a sole agreement, contrary to bond issues. In that case, there is a contractual instrument for each step of the operation[242]. This unique instrument suffers from an inflation of words: each situation requires an express stipulation[243]. Indeed, one must distinguish Eurobanks practice from sovereign borrowers that remain diverse and fundamentally dispersed. In addition, each particular crisis, specifically the latest one in Europe, increases the size of contractual clauses[244].

The only *instrumentum* legally tying all signatory members generally stipulates a clause of applicable law, since the determination of the law applicable to an international contract is complex. When it comes to a sovereign borrower, these international private law contracts can theoretically be governed by the application of the law of the sovereign borrower. However, contractual practice demonstrates that the law applicable to Eurocredit conventions is generally either the law of England or the State of New York, both applied by international syndicated banks. When the leader of the syndicate is French, French law applies.

2.1.3. Standard covenants applied to sovereign borrowers

Covenants from Anglo-American law are standard safeguard clauses inserted in banking contracts. They allow an acceleration of repayment in case of contractual breach. The concept of debt is important in two con-

---

242 See the model of Eurocredit contract between a state and a banking syndicate, Annex IV Jean-Bernard Blaise, et al., Les euro-crédits, un instrument du système bancaire pour le financement international (Librairies techniques. 1981), pp. 725-741.

243 "*The parties are considered, unless otherwise agreed, to have impliedly made applicable to their contract or its formation a usage of which the parties knew or ought to have known and which in international trade is widely known to, and regularly observed by, parties to contracts of the type involved in the particular trade concerned*". Article 9 (2) of the United Nations Convention on Contracts for the International Sale of Goods, adopted on 11 April 1980.

244 Mohamed A. El-Erian, *Lorsque la dette souveraine des économies occidentales devient risquée*, 16, Revue de la Stabilité Financière (2012).

tractual clauses: event of default and cross default. Far from competing, bank operators integrate the same clauses, as the practice followed in times of crisis demonstrated.

Safeguard clauses are alike in financing agreements. To take into account all commitments of the borrower towards credit institutions, the negative pledge is inserted. It is limited to external debt. This clause forbids the creation of securities in favour of other creditors. The negative pledge below is used in a World Bank loan[245]:

> "*if any lien shall be created on any public assets* (as hereinafter defined), as security for any External Debt, which will or might result in a priority for the benefit of the creditor of said External Debt in the allocation, realization or distribution of foreign exchange, *such lien shall*, unless the Bank shall otherwise agree, ipso facto and at no cost to the Bank, *equally and ratably secure the principal of, and interest and other charges on, the Loan, and the Guarantor*, in creating or permitting the creation of such lien, shall make express provision to that effect; provided, however, that, if for any constitutional or other legal reason such provision cannot be made with respect to any lien created on assets of any of its political or administrative subdivisions, the Guarantor shall promptly and at no cost to the Bank secure the principal of, and interest and other charges on, the Loan by an equivalent lien on other public assets satisfactory to the Bank" (we emphasise).

The latter is often associated with a cross-default clause[246]. This clause aims at detecting a default on financial obligation outside of the signed contract. Failure to fulfil such obligations constitutes an event of default. The frequent insertion of this provision reflects the lenders' desire to act as soon as another lender has a legal right of action. A control line is negotiated. However, for a sovereign borrower, cross-default mechanism may be difficult to delimit. Indeed, the repayment capacity of such a borrower is not only a function of its commitments. Therefore, the clause is modified when the borrower is a State or a public institution. It may include, in addition to the usual case of default, the issuance of a debt moratorium or the occurrence of political, economic, financial or military events of certain gravity.

---

245 Treaty Series, Volume 2153, I-37591, pp. 215-216.

246 Example of a cross-default clause for corporate borrowers: "*The borrower fails to pay other financial debt when due, or other financial debt is accelerated, or a commitment to lend other financial debt is cancelled, an event of default occurs in relation to any other financial debt, or collateral security for financial debt becomes enforceable or is enforced*" see Wood, International Loans, Bonds, Guarantees, Legal Opinions. 2007, pp. 103-104.

Another interesting clause is the *pari passu* clause. It is intended to ensure equal treatment among creditors of the banking union[247]. The *pari passu* clause integrated in the guarantees of the Peruvian State for international borrowing through Banco de la Nación and Banco Popular de Perú was[248]:

> "The obligations of the Guarantor hereunder do rank and *will rank at least pari passu in priority of payment with all other External Indebtedness of the Guarantor*, and interest thereon" (we emphasise).

Since the Elliott cases against Peru, the interpretation of this clause is unclear[249].

Combined with the creation of securities and guarantees on first applications, Eurobanks are implementing a contractual arsenal to recall their loans. The penalty for failure in the event of default is automatically triggered in case of conventionally prescribed failures.

These clauses can sometimes seem superfluous when applied to sovereign counterparty. They are nevertheless necessary for the creditor. It may, even if the borrower is not technically in default, terminate prematurely on the basis of these contractual provisions, regardless of the economic situation of the borrower. This contractual conformity is strengthened by crises.

The economic crises, combined with tensions in the interbank markets and the uncertainties resulting from the liquidity crisis, are changing these clauses in one direction. The borrower must now endorse more legal risks, while the bank retains the power of modifying clauses, almost unilaterally. Two clauses are inserted: the clause for exceptional circumstances and the clause on change of applicable law. They allow the borrower to bear any legislative or tax risk by integrating the time factor in the contract. The reintegration of material adverse change clauses is part of this trend. Initially inserted after 9/11, these clauses allow the termination of lenders' commitment in the event of adverse events affecting borrowers' business,

---

247 Georges Affaki, *Du sens des mots et du bon sens : de la bonne interprétation de la clause pari passu*, *in* Mélanges en l'honneur de Philippe le Tourneau (2007), p. 2.

248 William W. Bratton, *Pari Passu and a Distressed Sovereign's Rational Choices*, Vol. 53, Emory Law Journal (2004).

249 Egalité de traitement ou hiérarchie entre créanciers? (2013).

finances, patrimony, or in case of serious disruption of financial markets[250].

2.2. Disintermediation of debt market

The sovereign debt system remains fundamentally managed by private operators (2.2.1.). However, commercial banks no longer hold the majority of debt products (2.2.2.).

2.2.1. A debt system organised by private operators

While commercial banks still dominate the primary market, investment banks have reinforced their status since the 1990s. They are taking advantage of banking integration and debt market disintermediation.

In the syndicated loan market, there are coalitions of international lender banks. As previously analysed, this concentration of interest is characterised by the insertion of restrictive safeguard clauses encouraging credit discipline. These clauses prevent default debtors to access refunding in the banking market[251]. This strategy encourages contractual renegotiation by increasing the cost of a potential default for borrowers.

In addition, there is a contractual cooperation between syndicated banks in case of default through sharing clauses. The aim of these clauses is to discourage individual actions. Indeed, a sharing clause stipulates that each syndicated bank shall share with the other members of the syndicate any payment received by means of settlement or legal procedure[252]. Sharing

---

250 Thierry Arachtingi, *Les contrats de crédit syndiqué à l'épreuve de la crise*, 62, Revue Lamy Droit Civil (2009); Richard Marty, *Les clauses d'événements défavorables et de déchéance du terme dans les contrats de financement. Material adverse change and Cross default clauses*, n° 12, La Semaine Juridique Entreprise et Affaires (2011).

251 Bankim Chadha, et al., *The Evolving Role of Banks in International Capital Flows*, *in* International Capital Flows (Martin Feldstein ed. 1999).

252 See the jurisprudence of Allied Bank syndicate of 39 banks that lent to Costa Rica – see in particular the sharing clause: *Allied Bank International v Banco Credito Agricola de Cartago* 566 F. Supp. 1440 (S.D.N.Y.) 1983; 733 F. 2d 23 (2d cir. 1984); No. 83-7714 (2d cir. 18 March 1985).

potential profit obtained through courts does not prevent the use of litigation[253]. However, it is a discouraging factor against holdout strategies[254].

Depending on good or bad times, the nature of credit has been changing. Banks acted as last resort lenders in times of crisis. In 1980, syndicated bank loans accounted for more than a half of the international sovereign debt. These loans gradually declined, while the volume of international bonds increased. Yet during the 1994 Mexican crisis, the fear of a contagion effect contracted the bond market. Developing countries used syndicated loans. When the crisis was solved, developing countries returned to the bond market. This banking change highlights certain flexibility. In case of difficulties on the financial markets, banking funding may be available.

Thus, history conveys that bank financing follows a logical cycle. Although there is a quantitative decline in bank loans, competition in the financial market through the issuance of bonds is not irrevocable. The alternation between these debt products follows the evolution of debt crises that recur, regularly echoing the Kondratieff Cycles or Kuznets Cycles, as described by economics[255]. In times of growth, these international obligations and financial products have increased.

2.2.2. Disintermediation of debt products

The change of debt composition is a result of the explosion in the secondary public debt market and the appearance of banking conglomerates.

There are several factors behind the growth of the sovereign bond market. The erosion of the quality of bank assets following the 1982 crisis and the explosion of debt securitisation on the aftermarket clarify how States and public entities were able to obtain cheaper financing in the market. In 1980, the developing countries were still dependent on bank loans. How-

253 Michael Waibel, Sovereign Defaults Before International Courts and Tribunals (Cambridge University Press. 2011).

254 Lee C. Buchheit, *The Sharing Clause as a Litigation Shield*, 9, International Financial Law Review (1990).

255 See Christian Suter, Debt Cycles in the World- Economy: Foreign Loans, Financial. Crises, and Debt Settlements, 1820-1990 (1992).

ever, the generalisation of bond in the 1990s explains that bonds have become their primary source of financing, such as developed countries[256].

Syndicated loans are more easily traded on secondary market. This is due to the standardisation of legal documentation by professional associations. All participants on the secondary marker are usually interested in sovereign products: market-makers (major commercial and investment banks), traders (commercial and investment banks specialised in distressed debts) and occasional investors (insurance companies and institutional investors).

Banking mergers and acquisitions result from the development of investment banks and secondary market. Due to the market liberalisation, the cyclical deterioration in bank balance sheets and the prevalence of bonds over loans, banks have become purveyors of derivatives. International finance has been transformed. Banks continue to play an important role but with a double function of investors and advisors, through two activities: deposit banking and investment.

Unlike commercial banks that can rely on their retail banking business to structure their lending, investment banks finance themselves exclusively via the financial markets. The new financing techniques, initiated in the United States and introduced in other markets, offer a variety of products on the secondary market[257].

*

Since the mid-1960s, multinational banks have contributed to build a private monetary system where Eurocredits are central. A transnational hybrid monetary system has been gradually formed[258]. The public monetary system, consisting of interstate rules and principles, is exposed to the private Euromarkets monetary system organised by private rules.

Far from seeing a decline of sovereignty, we consider that borrowing is a sovereign privilege. This privilege depends on internal economic and fiscal policy. Reimbursement is a contractual obligation for the sovereign

256 In 1980, 55 % of developing countries financing came from bank loans, while in 1993 40 % of funding are bonds.

257 For example: currency swap, high yield, book-building, green shoe. See Michel Fleuriet, *La localisation des activités de banque d'investissement*, 57 Revue d'économie financière (2000).

258 Dominique Carreau, *Monnaie*, Dalloz – Répertoire de droit international (2009).

borrower. From the international law point of view, there is no general trend of applicable rules due to the variety of debt instruments.

This second chapter on private debt highlighted the way creditors and applicable law have been privatised, as well as how this affects borrowing sovereignty. When the State borrows, it is subject to market rules, which dictate the insertion of contractual clauses.

Title I. CONCLUSION

Sovereign debt is at the intersection between private agreement and sovereignty[259]. Our analysis developed in this first part is based on the notion of privatisation. This privatisation is indeed affecting both the use of private law and the transfer to the private sector[260].

Sources of international law are provided by States for States. However, international economic law is not limited to inter-state law as private entities are directly affected by measures taken by States. The international financial system is not yet structured with a system of law. Therefore, debt instruments are subjected to domestic laws.

Banking intermediation, by its action on debt contracts, illustrates the globalised law phenomenon by the convergence of conditions aligning standards and dominant models. Debt supports are modelled, standardised, and imposed on operators if they are proven to be safe and effective.

259 Strupp, L'intervention en matière financière. 1925.

260 Régis Bismuth, *La privatisation des organisations internationales*, *in* Droit des organisations internationales (Evelyne Lagrange & Jean-Marc Sorel eds., 2013).

Title II. IMPACT OF DEBT PRIVATISATION ON SOVEREIGN DEBT DEFAULT

Finance markets exert unprecedented influence on States indebtedness. States no longer borrow with specific benefits based on sovereign privileges. There has been a reorganisation of sovereignty in the matter of sovereign funding. Practices and debt products have changed. The dematerialisation of debt instruments and the professionalisation of debt markets lead to a privatisation of sovereign debt. This privatisation levels the borrowing conditions by applying market rules (Chapter 3).

The financialisation of sovereign debt is at the heart of the reinforcement of sovereign debt crises. The following medical analogy perfectly adapts to the economic phenomenon in general, and in particular to sovereign debt. The circulation of wealth and money, which refers to the blood system, is transposed to the social organisation[261]. It follows a repeated cycle such as the one described in the mid-nineteenth century by the economist Clément Juglar[262]. Thus, the financialisation of sovereign debt and the widespread of market practices are key factors on the multiplication and extension of recent sovereign debt crises (Chapter 4).

---

261 « *[C']est cette avancée et cette rentrée continuelle des capitaux qui constituent ce qu'on doit appeler circulation de l'argent, cette circulation utile et féconde qui anime tous les travaux de la société, qui entretient le mouvement et la circulation du sang dans le corps animal. Car, si par un dérangement quelconque dans l'ordre des dépenses des différentes classes de la société, les entrepreneurs cessent de retirer leurs avances avec le profit qu'ils ont droit d'en attendre, il est évident qu'ils seront obligés de diminuer leurs entreprises, que la somme du travail, celle des consommations des fruits de la terre, celle des productions et du revenu seront d'autant diminuées, que la pauvreté prendra la place de la richesse et que les simples ouvriers, cessant de trouver de l'emploi, tomberont dans la plus profonde misère.* » in Anne-Robert-Jacques Turgot, Réflexions sur la formation et la distribution des richesses (1766), pp. 161-163.

262 « *Les crises, comme les maladies, paraissent une des conditions de l'existence des sociétés où le commerce et l'industrie dominent. On peut les prévoir, les adoucir, s'en préserver jusqu'à un certain point, faciliter la reprise des affaires; mais les supprimer, c'est ce qui jusqu'ici, malgré les combinaisons les plus diverses, n'a été donné à personne.* » Clément Juglar, Des crises commerciales et de leur retour périodique en France, en Angleterre et aux États-Unis (1862).

CHAPTER 3. Financialisation of Sovereign Debt and Imposition of Market Practices

In the 1990s, finance has globalised through the deregulation of capital markets and the opening of national financial systems. This general de-compartmentalisation, under the impetus of financial liberalisation, has significantly altered public debt. Supply and demand of debt were directly confronted. Financial markets have become central to State, both in terms of funding and refinancing.

Moreover, sovereign debt is intrinsically linked to financial industry: sovereign debt is central for market development because it constitutes a reference for the pricing of other products (1.).

Sovereign debt is still based on intermediation. This intermediation has significantly changed. Financial markets serve both as intermediary and as regulator. Indeed, finance is based on a standardisation of securities (2.).

1. Internationalisation of sovereign debt instruments

States seek rapid and low-priced finance predominantly through the use of bond. These bonds are issued on currency and capital markets (1.1.). On the derivatives market, sovereign debt instruments expanded. This is a characteristic of the internationalisation of sovereign debt instruments (1.2.).

1.1. Configuration of sovereign debt primary market

States can use loans from syndicated commercial banks or bonds issued on financial markets to finance projects[263]. Bonds have always been used, even before becoming current's most known practice (1.1.1.). Launch of bond varies from one State to another, but all can be found on the markets. Sovereign debtors behave like any financial operator in order to receive the best conditions at lower cost (1.1.2.).

---

263 Wood, International Loans, Bonds, Guarantees, Legal Opinions, 2007, pp. 193-209.

1.1.1. Predominance of sovereign debt bonds

Financial engineering is as old as the will to spread the sources of sovereign debt. Thus, offering debt products to new investors is a common technique used to diversify the types of lenders. Using individual savings to manage sovereign debt is an option. This option allows the State to reduce its dependence on bankers. However, risk is not reduced. The French example of the 'tontine' in the seventeenth century provides an interesting historical perspective. Denmark released its first tontine in 1653, the United Provinces of the Netherlands several between 1670 and 1680[264]. France took its time to implement the 'Royal Tontine'. This sovereign debt product, defended by Lorenzo de Tonti against Mazarin, is an annuity bond issued by the State. This bond categorises its subscribers by age group[265], reverting the debt to the survivors[266]. In 1653, the decree to implement it was rejected by the Parliament for reasons of cost and technicality[267].

The modified project was issued in 1689 through the Paris 'Hôtel de Ville'. It consisted of a classic loan with a conventional annuity rates based on age. The French State was guarantor for public bonds and prime contractor of the debt service. The funding collected by these 'constitutions' – as bonds were called at that time – was used to finance war and avoid tax increasing. They also served to promote savings among middle classes. The edict of issuance specified that in case of litigation, the Provost of the Merchants of Paris was the judge of first instance, whose decisions were subjected to appeal to the Parliament of Paris. As for the *instrumentum*, the style of the edict was similar to contemporary issuances

264 Georges Gallais-Hamonno & Jean Berthon, Les emprunts tontiniers de l'Ancien Régime. Un exemple d'ingénierie financière au XVIIIe siècle (Publications de la Sorbonne. 2008), pp. 7-23.

265 Life annuity is a type of insurance product. Life annuity refers to the difference between life expectancy of the subscriber and the number of years of effective life of the same subscriber. If the subscriber lives a long time, the life annuity is at his or her benefits. If the subscriber dies earlier, the issuer makes more benefits.

266 Arrears of dead policyholders did not benefit the State since they are distributed among the survivors of their age group, until death of the last purchaser. The last purchaser extinguished the debt of the State *vis-à-vis* this group.

267 The loan was considered too expensive, its cost difficult to assess because of its technicality. In particular, the paid annuity rate was the same regardless of the age at the time of subscription. This computation was inequitable.

of treasury bonds[268]. Under the terms of Article 3, only inhabitants[269] residing in the French Kingdom could subscribe to this loan, regardless of their age, gender, quality or condition.

The three tontines issued at the end of the reign of Louis XIV were a failure for the State. Indeed, it collected only a fifth of the expected sums. Due to the absence of knowledge about the life duration of policyholders and the real cost of the loan, this technique was expensive. Under the reign of Louis XV, the seven tontines issued were more successful, albeit after various changes. This instrument is considered as the beginning of financial engineering. It is symptomatic of the willingness of States to diversify their creditors. At that time, bankers' conditions were not easily negotiable and debt products subscribed by investors were more flexible.

This historical example demonstrates that the existence of bonds is far from being a contemporary phenomenon. Current capital markets represent the most complete stage of lenders diversification. Lenders are organised between the currency market, the financial market, and the foreign exchange and derivatives markets[270]. They are multiple: hedge funds, pension funds, insurance companies, investment banks, and individual investors. These markets operators are gathered within the International Association of Capital Markets (IACM). This association is a forum for discussion[271] and self-regulation[272].

---

268 See the text of the 1689 edict, collection des Actes royaux, BNF, F-23614 (653, 654, 655): « *portant création de quatorze cens mille livres de Rentes Viagères sur l'Hôtel de Ville de Paris* » signed at Versailles in November 1689, registered by the Parliament in December and « *crié par les rues le dimanche 4 décembre* ».

269 Only the King's subjects were concerned. Foreigners and non-residents were excluded for reasons of fraud in the certification of the annuitant's death. Indeed, for French residents, priests were in charge of reporting every six months any dead policyholders. False statements from policyholders were punished.

270 Exchange market refers to currencies. Derivatives markets come from the exchange of products from other markets.

271 "*ICMA's primary objective is to support the creation of orderly and well-functioning international capital markets. In line with ICMA's mission, this involves setting standards of best market practice, through contract reform and practical improvements to standard form market documentation*". See ICMA Sovereign bond consultation paper (2013). ICMA Sovereign bond consultation paper supplement (2014).

272 Professional organisations gathering market participants offer standard contracts adapted to the conditions discussed between financial operators: derivatives by the ISDA, securities by the ICMA and syndicated loan agreements by the LMA.

In terms of sovereign financing, the State uses treasury bonds issued on the currency market for short-term funding. For medium and long term funding, bonds are issued in regulated markets, whereas tailored products are issued in the over-the-counter market (OTC)[273]. Bond issuances are statistically distributed between domestic and international bonds. This qualification depends on the nationality of the issuer, the currency and the place of issuance[274].

Contemporary prevalence of bonds dates from the early 1980s, when international obligations took precedence over Eurocredits. Restrictive monetary policies compared to opportunities offered by financial markets encouraged operators to issue bonds. Indeed, even if all States do not enjoy the same conditions, and even if restrictions of bonds issuance exist, financing is generally facilitated due to a rapid market access. For developing countries, it gradually changed from a development finance phase[275] to an explosion of emerging financial markets. Direct investment through markets has become the prevailing financing technique, despite of a more favourable treatment for developed countries.

Indeed, price of products and regulations of banking and financial activities reflect the preference for developed countries' bonds. These bonds are reference on the financial markets. This reference is however particular because each bond value is directly correlated to the situation of the sovereign borrower. The choices made in terms of public finances remain sovereign. The level of indebtedness of the United States, England, Japan or the Eurozone Member States can be classified according to defined criteria. However, their situation is not comparable[276]. This reality has been

273 In financial markets, stocks and bonds are traded, while negotiable debt and treasury bills are in the currency market. Derivatives are traded in organised derivatives markets or over-the-counter. Derivative market was unorganised and dominated by a small number of operators called primary dealers. After the financial crisis in 2008, the standardisation of certain products was imposed, as well as the establishment of a clearing and confirmation platform. See Christian de Boissieu & Jézabel Couppey-Soubeyran, Les systèmes financiers. Mutations, crises et régulation (Economica, 2013), 288p.

274 See Guide to the international financial statistics (2009).

275 Between 1950 and 1990, a 'development finance' was promoted by the International Finance Corporation and the World Bank to increased living standards in developing countries through capital invested for economic assistance.

276 The statistics provided by the BIS, the IMF, the OECD and the World Bank through the Joint External Debt Hub bring numbered information on external debt from assets held by international creditors or national debtors.

highlighted by the crisis that severely affected these States. The current rebalancing of their public finances is treated differentially. Nevertheless, we insist on the fact that bonds can be found in the primary market after the first issuance. We will now analyse this issuance.

1.1.2. Heterogeneous bond issuance practices

To understand how indebtedness works, we will begin with the bond issuance process. The monetary market – for short-term debt – and the bond market – for medium and long-term debt – are the largest international financial markets in terms of trading volume. The bonds issuance generally takes the form of an auction on the primary market. The level of risk perceived by investors will determine the interest; the higher the risk, the higher the interest rate will be. For sovereign borrowers, the entry into the international financial market is a tactical analysis based on strategic points. Any emission error can have a crucial impact on its public finance and repayment capacity. The prospectus of bonds generally contains the same information about the borrower as the one included in syndicated loan documents. The main interest of financial market is to benefit from funding sources and refinancing by matching capital suppliers and capital seekers. The issuance of sovereign bonds allows a faster raise of funding. This promptness explains the recourse to the financial markets.

In practice, the first issuance is generally performed in the context of an investment project or a change in the debt composition. The size must take into account the need for funding. Maturity and repayment structures are designed to set a reimbursement final date, maturities and currencies. Beyond these financial aspects, States should also choose their target and answer to investors' demand. Bond issuance must be preceded by an introduction of the country's situation to investors. It means that a rating agency is needed. Once these factors are defined, the State chooses the banks gathered in a syndicate that will place bonds on the international Eurobond market[277]. These banks can sell sovereign bonds simultaneously in the markets of at least two countries. Bonds may be denominated in a currency. It can be the borrower's currency, the creditor's currency, or the com-

277 Jacquillat, et al., Marchés financiers : Gestion de portefeuille et des risques, 2009, pp. 7-61.

bining of several currencies, as in the case of Eurobond issuance. These technical procedures combine techniques previously used in banking syndication for loans.

Despite their international nature, bonds are subjected to the domestic law chosen by the parties according to the criteria of transparency and legal certainty. The law applicable to bonds is often English law, the State of New York law or any domestic law[278]. The following clause illustrates it:

> "This Agreement and the rights, obligations and duties of the Parties hereunder shall be construed and *interpreted in accordance with Law (i.e. the laws of the country)* and by such rules and principles of generally accepted international law as may be applicable, particularly with regard to an investment by nationals of one country in another country. *Notwithstanding the foregoing, in the event of a conflict between this Agreement or the rights, obligations and duties of a Party under this Agreement, and any other Law, including administrative rules and procedures and matters relating to procedure, and applicable international law, then this Agreement shall govern the rights, obligations and duties of the Parties*" (we emphasise).

The determination of the applicable law depends on the economic context. Currently, domestic debt is increasing[279]. In that case, domestic law governs bonds[280]. As we previously underlined, the State is not a regular borrower due to sovereign privileges such as inalienable public property and tax authority[281]. However, when it contractually waives its jurisdictional immunity, it abandons the capacity to prevail on any action against it and resigns to unprotect its property[282]. A typical example is the Argentine waiver of immunity contained in contracts held by the fund NML:

> "To the extent that the government may in any jurisdiction claim for itself for its assets or revenues immunity from suit execution, attachment (whether in aid of execution, before judgment or otherwise) or other legal process and to

278 Fui S. Tsikata, "Investment Protection Provisions & their Implications", UNCTAD Workshop Natural Resources & Economic Development, 12-16 July 2010.

279 United Nations, General Assembly report on "Recent Developments in external debt", UN Doc. A/62/151, 2007, pp. 14-17.

280 Anna Gelpern & Brad Setser, *Domestic and External Debt: The Doomed Quest for Equal Treatment*, 35, Georgetown Journal of International Law (2004).

281 Dominique Carreau, *Dette d'État*, Dalloz – Répertoire de droit international (2009), 11p.

282 Supreme Court of the United States, Republic of Argentina v. NML Capital, LTD., 695 F. 3d 201, affirmed, No. 12–842, Argued April 21, 2014 – Decided June 16, 2014.

the extent that in any such jurisdiction there may be attributed to government or its assets or revenues such immunity (whether or not claimed) *government agrees not to claim and irrevocably waives such immunity to the full extent permitted by the laws of such jurisdiction*" (we emphasise).

Under customary international law, as reflected in the UN Convention on Jurisdictional Immunities of States and their Property of 2 December 2004, this waiver is possible insofar as it refers to *jure gestionis* acts. In terms of sovereign financing, contractual rules of the financial markets take precedence over State sovereignty via the end of sovereign immunity[283]. However, this question of immunity is currently debated, as the NML case against Argentina brought before the French Court of Cassation revealed it[284].

The State submits its bonds issuance to market conditions and to the principle of free competition. The issuance agreement corresponds to an ordinary debt contract. It states the issuance price, the annual interests[285], the periodicity, the price and the reimbursement terms. We can object that there may be a general impression that obligations have priority over bank loans. This perception comes from the differences between these two legal instruments – the way they are sold, managed and addressed in the restructuring. Subsequently, bond investors expect that the sovereign borrower will turn to banks to refinance or restructure its banking debt before it restructures its bonds. This is why some bonds, especially those governed by English law, are designed to facilitate restructuring[286].

Risks of purchasing sovereign debt contracts are known. Parties are notified to take them into account when negotiating the terms of the agreement. Risks of sovereign default are not necessarily superior to those of other contractors. However, the success of suing a sovereign borrower in

283 « *Traditionnellement, le droit accordait une protection quasi absolue aux emprunteurs souverains aux termes des principes d'immunité ou d'International comittee ou encore d'Act of State. Depuis quelques années, les tribunaux américains et anglais principalement n'ont eu de cesse que de limiter la portée de ces principes afin de mieux protéger les prêteurs.* » in Gilles de Margerie & Hubert de Vauplane, *Les défauts du défaut : Quelques clefs pour comprendre la crise de la dette souveraine*, 48, En Temps Réel (2011), pp. 11-20.

284 See Chapter 5.

285 Traditionally, bonds have a fix interest called 'coupon'. Historically, it was necessary to detach a coupon of the bond paper to receive payment.

286 Rieffel, Restructuring Sovereign Debt: The Case for Ad Hoc Machinery, 2003, pp. 149-177.

default is lower than in the case of non-sovereign borrowers. Thus, it is crucial to put into question the choice of applicable law and the competent courts. In case of default, the creditor will first sue the sovereign borrower in default and then try to seize its properties. Nevertheless, if a foreign court recognises a violation of the contractual terms, the enforcement of this decision can be problematic.

After this analysis, the jurist is blocked by the almost quasi-contracts that dominate bond issuance practices. Debt products contracts have very few distinct legal clauses. The choice of a particular legal system is possible through the clause of applicable law. This clause is inserted at the end of the contract. It is rarely negotiated as the attention is focused on technical aspects, leaving aside legal issues. This clause became some kind of standard for operators[287] who do not read it and do not seek to understand its consequences[288].

Yet the problem is often that the emission contracts refer to domestic law. The applicable language is usually the local language. Therefore, bond documentation, even if it tends to be standardised due to its use by market professionals, is nevertheless heterogeneous in its application. Mostly, it lacks transparency and systematisation[289].

The question of whether and when a sovereign issuer enters into default depends on contractual terms that describe the case of default and on the law applicable of the issuance contract[290]. In case of litigation, and before the adoption of collective action clauses, it was up to the judge to interpret

---

287 Favéro, Revue Trimestrielle de Droit Commercial (2003).

288 ICMA explains that "*earlier during the sovereign debt crisis, it appears that* some investors did not know whether the sovereign bonds they had bought were issued under national law or under foreign law and the implications for their holdings*; and that they were not familiar with the specific rights afforded to them as bondholders*" (we emphasise) in ICMA Sovereign bond consultation paper, 2010, p. 2.

289 The case of the evolution of Greek bonds illustrates it. We had access to two Greek bonds. The maturity of the first one was 20 March 2012. It was issued in euros and governed by Greek law. No clause of choice of jurisdiction was included. The maturity of the second bonds was June 2013. It was issued in dollars. The applicable law is English law. In case of litigation, English courts can be seized. Greece waives its sovereign immunity. Payment is made in Luxembourg. The *pari passu* clause stipulates that any advantage granted to other bondholders shall be extended to all bondholders of this particular bond issuance.

290 For example, in case of corporate default, clauses are the following: borrower's non-payment, interest or other charges concerning amount date, infringement of

these contractual terms. The law applicable is not necessarily that of the issuer and the competent courts are not always those of the country of issuance. Thus, it is important to be aware of the clause of applicable law and the competent courts.

1.2. Sovereign debt bonds on secondary markets

To understand the evolution of a bond contract after its issuance, we will go through the financial system. We will understand how sovereign debt bonds became investment instruments that were considered safe. The demand for such safe instruments structures the financial markets (1.2.1.). We will examine the development of financial products and particularly securitisation (1.2.2.).

1.2.1. A financial reference for markets

The secondary market is a second-hand market[291] where bond are exchanged between investors. The State may purchase its bonds in this secondary market to favour liquidity and debt reduction. These transactions are related to bonds' conversion or exchange. After the European sovereign debt crisis, the European Central Bank intervened through outright monetary transactions[292]. We will discuss this in the next chapter.

The current configuration of the sovereign debt market dates back to the development and the explosion of derivatives in the 1980-1990s. Developed in the early 1970s in the United States, the derivatives markets have spread in the financial world. It created, after the collapse of the Bretton Woods system, a new global financial situation. These derivatives markets are part of the outright markets. They are not related to capital or currency exchange but only to market risks. These derivative markets are

any other contractual commitment subscribed in the agreement, inaccuracy or repetition of a declaration made by the borrower, bankruptcy, liquidation of assets or judicial resolution of the borrower.

291 Valérie Lelièvre, *Economie monétaire et financière*, Paris, Bréal, 2000, pp. 191-192.

292 ECB, "Technical features of Outright Monetary Transactions", Press release, 6 September 2012.

split between regulated markets and over-the-counter markets. Regulated markets are considered secure. They are structured by a clearing house and based on standardised contracts. OTC markets do not follow this structure; the higher the risk of their products, the bigger the growth will be[293].

Products traded on capital markets have diversified due to financial innovation. Credit derivatives, a term used for the first time in 1992 by the ISDA, have grown exponentially in response to a request for protection against risk. Three main types of instruments are now available: futures, options, and swaps[294]. They allow operators to cover risks, arbitrate or speculate[295]. These instruments increase liquidity and serve as tools for qualitative discrimination between issuers[296]. With these derivatives, debt remains legally owned by the purchaser who is nevertheless protected against credit risk.

Securitisation is seen as the final stage in promoting financial liquidity. Indeed, bank loans previously illiquid are securitised and traded in markets[297]. Securitisation operates in several stages. First, the bank selects the assets that it wants to shift off its balance sheet. Then, it brings them together in special purpose vehicles (SPV). These SPV issue new securities used by those banking assets. The buyers of these securities receive interest and principal repayments of the underlying loans. These securities are structured into different facilities: the safest (senior and super senior) are highly rated, while intermediate (mezzanine) are lower-rated and the low-

293 A new category has emerged after the financial crisis. Some OTC markets are regulated by a clearing house or the rules of organised markets are applied to ensure the solvency of the operator. See Frédéric de Brouwer, *EMIR : état des lieux de la mise en œuvre et défis majeurs à venir*, 4, Bulletin Joly Bourse 237 (2014).

294 In a futures contract, buyer and seller agree to a transaction whose price and date are fixed in advance. In an option, the buyer decides whether or not to exercise its option. The contractual asymmetry is compensated by the price paid to the seller. The swap refers to an exchange. Swaps are traded on OTC markets, while futures and options can be either on regulated markets or OTC. In terms of vocabulary, futures are standardised contracts, forwards are sold on OTC markets, and warrants are similar to standardised options on OTC markets.

295 The cover provides protection against adverse movements in the markets. Arbitration relates to perform operations bringing profits without risks. Speculation refers to deliberate risk taken to improve benefits.

296 Scialom, Économie bancaire, 2013, pp. 7-24.

297 André Orléan, De l'euphorie à la panique : penser la crise financière (Éditions Rue d'Ulm, 2009), pp. 53-58.

est (equity) are not rated. The development of these tools has allowed a growth of liquidity that benefits borrowers, especially States.

1.2.2. Sovereign financing securitisation

Securitisation has brought assets liquidity and opened new possibilities. After the granting of a loan, banks can cede the risk to investors. This operation allows them to enhance their balance sheet[298]. The development of financial techniques in financial markets increases liquidity. Due to these increasing opportunities, capital seekers have borrowed more and investors have taken more risks. Derivatives have been developed by investors to reduce their exposure to sovereign risk. The use of these hedges ensures the liquidity of the market. Consequently, some investors considered developed countries' sovereign debt as risk-free assets. In addition, coupon payments and capital reimbursement are separated. Thus, operators can independently invest in securities and hedges.

Among many existing derivatives, credit default swaps (CDS) and collateralized debt obligations (CDO) have been particularly highlighted during the recent financial crisis. Traded over the counter, these credit derivatives are sold by banks, insurance companies and some investment funds. A CDS contract is designed to compensate a buyer in the event of a default. The buyer of the CDS receives compensation and the seller takes possession of the defaulted contract. A CDO is a structured financial product that pools together assets such as mortgages, bonds and loans. The portfolio is divided into different credit risk levels, from senior to equity. The excellent rating of the first level, while the following may be risky due to insolvent mortgages and companies in default, explains the billions of loss of CDO holders since 2007[299].

CDO generated the 2007-2009 credit crisis that has contaminated States through multiple channels[300]. Lack of transparency is at the heart of the problem of these hedging. They were sold independently of the underlying contracts they guaranteed. They were used both as indicators of the quality

298 Banque de France, *De la crise financière à la crise économique*, 3, Documents et débats (2010), pp. 9-10.
299 Banque de France, *La crise financière*, 2, Documents et débats (2009).
300 La crise des subprimes, 2008, 284p. See Chapter 4.

of underlying products[301] and as speculative products[302]. Moreover, the definition of credit event was problematic[303].

This detour of law through financial engineering is necessary to understand debt mechanisms. Without considering this functioning, it is not possible to envisage a legal framework adapted to this reality. We consider important to analyse these financial techniques in order to recommend regulatory solutions. Currently, debt instruments are becoming more complex as they can be quickly exchanged in the financial markets. However, the contractual legal clauses do not seem to be negotiated. This observation will be discussed in the following section. We will consider the operators that are involved in the functioning of sovereign financing.

2. *Internationalisation of sovereign debt operators*

The Eurobond market is composed of a multitude of international operators. Due to the widespread use of bonds, sovereign financing is now internationalised. International securities demand is driven by sovereign debt managers who work with different market operators – fundraisers, fund managers, financial analysts, brokers and traders (2.1). Far from a substitution of public officials by private operators, governments, central banks and regulators establish market finance's structures and rules (2.2.).

2.1. Professionalisation of debt operators

Under the auspices of financial liberalisation, the international mobility of operators and resources was facilitated by disintermediation, decompart-

---

301 Intraday dynamics of euro area sovereign CDS and bonds (2013).

302 Propositions to establish a legal framework emerged. After the German initiative in 2010 to ban the short sale of CDS based on speculation, the Member States of the European Union adopted Regulation (EU) No 236/2012 of the European Parliament and of the Council of 14 March 2012 on short selling and certain aspects of credit default swaps (OJUE L 86/1).

303 For a sovereign CDS, it is not bankruptcy but default on reimbursement of interest or principal: Jérôme Da Ros, *Incidence des Credit Default Swaps sur les dettes des États : bilan et perspectives*, *in* Insolvabilité des États et dettes souveraines (Mathias Audit ed. 2011), pp. 81-101.

mentalisation, deregulation[304] and dematerialisation, all of which have connected markets in real-time. The increase and diversification of investors had the benefit of reducing the cost of sovereign borrowing. Nevertheless, this internationalisation, due to the dispersion of securities in markets, complicates the identification of bondholders (2.1.1.). To attract private investors, debt managers seek to maintain public debt securities competitive. This imperative has become indispensable for States that play a central role in financial market development (2.1.2.).

2.1.1. Concentration of operators and dispersion of investors

The economic role of financial markets in sovereign debt has generated an internationalisation of the stakeholders involved in sovereign financing. Financial globalisation has increased concentration of market infrastructure. Central securities depositary in charge of holding securities for banks and brokers are no longer local but international, such as Euroclear and Clearstream. International institutions such as LCH Clearnet also offer compensation mechanisms. The concentration of market infrastructure has also led to the privatisation of institutions whose functions were previous-

304 Henri Bourguinat, Finance internationale, 4e éd. (Presses Universitaires de France, 1999): « *La déréglementation conduit à la suppression progressive des règlements et des contrôles en matière de fixation des prix des services bancaires, avec l'abolition du contrôle des changes, la libéralisation des taux d'intérêt à long terme, la création de nombreux produits financiers et le développement des marchés dits dérivés, malgré les risques que leur gestion comporte. La désintermédiation constitue un recours direct des opérateurs aux marchés financiers, sans passer par les intermédiaires financiers et bancaires. Le décloisonnement des marchés nationaux implique la suppression des frontières entre des marchés séparés régionalement, nationalement, entre les titres à court, moyen et long terme ou sur le marché des changes. Il conduit à la progressive indifférenciation entre le long et le court terme, à l'effondrement de la barrière du marché des changes et des marchés financiers et à l'ouverture de la bourse et du marché des créances des États et des grandes firmes aux opérateurs étrangers* ». Cited by Jacques Fontanel & Fanny Coulomb, *Spéculation internationale et régulation financière*, Vol. VII, Annuaire Français de Relations Internationales (2006).

ly managed by public authorities[305]. States are now involved only through regulatory authorities or domestic law to improve the system[306].

This concentration of private operators is decisive in the case of rating agencies. US rating agencies started to rate external debt in 1918[307]. Their relation with sovereign debt is fundamentally linked to the financialisation of this debt. In fact, banking intermediation historically assessed the creditworthiness of borrowers and project financing[308]. With the generalisation of bond issuance, the buyer of a debt security is using new intermediaries to assess risk. This task, previously attributed to bankers, is now given over to rating agencies. Rating agencies synthetise a wide range of information and simplify reality by giving a single score. Yet in regard to sovereign debt, State public finances are not only analysed by these private entities, but also by multiple national institutions, such as central banks, governments, regional and supranational institutions. They may have more resources and legitimacy than rating agencies[309].

Bonds issuance changes the types of investors. Bank loans are associated with a limited number of creditor banks, while bonds are more dispersed among various investors (investment funds, institutional investors, pension funds, insurance companies, or investment banks). This quantitative distinction is reinforced by a difference in the trust between lenders and borrowers[310]. Bondholders are more instable. They are located in several places and operate in multiple markets, which implies a dispersion and dilution of debt supports[311]. For example, in France, non-residents

---

305 La gestion de la dette publique et les marchés des valeurs d'État au XXIe siècle (2002).

306 See Regulation (EU) No 909/2014 of the European Parliament and of the Council of 23 July 2014 on improving securities settlement in the European Union and on central securities depositories and amending Directives 98/26/EC and 2014/65/EU and Regulation (EU) No 236/2012.

307 To err is human: rating agencies and the interwar foreign government debt crisis (2010).

308 Norbert Gaillard, A century of sovereign ratings (Springer, 2011), pp. 3-11.

309 Jean-Pierre Landau, *Quelle politique pour la dette souveraine?*, 16, Revue de la Stabilité Financière (2012).

310 Issam Hallak & Paul Schure, *Loans versus Bonds: The Importance of Potential Liquidity Problems for Sovereign Borrowers*, *in* Sovereign Debt: From Safety to Default (Robert W. Kolb ed. 2011).

311 In 2009, the US had a sovereign debt of 12 billion dollars. 43 % were held by federal government agencies (Federal Reserve and Social Security Trust Funds),

held 64.6 % of negotiable debt in the first quarter of 2014[312]. This internationalisation is one of the factors explaining the contagion carried from financial and economic crisis to sovereign debt crisis. Other States face different situations. For instance, the Japanese Government Debt to GDP ratio was 230 % in 2014. However, only 6 % of debt holders were foreigners. Japanese public entities and Japanese private investors mainly subscribe bonds[313].

Securities are part of the financial markets and can be acquired by any type of creditor, such as sovereign wealth funds. These funds hold, manage or administer sovereign assets for defined goals. They invested for the short or long term depending on the interests and objectives of a government[314]. Securities are a financing and investment tool for the State. The first sovereign wealth fund, created in 1953, was the Kuwait Investment Authority. China, with its trade surpluses, has four sovereign funds, all created over the past ten years[315]. These entities follow specific investment guidelines. For example, the Government Pension Fund of Norwegian has an ethics committee in charge of validating investments. Investments in companies producing tobacco, weapons, involved in corrupt activities, engaging in massive violations of human rights or damaging the environment are excluded[316]. These sovereign wealth funds allow the

27 % by domestic private creditors (pension funds, insurance companies, local governments) and 30 % by foreign governments and international private investors. See Holley H. Ulbrich, Public Finance in Theory and Practice (Routledge, 2011), p. 138. The US Treasury Department publishes a regularly updated list of the largest holders of the US debt.

312 Source Webstat – Banque de France.

313 Anton Brender, et al., The Sovereign Debt Crisis: Placing a Curb on Growth (Editions La Découverte, 2012), pp. 41-57. An updated version of the data is available online at tradingeconomics.com.

314 Régis Bismuth, *Les fonds souverains face au droit international. Panorama des problèmes juridiques posés par des investisseurs peu ordinaires*, Annuaire Français de Droit International (2010).

315 The most important sovereign funds are Safe, CIC, National Social Security Fund and the China Africa Development Fund. See Pascale Massot, *Globalisation économique et fragmentation de la décision politique : le cas des fonds souverains chinois*, Vol. 18, Revue internationale de politique comparée (2011).

316 Simon Chesterman, *The Turn to Ethics: Disinvestment From Multinational Corporations for Human Rights Violations – The Case of the Norway's Sovereign Wealth Fund*, 23, American University International Law Review (2008).

State to play an important economic role. This State capitalism refocuses international balance of power to new poles.

Investment funds have also attracted attention after the Argentine economic crisis in 2001 due to the legal battle to recover debts. They have various characteristics. For instance, pension funds collect employees' contributions to invest them. "Vulture" funds buy debt securities on the secondary market and sue sovereign debtors. Some of these funds have hit the headlines in recent years: Elliott Associates and its affiliate NML Capital, Pravin Banker, LNC Investments, FG Hemisphere, Donegal International, amongst others[317]. They are demanding the full payment of the interest rate of their debt securities. Peru, Nicaragua, Argentina, the Democratic Republic of Congo and Zambia are those States suffering the most from this phenomenon, as we will further analyse.

2.1.2. Professionalisation of debt management

In the 1970s, inflation and unemployment increased due to the oil shocks. Consequently, budget deficits increased and States borrowed to handle the unstable situation. Governments supported by international financial institutions focused on the question of sovereign debt management through new regulations, structures and institutions. New market techniques were ultimately developed, leading to a globalised financial market. Thus, bank operators started to work with State officials. The professionalisation of debt managers is based on this cooperation.

Before the generalisation of auctions, States used the underwriting system to issue bonds. The mandated banks gathered in syndicates bought the entire loan to invest it afterwards. From 1985, financial markets specialised in auction. Auction is a sale technique used by the Treasury to finance sovereign debt. Syndication continues to be used. However, auction has become the main technique. In France, private investors have no access to debt securities on the primary market[318]. Only credit institutions with accounts at the Bank of France can participate and buy.

---

317 Patrick Wautelet, *Les fonds vautours. Vulture Funds, Creditors and Sovereign Debtors: how to find a Balance?*, *in* Insolvabilité des états et dettes souveraines (Mathias Audit ed. 2011).

318 Individuals may buy sovereign debt on the secondary market, on stock exchange or from a specialist in treasury values.

We can take the case of the French sovereign debt issuance to illustrate the functioning of sovereign bonds issuance. The French Parliament decides each issuance[319] while the *Agence France Trésor* (AFT) manages it. The French State intervenes on the financial markets through the AFT[320]. This administrative agency handles negotiable debt. Non-negotiable debt belongs to the *Direction générale de la comptabilité publique*[321]. The Bank of France holds the Treasury account. The *Caisse de la dette publique* conducts debt operations on financial markets to ensure liquidity, in particular on the secondary market. This structure is based on the United States financial products that are used as model[322].

The mission of the AFT is to place funding at the best rate when the balance is positive, and to borrow when it is negative. Consequently, the AFT has a continued presence on the financial markets. A continuing issuance of sovereign debt bond is imperative to achieve economies of scale. This economy of scale allows the State to establish some kind of *affectio Etatis* between the State and its investors. To maintain this privileged relationship, transparency is fundamental in the management of public debt. All management functions delegated to a public entity linked to the Ministry of Finance or the French Central Bank should be oriented towards more autonomy and more transparency[323]. The Parliament's role is also to review and control these stages of proceeding[324].

---

319 Article 26 of the Organic Law on the Finance Laws of 1 August 2001 (*loi organique relative aux lois de finance*): « *4° L'émission, la conversion et la gestion des emprunts sont effectuées conformément aux autorisations annuelles générales ou particulières données par la loi de finances de l'année* ». See Paul Amselek & Pierre Lavigne, Le budget de l'État sous la Ve République, Bibliothèque de science financière, L.G.D.J., 1966, pp. 267-268.

320 The capital market is divided between short-term capital on the monetary market, and long-term capital on the financial market. The financial market is the place of negotiation of securities, mainly stocks and bonds. It allows the confrontation of agents seeking for financing, borrowers, issuers, and investors. It is divided into primary and secondary markets.

321 Negotiable debt is contracted in the form of financial instruments traded on the financial markets. It is different from the non-negotiable debt, which corresponds to deposits made by certain bodies (local and regional authorities, public establishments) into the Treasury's account.

322 Lemoine, Sociétés contemporaines, (2013).

323 Rôle et structure des offices de gestion de la dette, pp. 109-147 (2002).

324 Eckert, Revue française de Finances Publiques, (2013).

As for the operational management, selected banks act as official intermediates and institutionalised partners between the government and investors. These selected banks are gathered in a group specialised in Treasury securities. This group consists of the twenty major international banking institutions selected by the AFT for a three years mandate. They act on global bond markets. They participate in the AFT auctions, place Treasury securities and ensure the liquidity of the secondary market. Their mission is defined in a charter[325]. This charter summarises the conditions applicable to banks to join this prestigious private club and the AFT expectations regarding these professionals. After being selected, each bank is required to participate in State auctions, to join meetings at the French Ministry of Finance and to invest all its resources to assist the State.

To conduct their operational management mission, debt managers usually enjoy a relative autonomy from the political sphere. Their empowerment began in the 1990s and has been associated with the inclusion of debt assessment and risk management in the practice of monitoring financial markets. Overall, both institutional and operational managers face new challenges in sovereign debt. The priority is the identification, assessment and management of these new risks[326].

The sovereign debt market has seen an improvement of its functionality due to an introduction of clearing via its internationalisation. Deregulation has also opened funding opportunities. It has facilitated the development of financial products. Thus, dematerialisation of securities combined with debt auction, debt management professionalisation and expansion of international financial markets have helped to radically change investors' interests concerning sovereign debt. It has also facilitated the emergence of

325 Charte Spécialistes en valeurs du Trésor (SVT), (2012). "*This charter is prepared in the parties' common interest, which is to ensure the following, in compliance with applicable regulations and industry agreements: – Smooth progress of primary issuances; – greater liquidity of the secondary market for French Treasury securities1 and maintenance of their status as the most liquid securities of the euro area; – promotion of euro-denominated fixed income markets in general and of French Treasury securities in particular; – ongoing supply of high-quality advisory services to AFT and more broadly to the French Ministry in charge of the Economy as regards the policies governing issuances, debt management, promotion of the State's credit quality, hedging of the State's financial risks, regulation of fixed income markets and management of public finance; – mechanism allowing for an objective and transparent assessment of services supplied*".

326 Lemoine, Sociétés contemporaines, (2013).

new professionals of debt market. We consider that understanding the organisation of debt managers is fundamental to comprehend how States can regulate this matter.

2.2. States and international institutional regulators

When regulating financial markets worldwide and promoting new instruments of credit, States support financial innovations. This support is possible through legislative and regulatory redevelopment intended to reorganise complex financial activities (2.2.1.). We will determine how institutional regulators and central banks also play an active role in sovereign debt management (2.2.2.).

2.2.1. States and organisation of financial markets

Private agents seem to have supplanted public operators on sovereign financing. Nonetheless, State intervention remains at the centre of the functioning of the economic and financial spheres. Most historians of the financial globalisation emphasise the influence of technological changes and market development. This emphasis disregards States' role in the process of globalisation. Financial liberalisation remarkably involves the State. The so-called developed countries have played an important role in this process of globalisation since the late 1950s. Developed countries have increased financial market participants' freedom and have deliberately chosen not to implement more constraining practices to control capital. Indeed, they always had legal authority and technical expertise to intervene[327].

Their power has not disappeared but rather transformed into acts of government or legislative changes that affect private operators. Nowadays, States are *de facto* ultimate funds providers of the banking system. In case of financial crisis, States intervene to stabilise national operators. States act as last resort bail out. The State is not anymore considered as a dominant entity but rather as a partner. Subsequently, the overall privatisation of debt has an impact on the economic, fiscal and social policies. Political

---

327 Eric Helleiner, States and the Reemergence of Global Finance: From Bretton Woods to the 1990s (Cornell University Press. 1994), pp. 619-636.

issues are guided by financial market conditions since sovereign debt has carried out more than eighty percent of market participations. The paradox lies in the fact that States build and safeguard a system, and then are sanctioned or excluded. As a result, sovereign initiatives aim at regulating private operators and market functioning[328].

2.2.2. Debt management by central banks and supervisory authorities

Central banks are responsible for ensuring price stability and proper functioning of the payment system. This action is possible through the establishment of bank-refinancing rates. Sovereign debt management and monetary policy are conducted separately by the central bank. As a result, information on interest rates does not influence decisions regarding debt management. This banking supervision is complicated due to the behaviour of operators. In particular, market operators must take quick decisions on considerable amounts of money, while remaining compliant with prudential rules.

In times of abundant liquidity and low rate, investors seek higher remunerations and take more risks. Therefore, financial institutions have moved away from their risk assessment to issue innovative complex securities with higher rates. Alignment between operators is common and such reaction can have disastrous consequences[329]. International banks are subjected to moral hazards in their international lending activity. Subsequently, as soon as they see that their international loans have not been reimbursed, they incur a systemic risk that affects the financial system. This systemic risk can lead to an international bailout[330].

Therefore, regulatory institutions are particularly important to manage sovereign debt. They monitor the banking and financial system and enforce regulations, as we will examine in the second part of this dissertation. This monitoring is facing multiple business diversifications. The

328 See Part II.

329 Jean du Pré de Saint-Maur, *Perspectives du marché des euro-crédits*, *in* Les euro-crédits, un instrument du système bancaire pour le financement international (Jean-Bernard Blaise, et al. eds., 1981).

330 See Chapter 4.

main obstacle is the externality posed by the proliferation of operators; any negotiation to regulate an area is costly in time and energy[331].

The financial analysis of debt conducted in this part of the dissertation is essential. By segmenting disciplines, research possibilities are compartmentalised, thus limiting the examination for innovative solutions. This limitation also obstructs the sovereign debt functioning.

*

Methods of international public indebtedness are marked by a quantitative decline of bank lending, either for loans made by multilateral development banks as for those granted by banking unions. States and public entities use capital markets to rise ten times more fundings than the loans provided by original lenders. Following a logic of opportunity, this evolution swept all the existing financing structure to establish market law. Such transformation is at the heart of the current crisis, as we will consider it in the following chapter.

CHAPTER 4. Reinforcement of Sovereign Debt Crises

Based on the idea that any phenomenon is complex, relative and contingent[332], we will establish how the changing structure of sovereign debt analysed in the previous chapters has led to a crisis. The recent sovereign debt crisis is the first of its kind in recent decades that has affected States with a mature market economy. Initiated in 2007, this financial and economic crisis demonstrates that States have faced a poor financial regulation. Far from any notion of accident[333], the financial crisis has spread to the economic sphere. To rescue the financial system, States have borrowed to recapitalise failing banks. Therefore, States solvency deteriorated. It in-

---

331 See Chapter 6.

332 Edgar Morin & Jean-Louis Le Moigne, L'intelligence de la complexité (L'Harmatan. 2000), pp. 52-97.

333 Juglar, Des crises commerciales et de leur retour périodique en France, en Angleterre et aux États-Unis, 1862, pp. 7-26: « *Une crise ne survient jamais à l'improviste, elle a toujours été précédée d'une période de grande prospérité et d'un grand mouvement d'affaires qui n'a pu avoir lieu sans une progression, pour ainsi dire, continue de hausse.* ».

duced a crisis of confidence *vis-à-vis* their ability to ensure debt service[334] (1.).

However, weaknesses in banking and financial regulation are not the sole cause of sovereign debt crisis[335]. Other aspects of its general structure as well as financial markets functioning exist. For States, the costs of the crisis are important and multiple: financial losses have led to restrictions to access financial markets and procedural threats through sovereign debt litigation (2.).

1. Sovereign debt crises

Sovereign debt is the contemporary paradigm that connects economic crisis and financial crisis. After 2007, the contagion has spread to banks and markets, and finally to the real economy (1.1.). The multiple origins of the crisis have been clearly identified. Deficiencies are numerous. The whole system is affected by imbalances such as the absence of a lender of last resort and the lack of banking supervision, (1.2.).

1.1. From financial crisis to sovereign debt crisis

The crisis started in 2007 in the United States with the dissemination of subprime mortgages through securitisation. As these mortgages were insolvent, the derivatives structured with such products collapsed. This collapse was then transmitted to the public sphere through the banking and financial system, and to the real economy (1.1.1.). Factors behind this contagion are multiple. They highlight the weaknesses of the financial system (1.1.2.) and put into question the solvency of the developed market economy (1.1.3.). The objective of this concise presentation of sovereign debt crisis is to identify structural factors at the origin of these imbalances and their strengthening.

---

334 Régis Breton, et al., *Les banques, l'aléa moral et la dette publique*, 16, Revue de la Stabilité Financière (2012).

335 Régis Bismuth, *L'émergence d'un "ordre public de la dette souveraine" pour et par le contrat d'emprunt souverain ? Quelques réflexions inspirées par une actualité très mouvementée*, LVIII, Annuaire Français de Droit International (2012).

1.1.1. Anatomy of the crisis and analysis of a contagion

Before the outbreak of the crisis, derivatives have largely been developed. They became more and more complex as we confirmed it in the previous chapter. Since 2004, subprime mortgages had become popular within US banks that benefited from low interest rates and high capital liquidity. They granted loans to individuals that were too insolvent to be granted conventional mortgages. Risks associated to subprime mortgages were known. However, US banks securitised those loans to rebalance their balance sheet[336]. These subprime mortgages were combined with other products to offer an attractive investment. Due to their excellent rating, banks bought these products. However, the initial borrowers, who did not possess enough incomes, did not repay their loans. Creditors seized their properties but banks faced investors' distrust in July 2007 as they did not have provisions to manage losses on these products. Banks recovered credit or other guarantees, aggravating the financial situation of banks' capital and causing a drying up of liquidity. The loss of confidence led to a liquidity crisis. The banking circuit was then closed. The financial crisis emerged with a devaluation of US real estate securities transmitted to real economy by the interruption of bank lending activity[337].

From summer 2007 to summer 2008, investors were concerned by the viability of financial institutions. In September 2008, the US investment bank Lehman Brothers filed for bankruptcy. To avoid a total collapse, States provided support to the affected financial institutions in form of asset purchasing programmes or capital injection[338]. This assistance to the financial system affected public finances that were already unbalanced[339].

---

336 See Artus, et al., La crise des subprimes, 2008.

337 France, Documents et débats, (2010), pp. 5-37.

338 An Assessment of Financial Sector Rescue Programmes, (2009).

339 For the Member States of the European Union, aid to rescue banks must be authorised by the European Commission according to its rules on State aid: see Directive 2014/59 / EU of the European Parliament and of the Council of 15 May 2014 establishing a framework for the recovery and resolution of credit institutions and investment firms and amending Directive 82/891 / EEC and the European Parliament and Council Directives 2001/24 / EC, 2002/47 / EC, 2004/25 / EC, 2005/56 / EC, 2007/36 / EC, 2011/35 / EU, 2012/30 / EU and 2013/36 / EU and the regulations of the European Parliament and of the Council (EU) No 1093/2010 and (EU) No 648/2012. See also Sharon E. Foster, *Too Big to Fail – Too Small to Compete: Systemic Risk Should Be Addressed through Antitrust Law*

The growing indebtedness of some States gradually affected their ability to assume future financial obligations. Subsequently, on the financial markets, concerns were paradoxically focused on the sovereign solvency.

The crisis affected all the interactions between borrowers and lenders. Risks from the financial sector were transmitted to sovereign borrowers, whose risks were again transferred to the financial sector. Indeed, banks were exposed to sovereign risk. Their balance sheets were severely challenged due to the purchase of sovereign bonds or sovereign CDS. Their capital, financial results and shares decreased, while their financing burden increased. This rapid contagion from the financial sphere to the economic sphere, due to a general lack of fundings of undercapitalised banks and States' budget limitations to face crisis, reveals how the system is connected.

Sovereign solvency is questioned due to this contagion. Theoretically, tax revenues are *in fine* at the origin of the funding used during the crisis. We previously pointed out that part of the economic analysis considers that State is always a creditworthy borrower. It is due to its power to raise taxes as much as needed to repay its debts. Still, State keeps ensuring the functioning of its public services and welfare payments. Fundings available for crisis management are therefore limited by these financial obligations. As long as sovereign expenses are below generated revenues, State is considered solvent due to its ability to repay. As soon as there is a risk of lacking resources, various possibilities are conceivable.

The first possibility is to default. This term taken from the business world does not mean that a State may go bankrupt like a company. Default relates to a sovereign decision to suspend payments or to repudiate its financial commitments in order to reduce the debt value. Such reduction is carried out at the expense of debt holders. The majority of creditors are financial institutions investing in sovereign assets due to their safe reputation. Subsequently, the entire financial system is affected by a default, as well as the real economy. For sovereign bonds, the impact is directly negative. While States deemed safe were receiving favourable treatment and lower prices, the current crisis engraves the principle that no asset can be considered safe.

---

but Such a Solution Will Only Work if It is Applied on an International Basis, 22, Florida Journal of International Law (2010).

Another option is to use inflation. By influencing currency, the value of the securities issued by the State can be reduced. Newly issued money results in a reduction in the stock of the State. Debt burden diminishes through inflation. Deficits are monetised through the action of central bank acting as intermediary. This operation directly reinstates creditors' confidence. Nevertheless, risks are transferred to the central bank. This option does not favour financial consolidation since it is based on a short-term vision. In the medium term, this measure can destabilise the financial system[340].

A third possibility is to improve public finances to achieve a budget surplus. However, the reduction of public spending, the increase of taxation and the introduction of structural reforms are politically difficult to implement. In the absence of effective reforms, only a choice between inflation and instability of the financial system exists[341]. Reducing State's operating costs in order to increase growth currently remains merely wishful thinking[342].

1.1.2. Result of a predictable situation

The economic and financial crisis has aggravated a situation that was in advance structurally unbalanced due to a general deterioration of public finances and excessive debt. The situation was examined since the 1980s, when developing countries defaulted[343]. Disastrous market scenarios were established through the analysis of Eurocredits[344]. Nonetheless, the atten-

340 History is filled with examples of inflation due to States budget financing by the central bank. In the early twenties, there was even a hyperinflation situation in Austria, Hungary, Poland and Germany.

341 Masaaki Shirakawa, *Soutenabilité de la dette publique : condition préalable à la stabilité du système financier et des prix*, *in* Dette publique, politique monétaire et stabilité financière (Revue de la stabilité financière ed. 2012).

342 Dominique Carreau, *La surveillance internationale des politiques budgétaires*, *in* Quelle souveraineté budgétaire pour les États ? (Jean-Marc Sorel & Régis Chemain eds., 2013).

343 See Vinod K. Aggarwal & Brigitte Granville, Sovereign debt: origins, crises and restructuring (Royal Institute of International Affairs. 2003); Nouriel Roubini & Brad Setser, Bailouts or Bail-ins? Responding to Financial Crises in Emerging Economies (Peterson Institute for International Economics. 2004).

344 See Blaise, et al., Les euro-crédits, un instrument du système bancaire pour le financement international, 1981, pp. 341-342.

tion remained focus on developing countries[345]. The idea was to find a solution for indebted countries[346] without considering that it could also apply to developed countries. The analysis was based on non-payment episodes during the nineteenth century. At that time, States mainly borrowed under their domestic law. This phenomenon of non-payment was accentuated in the second half of the twentieth century with the development of modern financial market[347]. The history of these sovereign defaults seemingly remained confined to an over-indebtedness problem of developing countries[348], or was completely ignored[349]. However, the crises of the 1980s affected countries with structural policies that were estimated unbalanced. In the 1990s, financial and banking areas of Asian countries were affected, while they were considered well managed[350]. These observations prove that so-called developed countries can also be affected by a sovereign debt crisis. However, few observers have anticipated the current crisis[351].

The crisis invalidated two economic dogmas. First, the securitisation of risky private debt has not provided quality assets. Secondly, there is no safe financial assets since sovereign debt of developed countries are also risky. Retrospectively, European and Latin American countries defaulted almost the same amount of times. This cyclicality appears to be an immutable phenomenon inherent to State's existence. An analysis of debt cycles emphasises the link with banking crises. When the levels of external debt are very high, financial tensions may increase and lead to a banking

345 Pettifor, The coming First World debt crisis, 2006.

346 Living with debt. How to Limit the Risks of Sovereign Finance, (2006).

347 Sturzenegger & Zettelmeyer, Debt Defaults and Lessons from a Decade of Crises, 2007, pp. 3-10.

348 Monteagudo, The Debt Problem: The Baker Plan (1985) And The Brady Initiative (1989) – History, Experience, Practice And Prospects, 1995.

349 Sule Özler, *Have Commercial Banks Ignored History?*, 83 American Economic Review (1993). Peter H. Lindert & Peter J. Morton, *How Sovereign Debt Has Worked, in* Developing Country Debt and Economic Performance (Jeffrey D. Sachs ed. 1989).

350 Steven Radelet & Jeffrey Sachs, *The East Asian Financial Crisis: Diagnosis, Remedies, Prospects*, 29 Brookings Papers on Economic Activity (1998). See annex B presenting the Republic of Zaïre, the Republic of Peru, the Republic of Turkey, Jamaica, the Republic of Nicaragua, the Republic of the Sudan and the Republic of Poland in Rieffel, Restructuring Sovereign Debt: The Case for Ad Hoc Machinery, 2003, pp. 188-219 and 260-287.

351 Who saw Sovereign Debt Crises coming? (2008).

crisis[352]. In France, the *Pébereau report* already reported in 2005 a weak policy on public deficits. It stated that deficits have been accumulated over twenty-five years and were inappropriately managed. When the crisis began, deficits were high in many countries due to high expenditures, thus resulting in slow economic growth overall[353].

Nevertheless, it is not possible to establish a set of rules based on macroeconomic data to avoid crisis. Likewise, some attempts exist to define a sustainable limit of indebtedness, but a debt level can be sustainable for some States and intolerable for others. Thus, the debt-to-GDP ratio reveals major disparities between countries. For instance, we mentioned that Japan is much more indebted than the international average[354]. Yet Japanese domestic savings remain above the budget deficit and more than ninety percent of the bondholders are domestic investors. This structure avoids a debt dilution[355]. Intrinsically, the sustainability of sovereign debt depends on the policy implemented by States. For example, balanced public accounts in periods of instability are a positive sign for financial markets. However, the legal treatment of debt remains a critical factor for investors. When a State is committed to repay its investors, this policy inevitably reassures financial markets[356]. This commitment is legally reflected.

1.1.3. Criteria of sovereign default on the financial market

Like any other debtor, the State is financially committed to creditors through a series of loans. No creditor is immune to sovereign default. Therefore, financial markets' operators contractualise the notion of sovereign default in order to provide legal certainty to economic instability. According to the International Bond Market Association (ICMA), a default of a sovereign borrower is either a failure in the reimbursement to its

---

352 Carmen M. Reinhart & Kenneth S. Rogoff, *From Financial Crash to Debt Crisis*, 101 The American Economic Review (2011).

353 Banque de France, *La crise de la dette souveraine*, 4 Documents et débats (2012), pp. 5-9.

354 See the ranking of countries according to their public debt carried by the *World Fact Book of the Central Intelligence Agency*.

355 Shirakawa, Soutenabilité de la dette publique : condition préalable à la stabilité du système financier et des prix, 2012.

356 Landau, Revue de la Stabilité Financière, (2012).

creditors, or a breach of a material contractual obligation. A standard default clause of the ICMA states:

> "The bonds should entitle the bondholders to demand immediate repayment, prior to the contractual maturity date, *if: (i) the Issuer fails to pay any amount due under the bonds within 30 days of the due date for such payment; or (ii) the Issuer defaults in the performance of any of its other obligations under the bonds and (if the default is capable or remedy) fails to remedy the default within 30 days of being notified of it by any bondholders*. Acceleration of payment should be permitted provided holders of at least 25 per cent of the outstanding principal amount of the bonds vote in favour or such action" (we emphasise).

As seen above, the definition of default in such bonds only takes into account contractual obligations. The State is, therefore, in default on part of its bond contracts. Due to the mimetic functioning of markets, this may be enough to cause distrust. Consequently, the prices of CDS related to sovereign bonds rise. In these CDS contracts, the definition of default is wider and standardised[357]. Specifically, a credit event is contractually recognised when there is a breach of a reimbursement obligation, a moratorium, or a restructuring. This is the core definition of the functioning of this insurance. When an event is defined as a credit event, the CDS is triggered[358].

In the case of Greece, the scope of this definition is fundamental. In October 2009, when the newly elected government of George Papandreou announced that the country's public deficit had been undervalued for many years, market confidence gradually eroded. Operators were concerned about the sustainability of Greek debt. Rating agencies degraded their grade. In June 2010, Greece was excluded from capital markets[359]. Form the legal point of view, there was initially no default[360]. In 2011, the ISDA considered that the rescue plan negotiated with Greece did not con-

---

357 Most CDS on sovereign risks follow the 2003 ISDA Credit Derivatives Definition contract and its supplement in July 2009, updated in September 2014.

358 Virginie Coudert & Mathieu Gex, *Pourquoi le règlement des CDS grecs n'a pas conduit à la débâcle redoutée*, 17, Revue de la Stabilité Financière (2013).

359 Only four years later, in April 2014, Greece came back to the financial market. See Marie Charrel, *Grèce : le retour sur les marchés, une opération très politique*, Le Monde, 9.4.2014.

360 Hubert de Vauplane, *Pourquoi la Grèce n'est-elle pas juridiquement en défaut ?*, Revue Banque (2011), pp. 742-743.

stitute a default[361]. It is only on 9 March 2012, when the retroactive collective action clause forced all creditors to exchange their bonds, that rating agencies estimated that Greece was in default. Sovereign CDS were triggered[362]. Therefore, the concept of default remains entirely factual, whether legally or contractually stipulated.

This concept of sovereign default present in the markets differs from the one of the international financial institutions[363]. However, the same phenomenon of confusion was repeated in June 2015 when the IMF confirmed that Greece was in default[364]. This information was applied by the EFSF the next day. Several options were then considered[365]. This type of reaction was followed by legal provisions, as will be discussed in the second part of this dissertation.

---

361 On 31 October 2011, ISDA stated that: "*Based on what we know now, it appears from news reports that the Eurozone proposal involves a voluntary exchange that would not be binding on all holders. As such, it does not appear to be likely that the Eurozone proposal will trigger payments under existing CDS contracts. However, whether or not it does so will be decided by the [Determinations Committee] on the basis of the specific facts, if a request is made to them*" *ISDA, ISDA Statement on CDS Credit Event Process (2011).*

362 ISDA, ISDA EMEA Determinations Committee: Restructuring Credit Event Has Occurred with Respect to The Hellenic Republic (2012).

363 Default in Today's Advanced Economies: Unnecessary, Undesirable, and Unlikel, (2010).

364 International Monetary Fund, "Statement by the IMF on Greece", Press Release No.15/310, 30 June 2015: "*the SDR 1.2 billion repayment (about EUR 1.5 billion) due by Greece to the IMF today has not been received. We have informed our Executive Board that Greece is now in arrears and can only receive IMF financing once the arrears are cleared*".

365 EFSF, "EFSF takes note of Greece's non-payment to IMF", Luxembourg, 1 July 2015: "*propose one of the following three options:*
- acceleration of the loan: this means that the EFSF cancels the loan contract and requests immediate repayment of the principal and interest amounts;
- waiver of rights: this means that the EFSF irrevocably waives its right and remedies under the loan for this specific non-payment;
- reservation of rights: this means that the EFSF neither accelerates the loan nor waives its right to do so, but instead reserves the right to act at a later stage".

1.2. Challenges and pending questions

A general lack of transparency, an inadequate risk management and an underestimation of sovereign risk by the private sector were identified in the aftermath of the crisis (1.2.1.). Critics focus on market regulation, banking supervision, the lack of international lender of last resort (1.2.2.) and legal inconsistencies in sovereign financing system (1.2.3.).

1.2.1. Lack of international financial architecture

National and international financial regulation and market supervision take into account the lessons learnt from successive crises. After the 1929 crisis, banking supervision expanded through banking laws in key financial centres. After the collapse of the Bretton Woods system and the development of Euromarkets, the Basel Committee on Banking Supervision was created to regulate the banking system. In 1999, the concept of international financial architecture was created after the Asian crisis. The G7 and the Financial Stability Forum coordinated different entities to create financial standards. The purpose was to avoid gaps in supervision and regulation. International financial standards were created to prevent financial crises and to mitigate their effects[366]. They recalled the international financial architecture concept. After the last crisis, the G20 acted as a sponsor that establishes liability in the IMF and the Financial Stability Forum – which has become the Financial Stability Board in 2012[367]. This se-

366 International financial standards are one of the main changes following the financial crises of 1990 and discussions on a new international financial architecture. They include a set of measures to prevent crises and to mitigate their effects, generating more transparency in financial markets, especially on money laundering, terrorist financing or tax evasion. Douglas W. Arner & Ross P. Buckley, *Redesigning the Architecture of the Global Financial System* 11 Melbourne Journal of International Law (2010).

367 Financial Stability Board, Article 1 of the Charter of June 2012: "*The Financial Stability Board (FSB) is established to coordinate at the international level the work of national financial authorities and international standard setting bodies (SSBs) in order to develop and promote the implementation of effective regulatory, supervisory and other financial sector policies. In collaboration with the international financial institutions, the FSB will address vulnerabilities affecting financial systems in the interest of global financial stability*".

ries of measures demonstrate the absence of a system. It is rather a patchwork of measures taken during unstable times.

Every financial crisis refers to the basis of financial markets usefulness. These financial markets assist in making the real economy more productive by mobilising savings, allocating capital and managing risk[368]. Since the Asian crisis of 1997-1998, the idea of establishing a new international financial architecture has been considerably debated[369], with the concern of the efficiency of financial markets at the heart of the deficiencies that have been identified[370]. This issue directly affects States indebtedness. Indeed, financial markets freely determine payment interests on sovereign debt. Moreover, in times of great instability of international financial markets, much of the rapid contagion of financial crisis to sovereign borrowers was fundamentally based on an information problem among operators. Undeniably, the assessment of State creditworthiness depends on investors' judgments: if bondholders choose not to keep their bonds, they will sell them, other will imitate them and the price of government bonds will drop. Financing costs then increase as the probability of default increase. Thus, this behaviour leads to a sovereign debt crisis arising from a self-fulfilling process. The result is that from an initial limited unbalance, repercussions and losses are disproportionate[371].

Conflicts of interest between operators enhance this lack of information. For instance, on the Eurobond market, a banking syndicate is in charge of issuing, buying and reselling bounds to counterparty banks. All bond market operators meet in the ICMA[372]. The ICMA has a committee to determine default. Structurally, this default committee is led by members that benefit from the default. Indeed, commercial banks hold most

---

368 Joseph Stiglitz, Principles for a New Financial Architecture (The Commission of Experts of the President of the UN 2009).

369 Paul Krugman insisted that "*the first step of such reform is to find out who is responsible for that pompous phrase and punish him*" after he underlined "*The worst is now past, or so we hope. But what was it all about? How can things have gone so wrong so suddenly? And what should we do to prevent another financial crisis – or if one comes, what should we do to minimize it?*" Paul Krugman, *Analytical Afterthoughts on the Asian Crisis, in* Economic Theory, Dynamics and Markets: Essays in Honor of Ryuzo Sato (Takashi Negishi, et al. eds., 2001).

370 The High-Level Group Report on Financial Supervision in the EU. (2009).

371 Orléan, De l'euphorie à la panique : penser la crise financière. 2009, pp. 99-100.

372 Jacquillat, et al., Marchés financiers : Gestion de portefeuille et des risques, 2009, pp. 7-61.

sovereign debt bonds. Their exposure to the European debt crisis was considerable, with French and German banks holding large amounts of Greek, Irish and Portuguese sovereign debt[373]. Therefore, the conflict of interest in decision-making is undeniable.

Beyond a lack of information, there is a lack of transparency, as illustrated by the debate on the functioning of rating agencies[374]. While market tensions around sovereign debt appear, States' ratings are reassessed. It confirms that rating mechanism is driven by demand. Rating agencies are paid by the companies they rate[375]. On the financial markets, any decrease may cause a self-fulfilling prophecy by increasing distrust. The need for information is not questioned. It is the issuers' regulation of this information that is at stake. The growing use of ratings by regulators is explained by the fact that investors expect ratings. There is also a growing perception that ratings are more than an opinion because of their formal recognition by regulators. This leads to a vicious cycle of intrusive regulation to guide ratings towards regulatory requirements, and potentially changing the nature of ratings[376].

1.2.2. Lack of lender of last resort for States

The question on the need of a lender of last resort arises concerning the role of States[377]. This concept dates back to the eighteenth century when the banker Francis Barings referred in 1797 to the Bank of England as the last resource to obtain liquidity in times of crisis[378]. The lender of last resort is in charge of intervening through loans in the context of a systemic

---

373 Monitoring cross-border exposure: A primer on how to exploit the BIS banking statistics, (2010).

374 Agences de notation: pour une profession règlementée, (2012), pp. 113-169.

375 Charles W Calomiris, *The Subprime Turmoil: What's Old, What's New, and What's Next*, 15, The Journal of Structured Finance (2009).

376 Ratings and regulation, 2013, pp. 27-33.

377 Silvia Merler & Jean Pisani-Ferry, *Une relation risquée : l'interdépendance entre dette bancaire et dette souveraine et la stabilité financière dans la zone euro*, 16, Revue de la Stabilité Financière (2012).

378 Thomas M Humphrey & Robert E Keleher, *The Lender of Last Resort: A Historical Perspective*, 4, Cato Journal (1984).

crisis to save the financial system[379]. A single lender, a group of national lenders or a central bank in case of default of an institution can achieve this result. The purpose is to inject money to block the diminution of prices.

During the last crisis, the solvency of financial institutions was questioned. Their capital was affected by the contagion and the risks of insolvency of these institutions "too big to fail"[380]. States had to act as lender of last resort. This affected their solvency. Indeed, after announcing bank bailout, sovereign CDS increased[381]. Thus, States have held the role of lenders for financial institutions. No supranational central bank spontaneously imposed to alleviate the liquidity problems that States had subsequently encountered.

There is currently no such transnational authority taking the role of lender of last resort, even if the IMF has been envisaged to become the central bank for other banks. Indeed, its crisis management strategy moves away from the renegotiation of debt contracts to turn to the principle of lender of last resort[382]. This is analysed in the second part of this dissertation.

In the case of the European Economic and Monetary Union, States no longer have the monopoly of currency issuance. This is held by the ECB. States finance their expenses through taxes and bond issues. When joining the euro currency, States have chosen to restrict their monetary sovereignty. Monetary sovereignty allows a State to credit its accounts in its own currency. This facility disappears once the currency is fixed to another currency or in a monetary union. Ideally, the euro would inevitably stimulate

379 Michel Aglietta & Caroline Denise, *Les dilemmes du prêteur en dernier ressort international*, 14, Revue française d'économie (1999).

380 Intensity and Effectiveness of SIFI Supervision. (2010); Rosa María Lastra, *Systemic risk, SIFIs and financial stability*, 6, Capital Markets Law Journal (2011). Since November 2011, the FSB has published a list of banks "*too big to fail*". This list is annually updated and established following a strict methodology. See Banques d'importance systémique mondiale : méthodologie révisée d'évaluation et exigence additionnelle de capacité d'absorption des pertes, (2013).

381 Viral Acharya, et al., *A Pyrrhic Victory? Bank Bailouts and Sovereign Credit Risk*, The Journal of Finance (2013). Breton, et al., Revue de la Stabilité Financière (2012).

382 Stanley Fischer, *On the Need for an International Lender of Last Resort*, 13 Journal of Economic Perspectives (1999), pp. 85-104. Jeffrey Sachs, Do We Need an International Lender of Last Resort? (1995).

growth and the combination of convergence criteria and obligations imposed in Articles 123-126 of the TFEU[383] would be sufficient[384]. Under its statutes, the ECB is responsible for ensuring monetary and financial stability in the European construction. Its independence from States is essential to regulate. Financing public deficit is strictly prohibited.

Yet with the crisis, the purchase of public debt by the European central bank has been interpreted as part of the objective of monetary and financial stability. Avoiding a liquidity crisis was crucial to restore the proper functioning of markets. Sovereign solvency and the stability of the system were affected. The ECB monetised debt and acted as lender of last resort to support the prices of European sovereign debt securities. In September 2012, the ECB implemented a technical mechanism regarding outright transactions in secondary sovereign bond markets[385]. This mechanism of crisis resolution intended to reassure investors. It has been legally debated in Germany before the Constitutional Court in Karlsruhe[386]. This questioning of the constitutional law of the European governance is one of the consequences of the lack of a comprehensive legal framework[387]. The ECJ considered in June 2015 that:

> "This programme for the purchase of government bonds on secondary markets does not exceed the powers of the ECB in relation to monetary policy and does not contravene the prohibition of monetary financing of Member States"[388].

---

383 According to Article 123 TFEU, any overdraft or any other type of credit granted by the ECB or national central banks to public authorities are forbidden. Article 124 prohibits privileged access by public authorities to financial institutions. Article 125 provides that neither the Union nor the Member States meet the commitments of the authorities, public bodies or companies of a Member State. Article 126 provides for penalties for exceeding the deficit criteria.

384 Francesco Martucci, *Traité sur la stabilité, la coordination et la gouvernance, traité instituant le mécanisme européen de stabilité. Le droit international public au secours de l'UEM*, Revue des Affaires Européennes (2012).

385 Decisions of the Board of Governors of the European Central Bank in September 2012.

386 Eric Dor, *La Cour constitutionnelle de Karlsruhe suspecte les OMT d'être illégales*, 771, Revue Banque (2014). The ECB's Outright Monetary Transactions in the Courts (2015).

387 Hubert de Vauplane, *Le rôle du juge pendant la crise : entre ombre et lumière*, Revue des affaires européennes (2012).

388 Press release related to Court of Justice of the European Union, Judgment in Case C-62/14, *Gauweiler and Others v. Deutscher Bundestag*, 16 June 2015.

This broad interpretation of European texts and its case law indicates that there is no legally expected lender of last resort, despite its need and importance. States of the euro area, deliberately separated from their monetary sovereignty, cannot issue or depreciate their currencies. They are looking for a legal framework for sovereign debt, which, although national, binds them *in fine* through currency. In the absence of a lender of last resort, another idea may be introduced such as a common issuance of bonds. Various techniques have been studied to ensure their consistency with European law[389]. The purpose of such project is to take advantage of each State rating in order to launch on the markets a European debt that would promote financial solidarity among Member States. Solidarity can take the form of such common bonds, or a mutual fund, a joint liability mechanism for Member States in the event of default in the Eurozone, a debt cancellation or a bailout[390]. The debate remains suspended to political commitments. Since the crisis, the solidarity appears to be more amongst creditors.

1.2.3. Legal inconsistencies in sovereign financing

Market operators must redirect their investment strategies as sovereign bonds of developed countries are no more risk-free assets. Sovereign credit quality varies and high rates can be misleading. Changing the risk status of these securities implies, beyond the regulation of banking exposure levels, a structural change of products traded on financial markets. Moreover, the contractual terms and conditions imposed on States are essential. Amending them can redefine the contractual balance of bond contracts.

Yet the experience of previous crises brings only partial light to the current situation since debt instruments were syndicated bank contracts. Historical precedents in the nineteenth century and during the interwar period reveal that it is less complicated to solve a crisis based on syndicated loans than a crisis involving bonds. By definition, bonds do not bring together all debt holders as they are dispersed among investors. Bondholders acting as free riders have accentuated refinancing and restructuring problems.

389 Frédéric Allemand, *La faisabilité juridique des projets d'euro-obligations*, Vol. 48, Revue trimestrielle de droit européen (2012).

390 Jean Tirole, *La crise de l'euro : quelques éléments de réflexion sur la réforme institutionnelle*, 16, Revue de la Stabilité Financière (2012).

Without a viable mechanism to manage defaults based on bonds, financial growth inevitably leads to the current situation.

In the absence of a formal international legal framework, financial standards serve as safeguards to crisis. Since 1975, they have been developed in form of recommendations, principles, good practices or guidelines adopted by countries. These standards are not limited to soft law. The coefficient of 8 % of capital for international banks, decided by Basel II[391], is an example of binding standard that was reinforced with Basel III. For many standards, their purpose and aim is to prevent contagion. The twelve standards of the Financial Stability Board managed by the IMF through Reports on the Observance of Standards and Codes (ROSCs) and the World Bank Financial Sector Assessment Program (FSAPs)[392] may not prevent the US crisis, which has since turned into a global economic and financial crisis. Moreover, the anticipation of government support has somehow invalidated the need for such standards as losses were compensated by taxpayers and not by bondholders. With the absence of a clear regulatory framework, State decision regarding the bailouts for banks and the preservation of its credit rating is in favour of banks.

The financial crisis has tested the viability of banking markets and the regulatory framework. It highlighted an existing regulatory gap between the degree of financial integration of banking conglomerates and the limits of regulation. Serious lacks exist not only in the financial services industry, but also in regulatory and surveillance authorities at an international level[393]. Such exogenous shocks can also assist in the reform of the system

---

391 This coefficient of exposure implies that if more than 8 % of the loan is not repaid, the shareholders will rescue the bank. Mario Giovanoli, *The reform of the international financial architecture after the global crisis*, Vol. 42, N.Y.U. International Law and Politics (2009).

392 Thomas Hale & David Held, The Handbook of Transnational Governance: Institutions and Innovations (Polity. 2011).

393 "*This confidence, taken for granted in well-functioning financial systems, has been lost in the present crisis in substantial part due to its recent complexity and opacity,...weak credit standards, mis-judged maturity mismatches, wildly excessive use of leverage on and off-balance sheet, gaps in regulatory oversight, accounting and risk management practices that exaggerated cycles, a flawed system of credit ratings and weakness of governance*". See the G30 report cited by Larosière, The High-Level Group Report on Financial Supervision in the EU, 2009. Financial Reform: A Framework for Financial Stability (2009).

since the crisis highlights the weaknesses of the control and forces policy-makers to reconsider their positions.

Law must be taken into account in this current outlook[394]. Legal issues arise as the euro zone is different from the European Union. Eurozone members do not benefit from an institution that may strengthen emergency measures as it is the case for the European Union. Instead, the *modus operandi* among States of the euro zone is inter-governmental cooperation. Yet the legal framework of the European Union draws limits to this cooperation that may be in conflict with the rescue funds set up by the Eurozone members.

The paradox is strengthened by the denial of law and the need of a normative framework. This leads to a *sui generis* legal construction impossible to classify into any of the traditional categories of international law. We observe the presence of measures and at the same time regret the lack of legal rules. Informality is the main characteristic of the legal bases of this system, a characteristic that hinders the access and applicability of an international legal framework[395].

2. *Costs of default*

The non-payment of sovereign debt results in a number of economic and financial events that set default costs and restrict access to finance (2.1.). Default implies a jurisdictional cost. When defaulting, the State is sued to justify contractual violations (2.2.).

2.1. Restricted funding

Financial markets' sanctions have a direct negative impact for States. These sanctions drastically restrict the available financing or increase the cost of accessing to funding. In addition to these financial disadvantages, there is a subsequent reduction of State's economic and trade benefits

---

394 Christian Hofmann, *A Legal Analysis of the Eurozone Crisis*, *in* A Debt Restructuring Mechanism for Sovereigns. Do we need a legal procedure? (Christoph G. Paulus ed. 2014).

395 Michael C. Burda, *The European Debt Crisis: How Did We Get into this Mess? How Can We Get out of it?*.

(2.1.1.). The instability resulting from these various phenomena extends to the political sphere and partly explains why States mainly pay their debts (2.1.2.).

2.1.1. Financial, economic and commercial sanctions

Financial markets seriously affect defaulting States by excluding them[396] after each default during the period of negotiations for restructuring[397]. After this period, States can re-access markets and issue bonds. However, rising cost can durably affect a defaulted State. Market sanctions are in fact integrated in the risk premium. It consists of an increase of interest rates due to the deterioration of public finances. Credit risk refers to this risk of default of the bond issuer. Effect on the financing cost is similar to market exclusion. Borrowing becomes more expensive for States immediately after the implementation of a restructuring[398]. Therefore, maintaining a good reputation on financial markets is not necessarily correlated to the way the State is treated afterwards. Consequences of default do not last long and cost for borrowing is only temporarily affected.

However, other sanctions are more substantial. Creditors can sometimes impose direct sanctions on defaulting States. Beyond financial and economic costs, there is a commercial cost. Creditors can decide to sanction the State in default by stopping any business relationship or by decreasing trade[399]. Statistically, defaults reduce trade during long periods and causing effects close to an embargo. Restructuring plans of the Paris Club demonstrate a significant decline of bilateral trade[400], due to the way im-

---

396 The Costs of Sovereign Default (2009).

397 The average length of exclusion for a State is four years: see Sovereign Borrowing by Developing Countries: What Determines Market Access? (2004). The average length decreases as it was 5.5 years in the 1980s, 4.1 years in the 1990s and 2.5 in the 2000s. See Christine Richmond & Daniel A. Dias, Duration of Capital Market Exclusion: Stylized Facts and Determining Factors (2008).

398 Federico Sturzenegger & Jeromin Zettelmeyer, *Creditors' Losses versus Debt Relief: Results from a Decade of Sovereign Debt Crisis*, 5 Journal of the European Economic Association (2007).

399 The Cost of Aggressive Sovereign Debt Policies: How Much is the Private Sector Affected? (2009).

400 The decline amounted to 8 % per year. See Andrew K. Rose, *One Reason Countries Pay their Debts: Renegociation and International Trade*, 77 Journal of Development Economics (2005).

porters and exporters are losing their access to credit. This credit limitation partly explains the decline of trade.

Thus, economic activity can be affected by restrictions on sovereign financing. Sovereign defaults are often associated with a significant probability of a banking crisis and a decline of international direct investment or private investment[401]. Even in case of recovery, the economic situation remains difficult. States often need additional funding. This impact on economy and growth has provoked a lively debate, in particular among economists regarding the effects of deficits on growth[402].

The legal consequences differ according to the way a State defaults. If the State adopts a new legislation that amends the terms of the existing debt bonds, it is not clear if these new legislations are recognised or enforced. If the State forces its creditors to accept a debt reduction, creditors are not reimbursed according to initial conditions.

2.1.2. Political consequences

When the real economy is affected by a recession, political stability is jeopardised. The political consequences of a debt crisis are a warning sign to ministers and governments[403]. States are encouraged to repay their debts because the costs of default are huge for defaulting governments.

---

401 Carlos Arteta & Galina Hale, *Sovereign Debt Crises and Credit to the Private Sector*, 74 Journal of International Economics (2008).

402 Reinhart and Rogoff work highlighted a negative correlation between sovereign debt and economic growth. They claimed that "*when gross external debt reaches 60 per cent of GDP, annual growth declines by about two per cent; for levels of external debt in excess of 90 per cent of GDP, growth rates are roughly cut in half*". Carmen M. Reinhart & Kenneth S. Rogoff, *Growth in a Time of Debt*, 100 American Economic Review: Papers & Proceedings (2010). This numerical correlation, used by politicians and regulators, was methodologically criticised. Thomas Herndon, et al., Does High Public Debt Consistently Stifle Economic Growth? A Critique of Reinhart and Rogoff (University of Massachusetts 2013). The working hypotheses were also critised. Nersisyan & Randall, Revue de l'OFCE, (2011). The analysis was partially reviewed by the authors. See Carmen M. Reinhart & Kenneth S. Rogoff, Errata: "Growth in A Time of Debt" (Harvard University 2013).

403 Borensztein & Panizza, The Costs of Sovereign Default 2009.

All of these negative externalities encourage States to repay their debt as a default is more expensive than a debt service[404]. Since the costs of a sovereign default are particularly high and States have an incentive to repay, States seek *a priori* to reduce the risk of default. Globally, authorities are adopting macroeconomic policies and structural reforms to reduce the possibility of a crisis and to increase growth. The high cost of a default underlines the need of a crisis prevention system to avoid litigation.

2.2. Arbitrability of sovereign debt litigation

Creditors can file a lawsuit against States in a domestic court or arbitral tribunals to examine the alleged claims (2.2.2.). The waiver of jurisdictional immunity facilitates arbitration. It privatised the sovereign debt debate that seems to be dominated by profit-seeking operators (2.2.1.).

2.2.1. End of sovereign immunity on debt matters

Sovereign immunity plays a central role in the analysis of sovereign debt problem. According to this principle, States cannot be sued in foreign courts without their consent. Article 5 of the 2004 United Nations Convention on Jurisdictional Immunities of States and Their Property provides that:

> "a State enjoys immunity, in respect of itself and its property, from the jurisdiction of the courts of another State subject to the provisions of the present Convention".

Under international law, sovereign immunity derives from the acceptance of equality and the lack of hierarchy between States. According to the maxim *par in parem non habet jurisdictionem*, a State may not be subjected to judicial acts of another State. A doctrine of absolute immunity prevailed in the nineteenth century and in the first half of the twentieth century. This doctrine indicated that sovereign immunity applies even to interstate commercial transactions and transactions with an individual of another State. Private commercial interests did not come in the way of diplo-

---

404 Jonathan Eaton & Raquel Fernandez, *Sovereign debt, in* Handbook of International Economics (Ronald Winthrop Jones, et al. eds., 1995).

matic and political relations. Therefore, if a creditor may not successfully summon the defaulting State to the courts of this defaulting country, he was deprived of any legal remedy to obtain a reimbursement.

Contracts concluded by States in the field of financing may be subjected to judicial review. The doctrine of absolute immunity is now a concept of the past, as the aforementioned United Nations Convention on Jurisdictional Immunities of States enacted. Immunity can be waived and, in the case of a dispute relating to the contract, a sovereign can choose to enter into a contractual relationship and voluntarily submit itself to the authority of a foreign court. According to Article 7 of the UN Convention of 2004, a State loses its right to invoke its immunity if it has expressly consented to the exercise of jurisdiction[405]. Article 8 clarifies the effect of a State participation in the proceedings before a court. This participation characterises the State's consent to the exercise of jurisdiction[406]. Thus, States can be held legally responsible for violations of commercial contracts signed with foreign parties similarly to a private contractor.

---

405 Article 7 – Express consent to exercise of jurisdiction: "*1. A State cannot invoke immunity from jurisdiction in a proceeding before a court of another State with regard to a matter or case if it has expressly consented to the exercise of jurisdiction by the court with regard to the matter or case: (a) by international agreement; (b in a written contract; or (c) by a declaration before the court or by a written communication in a specific proceeding. 2. Agreement by a State for the application of the law of another State shall not be interpreted as consent to the exercise of jurisdiction by the courts of that other State*".

406 Article 8 – Effect of participation in a proceeding before a court: "*A State cannot invoke immunity from jurisdiction in a proceeding before a court of another State if it has: (a) itself instituted the proceeding; or (b) intervened in the proceeding or taken any other step relating to the merits. However, if the State satisfies the court that it could not have acquired knowledge of facts on which a claim to immunity can be based until after it took such a step, it can claim immunity based on those facts, provided it does so at the earliest possible moment. 2. A State shall not be considered to have consented to the exercise of jurisdiction by a court of another State if it intervenes in a proceeding or takes any other step for the sole purpose of: (a) invoking immunity; or (b) asserting a right or interest in property at issue in the proceeding. 3. The appearance of a representative of a State before a court of another State as a witness shall not be interpreted as consent by the former State to the exercise of jurisdiction by the court. 4. Failure on the part of a State to enter an appearance in a proceeding before a court of another State shall not be interpreted as consent by the former State to the exercise of jurisdiction by the court*".

The legal protections of sovereign debtors facing creditors' legal action have been significantly reduced since the 1980s. We will see that it is in large part due to a particular jurisdictional evolution. In addition to sovereign immunity, sovereign debtors used two legal principles in the 1980s and 1990s. First, the doctrine of the act of State emerged and provided that courts cannot judge the validity of the acts of a foreign State in its territory. Unlike sovereign immunity, the doctrine of the act of State relates to the inability to judge the actions of a foreign State. It creates a rule of abstention on the justiciability of the acts of a foreign State[407]. This doctrine is ineffective in practice since defaulting on international securities is not considered a sovereign act requiring legal protection[408]. Second, the principle of International Comity recognises legislative, executive or judicial actions of a State in another State's territory. However, this principle was unsuccessful among judges.

The end of sovereign immunity on debt matter includes seizure of property. When a creditor decides to execute a judgment in another jurisdiction in order to seize assets, the question of a contractual waiver of immunity from execution arises[409]. It is generally accepted that the assets of a State cannot be seized, due to their nature. In fact, these assets can be used to fill sovereign functions and public interest duties or for public purposes (*actiones iure imperii*). Public interest is strictly defined to prevent a sovereign debtor from losing its assets and keeping such assets from creditors. In many debt agreements, sovereign immunity waivers allow debtors to seize properties located abroad, allowing the enforcement of judgments on States. As the State has expressly waived its immunity from execution,

---

407 Philip J. Power, *Sovereign Debt: The Rise of the Secondary Market and Its Implications for Future Restructurings*, 64, Fordham Law Review (1996).

408 *Allied Bank International c. Banco Credito Agricola de Cartago*: the doctrine of the State act does not necessarily protect the States in case of default. See Otto Sandrock, *Is international arbitration inept to solve disputes arising out of international loan agreements?*, 11, Journal of international arbitration (1994). In *CIBC Bank and Trust Co. (Cayman) Ltd v. Banco Central do Brasil*, Brazil has neither invoked sovereign immunity nor the act of State doctrine in its defence. These principles have lost their protective power in the context of sovereign debt litigation. See Ugo Panizza, et al., *The Economics and Law of Sovereign Debt and Default*, 47, Journal of Economic Literature (2009).

409 Engela C Schlemmer, *The enforcement of sovereign debt*, *in* International monetary and financial law: the global crisis (Mario Giovanoli & Diego Devos eds., 2010).

it is possible to seize any property unless a national law allows special immunity[410], or if the State tries to limit its sizeable assets, traditionally by placing them outside the jurisdiction of the foreign courts[411].

2.2.2. Success of holdout creditors

The end of sovereign immunity is correlated to the success of holdout creditors. All State creditors' interests diverge in case of default. Banking institutions usually prefer negotiation to maintain their relationships with States and to avoid a default that would appear on their balance sheets. Non-institutional creditors may not follow this policy. With the creation of the secondary debt market, new investors have emerged, including companies specialised in the purchase of devalued sovereign debts. Called "vulture funds", these hedge funds are specialised in distressed debt funds. These funds purchase the debt of defaulting States at a low price and began proceedings against those States to recover the original price, normally negotiating a reimbursement through a court decision[412].

This type of litigation was rare in the 1980s due to the existence of significant contractual mechanisms and informal institutions such as the London Club, which promoted collective negotiations with debtors to avoid these vulture funds. Before the creation of the secondary debt market in the late 1980s, all sovereign debt holders were banks, forcing creditors to declare the debtor in default, and thus requiring full loan recall in accordance with contractual provisions.

Holdout creditors may sometimes receive better treatment. The case *Allied Bank International v. Banco Credito Agricola de Cartago* proved that such creditor could obtain a favourable sentence, even if it encountered problems in its execution[413]. In this case, the vulture fund finally received

410 This can be problematic under the rule of estoppel: the State cannot on one side waive its immunity in a contract while keeping its protective duty.

411 It can place them at the Bank for International Settlements to protect them against seizure.

412 Panizza, et al., Journal of Economic Literature, (2009). Fanny Giansetto, *Les fonds dits « vautours » et la dette souveraine. – Un nouvel enjeu de la régulation financière*, 6, Cahiers de droit de l'entreprise (2012).

413 Costa Rica had suspended payment of its debt to a syndicate of 39 institutions. A restructuring was organised between all banks except one, Fidelity Union Trust of New Jersey, that continued the proceedings before the United States authori-

no better results than other banks. The strategy of litigating creditors has been sophisticated with the case *Elliot Associates L.P. v Republic of Peru and Banco de la Nación del Peru* in 1998 and 1999. This case was critical[414]. After obtaining a favourable decision based on a broad interpretation of the *pari passu* clause[415], this vulture fund has subsequently developed a comprehensive strategy to seize sovereign assets abroad. This vulture fund solicited the courts to interfere in cross-border payments between the defaulted State and its other creditors that had agreed to a debt restructuring. Negotiations took place because the strategy of *Elliott Associated* threatened States[416]. This case has alerted observers because it demonstrated that litigating creditors may receive more than those accepting the restructuring, thus discouraging any future negotiations. *Elliott Associated* steered holdout creditors from the rank of minor nuisance to that of formidable obstacle to sovereign debt restructuring. Their action is a veto on the regularisation of relations between a country and its major creditors. Vulture funds hold influence over a State's return to international capital markets.

---

ties through an agent, Allied Bank. In first instance, the doctrine of act of State ruled in favour of Costa Rica. But in appeal in 1984, the argument was dismissed. Defaulting on sovereign debt is not an act of State. The debt restructuring of Costa Rica is similar to Chapter 11 of the United States Bankruptcy Code. The State had not repudiated its debt but had renegotiated in good faith. Yet in 1985, the case was again presented before a judge who considered, recognising the argument of the US Department of Justice, that Costa Rica had unilaterally decided to restructure its debt. The case ended with a settlement: the US government encouraged Fidelity Union to accept the offer that the rest of the banking union had accepted.

414 Eric Robert, *Rééchelonnement de la dette ou règlement judiciaire? Analyse de la jurisprudence interne et internationale au regard des enjeux de la renégociation de la dette, in* La dette extérieure / The external debt (Martinus Nijhoff Publishers ed. 1995).

415 Under this broad interpretation, the *pari passu* clause guarantees equal payment to creditors. A more conventional interpretation of the clause is that this clause provides equal rank among creditors. The interpretation of this clause is still debated.

416 See prologue Martial Heland, Restructuration de dette souveraine et défense contre les fonds vautours (Université Paris 1 Panthéon-Sorbonne 2011).

Other creditors have tried to imitate the legal strategy developed by *Elliott Associates*, albeit with mitigated success[417]. Thus, the effect of these vulture funds remains limited. Full repayment is exceptional and several funds receive nothing, while attempts on blocking the restructuring negotiations by lawsuit remain unsuccessful[418]. In addition, due to high legal fees, such strategies only make sense for highly specialised companies.

The case of Argentina illustrates the cost of default for a State. In January 2002, the Argentine State went to default on its sovereign debt after two restructuring plans negotiated in June and November 2001. The economy was already in recession and public debt deficit was critical. The government used domestic commercial banks to finance its deficit. In late 2004, more than 140 legal proceedings were in progress against Argentina, with fifteen class actions from vulture funds and retail investors in New York, Italy, Germany. The case *Abaclat and Others v. Argentine Republic* raised the question of whether sovereign bonds were recognised as an investment under the ICSID Convention[419]. Based on the definitions of bilateral investment treaties, the arbitral tribunal held that ICSID arbitration applies to sovereign debt contracts conflicts. The case *NML Capital c. Argentina* focused all attention due to the interpretation of the *pari passu* clause and its implications for the Argentine State. This is addressed in detail in the second part of this dissertation.

The current situation is not satisfactory, either for creditors or sovereign debtors. Creditors have *de lege lata* the right to enforce their trials but often fail to receive adequate reimbursement due to the lack of funds located outside the territory of sovereign debtors. States face legal action in case

---

417 In the case *LNC c. Nicaragua*, the Belgian Court of Appeal found that the *pari passu* clause did not give the right to seize LNC payments routed through Euroclear insofar Euroclear was not a party of the contract containing the clause *pari passu*. In *Kensington v. Republic of Congo*, an English judge dismissed the application of the *pari passu* clause. In *Red Mountain in Finance v. Democratic Republic of Congo*, the same clause was rejected but the judge ordered that payments made by the debtor should be proportioned between creditors. The DRC finally negotiated with Red Mountain.

418 Sturzenegger & Zettelmeyer, Debt Defaults and Lessons from a Decade of Crises, 2007, pp. 3-30.

419 *Abaclat and Others v. Argentine Republic*, ICSID Case No. ARB/07/5 (formerly Giovanna a Beccara and Others v. The Argentine Republic). See Michael Waibel, *Opening Pandora's Box: Sovereign Bonds in International Arbitration*, 101, American Journal of International Law (2007).

of non-repayment of their debt. As they are excluded from markets, they have no more access to financing. In such way, state interventions may then be counterproductive. Conversely, vulture funds respect law[420]: they serve in some way the cause of a more rigorous legal framework.

*

The subprime market crisis in the United States can be explained by imprudent lending to borrowers that were not falling under the usual criteria for creditworthiness. After being securitised, these loans were massively sold worldwide to banks and other financial intermediaries. When the subprime mortgage market eventually collapsed after the burst of the housing bubble, the related assets have become toxic due to their worthlessness. Still, a number of major banking institutions and other financial intermediaries around the world held these toxic assets.

The general banking distrust blocked the interbank market. An important governmental support to the financial sector helped to partially restore market confidence. However, the credit contraction resulting from the financial crisis has subsequently affected the economy in general, which has fallen into a deep recession. Government programmes to support the real economy, in addition to the aids already granted to the financial sector, have particularly increased sovereign deficits.

Massive steps have been gradually taken to solve this sovereign debt crisis. Reducing sovereign debt became imperative. Iceland defaulted while Greece has restructured its debt. Austerity was preferred by other States that implemented fiscal efforts, recovering their deficit and changing the labour market for more flexibility. Nevertheless, regulatory reforms are necessary to avoid a further major shock and to stabilise the global financial system.

---

420 Kunibert Raffer, *Improving Debt Management on the Basis of UNCTAD's Principles*, *in* Sovereign Financing and International Law. The UNCTAD Principles on Responsible Sovereign Lending and Borrowing (Carlos Espósito, et al. eds., 2013).

Title II. CONCLUSION

International public debt is characterised by a quantitative decline of loans from multilateral development banks and from banking syndicates. States and public entities substituted their fund raising by the capital market, which can exceed ten times the capacity of the original lenders. This development is opportunistic. Existing financing operators worked under the law of the market, i.e. private law. This transformation is at the heart of the current crisis. We may ponder over the ambivalence of these sovereign debt bonds, positioned between private contract and sovereignty. However, the real issue is whether the government can provide measures to solve the problems posed by this financialisation and privatisation of sovereign debt.

PART I. CONCLUSION

The first part of this dissertation laid the foundations of the organisation and operation of sovereign debt financing. The consolidation of the use of bonds implies a profound legal change. Private law contracts are prevailing in the sovereign debt structure. Debt bonds are not negotiated as international financial agreements are. The changing financial environment disrupts the application of law. It is neither domestic nor international, but adapted to financial and market purposes.

Analysing sovereign debt financing demonstrates that phenomena are intertwined with a new reality: private operators such as bankers, economists and lawyers delimit strategic decisions for State. Their broad power has serious consequences[421]. Legal difficulties posed by debt contracts and derivatives as well as methods used to regulate market operators are dependent on the political will.

Public intervention cannot intervene through tinkering to regulate permanently and stabilise markets. However, it is essential at least to redefine debt contracts with clear clauses, to regulate the determination of CDS credit events, and to set accounting standards to ensure transparency and effective information. These measures are all necessary, especially since rescheduling plans may entirely affect the phenomenon of sovereign debt.

421 Charles-Albert Michalet, *La dimension monétaire et financière du capitalisme mondial*, *in* Les euro-crédits, un instrument du système bancaire pour le financement international (Jean-Bernard Blaise, et al. eds., 1981).

PART II. PUBLICISATION OF SOVEREIGN DEBTMANAGEMENT

The first part of this study highlights the fact that financial and monetary imbalances are the cause of a failed operation of sovereign financing. Some of these imbalances arose from market failures. The usual causes are not only inappropriate regulations, but also a defective macro-prudential supervision. Without trying to definitively solve future crisis, we assume that an adequate regulation is still needed to stabilise the financial system[422]. This implementation is fully dependent upon the States.

Sovereign debt consists of a public/private inversion with few possibilities for State regulation[423]. Yet, examples of cooperation between public and private sectors are numerous, such as the prudential regulations of the Basel Committee[424]. In the field of human rights, States create legal systems from private foundations. In the case of marine insurance or Internet access, private operators are in charge of the regulation under States' control. It should therefore be possible for States and private stakeholders to create, implement and monitor standards and rules.

Yet, the number of international standards to regulate and manage sovereign indebtedness is inversely proportional to the challenge posed by international public funding. Without talking about a unilateral sovereign right to stop repaying debts[425], the fact that States have not yet developed a common regulation, or are still reluctant to address it, is central in the debate on publicising sovereign debt management. Since the last financial crisis, there has been a reflection on institutions and on the role of international law. The purpose is to rethink debt and its political implications[426]

---

422 Larosière, The High-Level Group Report on Financial Supervision in the EU, 2009, p. 16.

423 Horatia Muir Watt, *Conclusion générale*, *in* Insolvabilité des États et dettes souveraines (Mathias Audit ed. 2011).

424 Daphné Josselin, *Regime Interplay in Public-Private Governance: Taking Stock of the Relationship Between the Paris Club and Private Creditors Between 1982 and 2005*, 15, Global Governance (2009).

425 Georges Ripert, *Le droit de ne pas payer ses dettes*, Dalloz Revue hebdomadaire de jurisprudence (1936).

426 Claude Giraud, De la dette comme principe de société (Harmattan. 2009), p. 267.

in order to witness the emergence of a new public policy of sovereign debt[427]. While initiatives are mostly national, the progressive integration of standards allows the emergence of a public policy of sovereign debt to protect States' financial interests and international organisations. Although no ideal structure exists in such a complex system, mechanisms for consultation and legal tools can be used to reach a balance. Such structure should constantly be adapted to the reality and the on-going negotiations between operators.

Sovereign borrowers facing a critical financial situation evolve in a flexible legal world. They can use a mix of public, private, legal and political resources. This second part will examine the resolution mechanisms of current sovereign indebtedness and identify different modalities. Since the late 1970s, two approaches are typically offered in debt management and restructuring in case of sovereign default.

First, the vertical approach consists of renegotiating, restructuring and rescheduling debt. This renegotiation is often bilateral and conducted under the auspices of States' creditors, an *ad hoc* forum such as the Paris Club or an international financial institution like the IMF (Title III). Second, the horizontal approach favours interstate cooperation in various fora that work towards the establishment of standards and statutory rules (Title IV).

Informal clubs and holdout creditors preferred contractual solutions (Chapter 5). The World Bank and the IMF promote a comprehensive approach of debt (Chapter 6) that has allowed the emergence of some international framework proposals (Chapter 7). It is based on this work that an international economic law of sovereign debt emerged (Chapter 8).

427 Bismuth, Annuaire Français de Droit International, (2012).

Title III. INSTITUTIONAL FRAMEWORK OF CONTRACTUAL INSTRUMENTS

Under the vertical approach, the settlement of a sovereign default can take two forms. The first form is contractual and is based on negotiating a debt-restructuring plan between the sovereign debtor and its creditors. This plan is the result of an agreement between all or a majority of creditors. Contractual arrangements on collective treatment exist within several entities like the Paris Club and the London Club. The second form is judicial: creditors go to court asking for the payment of debt contracts. This strategy has generated an abundant case law examining the conditions of seizure of sovereign property. During the last crisis, the debate has moved towards the introduction of collective action clauses to facilitate the establishment of collective treatment (Chapter 5).

However, these negotiations do not allow a comprehensive treatment of sovereign default as creditors only seek to recover their investment. Subsequently, since the late 1990s, rescheduling under the auspices of international financial institutions promoted the development of legal tools to facilitate debt restructuring with the approval of a majority of creditors. The treatment of sovereign debt is made for and by public and private operators (Chapter 6).

CHAPTER 5. Choice of Contractual Measures for Debt Restructuring

In the absence of a legal framework for sovereign debt issues, legal issues encountered by creditors are multiple. There is neither a common definition of the concept of default, nor an automatic law applicable to a recognised default condition, nor identical rights for creditors that bought the same bonds. Everything should be defined. Debt restructuring has been made among *ad hoc* fora designed only to manage certain types of debts (1.).

Unanimity is rare and some creditors often prefer litigation. The integration of clauses in contracts ensures that a qualified majority will be contractually privileged to turn these strategies into collective treatment negotiations (2.).

1. Ad hoc restructuring fora for collective processing

Collective action is essential to any successful debt restructuring. Under the contractual approach, creditors and the sovereign debtor shall agree on a plan. The fora for negotiations on restructuring vary depending on the public or private nature of creditors (1.1.). The restructuring of Greek debt, undertaken by the Troika, proves that this contractual treatment is still in force thanks to its flexibility (1.2.).

1.1. Restructuring plans of the Paris and London Clubs

The Paris Club and the London Club are mechanisms that facilitate restructuring by supervising and organising negotiations between the sovereign debtor and its creditors. The Paris Club, founded in 1956, is an informal structure hosted by the French Ministry of Economy that brings together OECD members and other States' creditor (1.1.1.). The London Club, established in 1976, operates through *ad hoc* meetings of private banks that are States' creditors (1.1.2.).

1.1.1. The Paris Club, from restructuring to debt reduction

The Paris Club is a sovereign debt-restructuring forum. Its existence confirms the principle of a pacific settlement of debts raised in 1907 in the Drago-Porter Convention[428]. In the mid-1950s, the first club appeared in The Hague to renegotiate commercial debt. Brazil was negotiating the reorganisation of its debt with Germany, the United Kingdom and the Netherlands. Brazil was facing repayment difficulties, partly due to the collapse of its export incomes of coffee. The United Kingdom was plan-

428 See Chapter 1. Pursuant to this Convention, in the event of a dispute between two States on a contractual debt, the creditor must provide debtor arbitration to settle the dispute. If the debtor tacitly or expressly rejects the arbitration, the creditor may use armed force (Article 1).

ning to grant a new loan. This decision was taken in the context of commercial competition for Latin American markets. Such a loan was in fact a financial assistance in exchange of market segments' preservation. In July 1955, the three creditors reached an agreement to gradually settle the Brazilian commercial debt[429]. Following the success of this negotiation, Argentina submitted a debt-restructuring request to its European creditors. The Paris Club was formed on this occasion[430]. The Paris Club is a pragmatic solution to sovereign debt disputes. Due to its international nature, it joins together creditors of sovereign debtors without having the characteristics of an intergovernmental organisation. Indeed, there is neither a founding charter governing its establishment or operation, nor a legal personality[431]. The Paris Club is an informal entity that escapes international law. It is a legal paradox. On one hand, creditors of sovereign debtors reaffirm the principle *pacta sunt servanda*:

> "every treaty in force is binding upon the parties to it and must be performed by them in good faith"[432].

On the other hand, by agreeing to renegotiate a debt, creditors renounce to this contractual principle and to their right to go to courts. As for the sovereign debtors, renegotiation implies a *rebus sic standibus* renunciation[433]. They may no longer rely on Article 50 of the 1969 Vienna Convention on the Law of Treaties that is related to corruption of a representative of a State[434]. These States renounce the ability to invoke the invalidity

---

429 Holmgren, La renégociation multilatérale des dettes : le Club de Paris au regard du droit international, 1998, pp. 58-61.

430 Henry J. Bittermann, The Refunding of international debt (Duke University Press. 1973), p. 112.

431 Since 2003, the Paris Club communicates on its website. Information on the conditions of participation and results of each negotiation are published. However, negotiation minutes are not available.

432 Article 26 of the Vienna Convention on the law of treaties concluded at Vienna on 23 May 1969.

433 According to this clause, a fundamental change of circumstances may result in terminating or withdrawing from a treaty. See Articles 62 and 44 of the Vienna Convention on the law of treaties concluded at Vienna on 23 May 1969.

434 "*If the expression of a State's consent to be bound by a treaty has been procured through the corruption of its representative directly or indirectly by another negotiating State, the State may invoke such corruption as invalidating its consent to be bound by the treaty*". Article 50 of the Vienna Convention on the law of treaties concluded at Vienna on 23 May 1969.

of the financial agreement. While renegotiating, the sovereign debtors sign a debt rescheduling agreement that replaces the original agreement according to standards, rules and procedures that have been developed and codified since the early 1980s.

The aim of the Paris Club is to bring together the maximum of creditors of States to renegotiate arrangements for recovering sovereign debtors outside of any institutional framework. This *ad hoc* system of sovereign debt renegotiation is based on six principles: creditors' solidarity, comparability of treatment, conditionality, consensus, case-by-case decision and consensus[435].

Solidarity and comparability of treatment concern creditors and not sovereign debtors, which are not organised in groups[436]. Comparability of treatment means that debtors are treated in the same way by their creditors with the exception of multilateral financial institutions (whose debt is deemed a priority) and bondholders (which are considered unsecured creditors). According to the rule of conditionality, the sovereign debtor has to first conclude a stand-by agreement with the IMF in order to address the Paris Club. The consensus rule means that during the meetings, participants seek to reach a debt rescheduling agreement without the implementation of any constraint. All negotiations are at the discretion of the Paris Club. This system allows a political control over debtors reinforced by the IMF surveillance through stand-by agreements[437].

In 1994, the Paris Club defined modalities to deal with debt unsustainability. Progressively, the Paris Club evolved from a pure logic of restructuring to a debt reduction reasoning[438]. Standard terms of treatment changed over the years[439] to gradually integrate a range of options for

---

435 See the six principles of the Paris Club available on its website.

436 The only attempt of organisation is the Cartagena Consensus in the late 1980s at the initiative of eleven Latin American States under the leadership of Uruguay. The initiative failed because larger States refused to diminish their power of negotiation by joining a group.

437 Loïc Grard, *Le club de paris et les dettes publiques des États in* La dette extérieure / The external debt (Martinus Nijhoff Publishers ed. 1995).

438 Innovation in the Sovereign debt regime: from the Paris club to enhanced HIPC and beyond (2002).

439 Four categories of treatment exist, ranked in order of concessionality: 1) Classic terms (standard treatment), 2) Houston terms (for highly indebted lower-middle-income countries), 3) Naples terms (for highly indebted poor countries), and 4) Cologne terms (for countries eligible to the HIPC initiative).

each case[440]. In 1996, the launch of the initiative for highly indebted poor countries (HIPC) under the auspices of the IMF and the World Bank consolidated the tailored treatment of debt. This initiative brought together international financial operators to manage the issue of some indebted countries. The programme has been strengthening by the Evian approach for non-HIPC states[441]. The purpose is to ensure long-term debt sustainability through a multi-institutional analysis based on a debt viability evaluation conducted by the IMF and the World Bank[442]. Based on this evaluation, the Paris Club creditors choose between a predefined treatment and the application of tailored measures.

Thus, the Paris Club is a particular entity for sovereign debt restructuring[443]. Its standards for public debt management are directly inspired by its practice. However, no international consensus has been reached to create and perpetuate this Club that brings together creditors of States and disregards sovereign debtors. This dichotomy demonstrates that this club is not *per se* a debt management institution as its purpose is not to solve over-indebtedness. Its standards of treatment have changed due to criticism[444]. Negotiations changed in particular when some sovereign debtors became creditors. It is the case for Russia and Brazil. Debt management within the Paris Club may be similar to an interstate agency of debt recovery. This *ad hoc* mechanism suffers from a lack of overall vision. It is

440 Forteau, Le défaut souverain en droit international public : les instruments de droit international public pour remédier à l'insolvabilité des États, 2011.

441 Until 2013, Paris Club creditors have provided debt treatment under the Evian approach to fourteen countries: Antigua and Barbuda (2010), Republic of Djibouti (2008), Gabonese Republic (2004), Georgia (2004), Grenada (2006), Republic of Iraq (2004), Republic of Kenya (2004), Dominican Republic (2004 and 2005), Kyrgyz Republic (2005), Republic of Moldova (2006), Republic of the Union of Myanmar (2013), Federal Republic of Nigeria (2005), Federation of Saint Kitts and Nevis (2012) and Republic of Seychelles (2009). See Paris, Rapport annuel d'activité, 2013.

442 Thomas A. Duvall, *Debt Relief for Low-Income Countries*, *in* Sovereign Debt Management (Lee Buchheit & Rosa Lastra eds., 2014). See also Chapter 6.

443 IMF Managing Director Christine Lagarde considers the Paris Club as « *le seul forum organisé mondial qui assure une coordination entre créanciers bilatéraux officiels en matière de restructuration de dette souveraine* ».

444 See "Club de Paris Comes Under Attack", Euromoney, IMF/WB Annual Meeting, Issue 2000, pp. 56-61.

strengthened by the fact that each renegotiation is considered exceptional[445].

1.1.2. The London Club, banking committees for restructuring

The private equivalent of the Paris Club is the London Club[446]. Constituted in 1975, it facilitates negotiations between commercial banks and sovereign debtors. The London Club is based on practice, similarly to the Paris Club. The restructuring of bank loans has increased in the 1980s because of the debt crisis. In 1976, due to the rising price of oil, Zaire (current Democratic Republic of the Congo) and Peru were the first sovereign debtors to renegotiate their bank debt. In 1977, Turkey and Sudan followed them, as well as Poland in 1981.

Unlike the Paris Club, there is no secretariat or membership status in this club of commercial banks. The London Club is organised in *ad hoc* banking committees, which gather representatives of banks exposed to defaulting sovereign debtors. The lack of secretariat to track the London Club's activity complicates the compilation of information. It is nevertheless possible to distinguish several distinctive elements. In the negotiations, commercial banks are organised in syndicates[447]. Generally, the most exposed bank organises and chairs the advisory committee. According to the rule of equal treatment, each bank takes part of a debt restructuring proportionally to its exposure. There is no consensus on the core principles of restructuring in the London Club because each negotiation is unique. Nevertheless, some principles apply such as the notion of case-by-case, the voluntary support and the market-based solutions. Conditionality rules generally include an agreement between the IMF and the debtor. This stand-by agreement precedes negotiations with private creditors. In this way, a private system based on consistent rules and procedures has

445 For examples of restructuring, see Sovereign Debt Restructurings 1950-2010: Literature Survey, Data, and Stylized Facts (2012).

446 The origin of its name remains unclear. The term seems to have been used for the first time by the financial press in 1980 due to the meetings in London, the choice of English law in Eurocredits and the use of LIBOR as reference for the interest rate. However, New York was the seat of multiple negotiations between sovereign debtors and commercial banks.

447 See the functioning of banking syndicates in Chapter 2.

gradually emerged to guide the restructuring. This system stabilises operators' behaviour during negotiations.

Regardless of the forum, case-by-case treatment is central to the negotiations with sovereign debtors. The concept of voluntary participation means that the terms of the restructuring are negotiated between banks and the sovereign debtor until a mutual agreement is reached. Reaching a debt relief is therefore not a unilateral creditor commitment. In a commercial context, creditors only consider negotiating when the alternatives are between not being paid at all or get some benefits such as liquidity or collateral[448].

The market-based approach implies that the agreed solution is flexible, pragmatic and apolitical. The repayment terms are indexed according to the debtor's ability to repay. A new loan is usually granted. Based on the concept of conditionality, debtors must seek an agreement with the IMF before starting negotiations with the London Club. Nevertheless, bank negotiations can succeed before the State has obtained the stand-by agreement of the IMF. Out-dated payments can then be promptly reimbursed. Imminent default is not a prerequisite for renegotiation.

Procedurally, when negotiations converge to a new contractual version, participants are invited to respond positively. If some banks are recalcitrant, other banks may invite them to reconsider their position. For smaller amounts, the State can repay through a new loan to facilitate the final agreement. The overall balance of the new contract is based on further cooperation with international institutions like the IMF and the Paris Club. The London Club reflect specific objectives to commercial banks. Instead of foreign policy, the pursuit of profit and risk management, economic development and regional stability lie at the forefront of these negotiations.

The Paris Club and the London Club have emerged in response to similar challenges and have analogous procedures. For example, the conditionality rule places the IMF in the middle of the restructuring. Sovereign debt treatment in these fora is a sort of sovereign reorganisation law in *statu nascendi*. However, this process of debt restructuring is related to exceptional measures and cannot be used as a permanent mechanism. The Paris Club and the London Club are not involved in the sense of *opinio juris* to define debt reorganisation mechanisms. Moreover, official and private

448 For private creditors, a negotiation is imposed when official institutions like the IMF or the World Bank intervenes or when the sovereign debtor offers them a take-it or leave-it proposal.

creditors share a reluctance to create a mechanism for restructuring sovereign debt that may legally recognise the doctrine of odious debt in international public law[449]. In recent years, these clubs have partially lost their relevance. Nowadays, bank loans are less used. The current problem is the restructuring of sovereign bonds. In fact, the original London Club disappeared at the end of the 1990s. The evolution has been from a homogeneous group of common creditors to a fragmentation of bondholders' interests and objectives. Hedge funds, pension funds and insurance companies are more interested in immediate profits and do not hesitate to act accordingly to maximise their investments, as exemplified by the vulture funds' strategies.

Opening the practice of these clubs arose as part of the reform proposals. The idea is to create a sovereign debt forum to provide an independent place in which creditors and debtors can voluntarily meet regularly to discuss difficulties related to sovereign debt[450]. Such a forum would also provide research and continuous reform on the issues of sovereign debt to go beyond specific actions taken in response to a crisis. This type of forum would provide an active engagement on debt treatment with new creditors, rather than waiting for a comparable implementation in conventional processes.

The pragmatism of these clubs may be used in the context of burden sharing. In commercial practice, creditors share losses in case of restructuring. Some creditors have a priority above others. This differential treatment is the result of both historical practice and extensive negotiations. In terms of sovereign debt restructuring, the favourable treatment remains highly debated[451]. The political dimension of the sovereign debtor treatment in the Paris Club is well known[452]. The London Club has a practice of renegotiating banking committees, which is politically oriented. The experience of the Brady Plan demonstrates that the US government overexposed itself to save US banks. It has played an important role in decision-

449 Anna Gelpern, *What Iraq and Argentina Might Learn from Each Other*, 6, Chicago Journal of International Law (2005).

450 A blueprint for a Sovereign Debt Forum (2014).

451 Structuring and Restructuring Sovereign Debt: The Role of Seniority (2005).

452 Debt Relief for the Poorest: An Evaluation Update of the HIPC Initiative, (2006). Leonie F. Guder, The Administration of Debt Relief by the International Financial Institutions: A Legal Reconstruction of the Hipc Initiative (Beitrage Zum Auslandischen Offentlichen Recht Und Volkerrecht ed., Springer-Verlag Berlin and Heidelberg GmbH & Co. K. 2010), pp. 172-194.

making and influenced the overall strategies of the debt crisis management adopted by international financial institutions. The same political dimension is found in the Greek restructuring.

1.2. Greek restructuring under the auspices of the Troika

The expertise developed by the IMF on financial crisis management convinced the ECB and the European Commission to work collectively under the name of Troika. Greece's membership in the Eurozone and the restructuring of Greek debt forced the EU to develop a legal framework to organise restructuring (1.2.1.). This restructuring involves private creditors (1.2.2.) and questions their preferential creditor status (1.2.3.).

1.2.1. Towards the establishment of a European legal framework for restructuring

We presented in the previous chapter how the Greek crisis became the first sovereign debt crisis in a mature market economy. The restructuring of Greek sovereign debt is the largest in history in terms of volume[453]. Legally, its sovereign debt was mainly constituted of bonds. Investors were not only private and domestic but also international and institutional. The Greek debt restructuring was carried out through *ad hoc* mechanisms. The high risk of contagion in the Eurozone and the threat to the banking system and the global economy led to manage debt through successive restructuring plans. In addition, the impact on the banking system imposed to recapitalise banks[454]. However, given the extent of the crisis, the succession of measures demonstrated that they were insufficient to install a permanent basis for the resolution of other financial difficulties faced by a Member States of the Eurozone. The evolution of the management of sovereign debt crisis in the Eurozone led to the development of a legal framework for sovereign debt management.

---

453 An exchange of 206 billion euros out of 305 billion euros of debt is considered. See Jeromin Zettelmeyer, et al., *The Greek Debt Restructuring: An Autopsy*, 28, Economic Policy (2013).

454 Christoph G. Paulus, *The Interrelationship of Sovereign Debt and Distressed Banks: A European Perspective*, 49, Texas International Law Journal (2014).

Following the approval of the first Greek restructuring programme, a mechanism was established in May 2010, comprising the European Financial Stabilisation Mechanism (EFSM)[455] and the European Financial Stability Facility (EFSF). Based on the observation that, within the European Union, there cannot be solidarity without responsibility, fiscal discipline and the Stability and Growth Pact were reinforced by the *Six Pack*[456]. The purpose was the preservation of the European financial stability in case of serious tensions in Eurozone sovereign debt markets. Financial assistance was granted to any Eurozone States facing budget problems[457]. These two mechanisms were provisional with a limit fixed on 30 June 2013. As they restored market confidence, they had to be perpetuated. Subsequently, the Treaty establishing the European Stability Mechanism (ESM) was confirmed on 2 February 2012. This permanent organisation has a legal personality[458]. The ESM provides loans by issuing bonds or negotiating loans with Member States, international financial institutions or third parties[459]. Specifically, the ESM:

---

455 Introduced by Council Regulation (EU) No 407/2010 of 11 May 2010, the EFSM is based on Article 122(2) TFEU. Nothing in this article excludes debt crisis of its scope to the extent that, when assistance is implemented, the Council is able to show that the crisis was caused by exceptional reasons beyond the control of the concerned Member State. See Alberto de Gregorio Merino, *Legal developments in the Economic and Monetary Union during the debt crisis: The mechanisms of financial assistance*, 49, Common Market Law Review (2012).

456 Martucci, Revue des Affaires Européennes (2012).

457 Ireland and Portugal benefited from this assistance. See for Ireland: James Croke, *Chuaigh Ar La – Debt of a Gaelsman: Ireland's Sovereign Debt Crisis, National and International Responses*, 32, Northwestern Journal of International Law & Business (2012).

458 Article 136(3) TFEU is the legal basis for the establishment of the ESM Treaty. Member States (and not the EU institutions) may establish a stability mechanism as recalled by the ECJ in the case *Thomas Pringle v Governement of Ireland* (ECJ, Case C-370/12). See Delphine Dero-Bugny, et al., *Chronique – Cour de justice et Tribunal de l'Union européenne*, 2, Journal du Droit international (2013). For a discussion relted to the amendment of the ESM Treaty to incorporate debt management, see Paulus/Tirado, Law & Economics Yearly Review 2013, 504 ff.

459 Article 3 of the ESM Treaty: "*For this purpose, the ESM shall be entitled to raise funds by issuing financial instruments or by entering into financial or other agreements or arrangements with ESM Members, financial institutions or other third parties*".

> "shall be empowered to borrow on the capital markets from banks, financial institutions or other persons or institutions for the performance of its purpose"[460].

A reserve fund receives:

> "the net income generated by the ESM operations and the proceeds of the financial sanctions received from the ESM Members under the multilateral surveillance procedure, the excessive deficit procedure and the macro-economic imbalances procedure established under the TFEU"[461].

The ESM has conventionalised the financial assistance[462] and provides a legal structure for Eurozone members[463]. All Members States of the Eurozone are ESM Members. To borrow, they must meet two requirements:

> "experienc[e], or [be] threatened by, severe financing problems, if indispensable to safeguard the financial stability of the euro area as a whole and of its Member States"[464].

The aid is conditioned by the ratification of the ESM treaty. Different types of assistance are available: credit lines granted on a precautionary basis[465], financial assistance to recapitalise financial institutions[466], ESM loans[467], a purchase of sovereign bonds on the primary market[468] and an exceptional system on the secondary market in case of financial stability risk[469]. This assistance may be presented as a State's aid. The legality of

---

460 Article 21 of the ESM Treaty.

461 Article 24 of the ESM Treaty.

462 Régis Bismuth, *L'assistance financière du FMI aux États membres de la zone euro : de l'inconcevable au conventionnel (ou comment "conventionnaliser" l'inconcevable)*, Revue des affaires européennes (2012).

463 Christoph G. Paulus, *Should Politics be Replaced by a Legal Proceeding?*, *in* A Debt Restructuring Mechanism for Sovereigns: Do we need a legal procedure? (Christoph G. Paulus ed. 2014).

464 The financial aspects of the functioning of the ESM have been widely presented and commented on ESM website. See also reports No. 4347 and 4348 of the French National Assembly of 14 February 2012 and No. 390 of the French Senate of 21 February 2012.

465 Article 14 of the ESM Treaty: the purpose is to assist a State which economic conditions are well to maintain access to financing on the markets. See *ESM Guideline on precautionnary assistance*, art. 1.

466 Article 15 of the ESM Treaty. See *ESM Guideline on financial assistance for recapitalization*, art. 1.2.

467 Article 16 of the ESM Treaty See *ESM Guideline on loans*, art. 1.

468 Article 17 of the ESM Treaty.

469 Article 18 of the ESM Treaty.

this new framework was debated[470]. Many commentators have noted that markets' short-time decision-making implies a rapid response, which results in risks of legal imperfections.

EU law is built on political pragmatism and economic realism. One can denounce it while also recognizing it as an adjustment force and an advantage in times of crisis. The integration of international public law to European law offers a pragmatic solution to Member States. The development of a legal framework for financial assistance and the strengthening of budgetary discipline are treaty based on international law developed by the EU Member States[471]. The European sovereign debt crisis has allowed the development of supporting tools. Moreover, by seeking to standardise sovereign bonds through the integration of collective action clauses, Article 12.3 of the ESM Treaty takes a step towards a joint management of European debt[472]. It is only a first step, because Article 125 TFEU provides that neither the Union nor a Member State can take charge of the commitments of another Member State. There is no possible bailout. Each State shall be accountable for its own commitments. The prohibition of financial solidarity between States is clearly affirmed[473]. The monetary union continues functioning without budgetary solidarity[474].

In front of all these provisions, the role of private creditors in debt restructuring is questioned. In Greece, negotiations took place between pri-

470 The ratification of the ESM Treaty was marked by the decision of the German Constitutional Court confirming the constitutionality of the mechanism, as previously happened with the EFSM and the EFSF. See Emmanuelle Saulnier-Cassia, *Le Traité instituant le mécanisme européen de stabilité et le Traité sur la stabilité, la coordination et la gouvernance au sein de l'Europe, sous contrôles constitutionnels*, 1, Revue Trimestrielle de Droit Européen (2013).

471 Martucci, Revue des Affaires Européennes (2012).

472 Article 12.3 of the ESM Treaty: "*Collective action clauses shall be included, as of 1 January 2013, in all new euro area government securities, with maturity above one year,* in a way which ensures that their legal impact is identical" (we emphasise).

473 Article 125 TFEU states that "*2. The Council, on a proposal from the Commission and after consulting the European Parliament, may, as required, specify definitions for the application of the prohibitions referred to in Articles 123 and 124 and in this Article*".

474 Jean-Marc Sorel & Régis Chemain, Quelle souveraineté budgétaire pour les États? (Pedone. 2013). Aurore Laget-Annamayer & Jean-Marc Sorel, *Le meccano de l'euro : les multiples contraintes d'une monnaie pas comme les autres*, 117, Revue générale de droit international public (2013).

vate creditors under the auspices of a representative committee, as well as between public creditors of different institutions. Coordination during these negotiations was delicate. If the market-based voluntary approach was more effective and appropriate than the imposed unilateral solution, the second package incorporated a significant participation of public and private creditors through debt exchange.

1.2.2. Unequal contribution of private creditors

During a corporate bankruptcy, shareholders lose their parts. In the event of a sovereign default, there is a debt haircut. The restructuring of the Greek external debt has involved lenders and depositors under the heading of Private Sector Involvement. Creditors' involvement means negotiating new conditions with the State[475]. The ESM Treaty is explicit in terms of private sector participation in its recitals[476]:

> "12) In accordance with IMF practice, in exceptional cases an adequate and proportionate form of private sector involvement shall be considered in cases where stability support is provided accompanied by conditionality in the form of a macro-economic adjustment programme".

This participation is strengthened by the inclusion of collective action clauses in European sovereign debt bonds with a maturity of one year from 1 January 2013.

This participation brings out the problem of holdout creditors refusing to renegotiate. Luckily, banks and other institutional investors held most of Greek bonds[477]. Thus, they were able to pressure holdout creditors through their regulators and governments. The committee of private cred-

---

475 About the participation of the private sector in general, see Private Sector Involvement in Financial Crises: Analytics and Public Policy Approaches, pp. 184-196 (1999). Haircuts: Estimating Investor Losses in Sovereign Debt Restructurings, 1998-2005, p. 68 (2005).

476 Article 12.2 of the original version of the ESM Treaty provided: "*[a]n* adequate and proportionate form of private-sector involvement *shall be sought on a case-by-case basis where financial assistance is receive by an ESM Member, in line with IMF practice. The nature and the extent of this involvement shall depend on the outcome of a debt sustainability analysis and shall take due account of the risk of contagion and potential spill-over effects on other Member States of the European Union and third countries.*" (we emphasise).

477 Large banks and institutional investors represent 60 % of all participants.

itors of Greece[478], similar to a modern London Club, also influenced private creditors. To convince the remaining creditors, the Greek government threatened to change the law to impose the bonds exchange to all bondholders under Greek law. At the same time, a financial benefit was proposed[479], coupled with legal and contractual terms for new bonds in case of another crisis. English law replaced Greek law in all bonds. A majority of creditors accepted the exchange[480].

The management of sovereign debt involves public-private cooperation. The more a sovereign debtor receives aid from public lenders, the more its ability to repay its private creditors is increased. Meanwhile, as more concessions are given to private creditors, there is less of a burden of restructuring for public creditors. The relationship between public and private creditors in the restructuring scheme defines the future of sovereign financing, especially in case of global financial crisis where resources are limited. Some tensions may complicate the implementation of collaborative approaches. In fact, business interests drive private creditors while public creditors generally consider foreign or domestic policy, and therefore give priority to partners States. In case of tensions, public creditors' financial assistance may be deviated by debtors to repay private creditors[481].

Thus, any renegotiation tacitly refers to responsibility, particularly in case of over indebtedness. The legal dimension is excluded when the notion of burden sharing is involved. Informality replaces responsibility. However, the respective responsibilities of sovereign debtors and public or private lenders arise. If the international responsibility of a sovereign debtor, which borrows excessively and deliberately, is not questioned by international law, some sovereign lenders have already officially and politically agreed to compensate for the damages caused[482]. For private lenders, investing in sovereign debt means to be repaid with public money.

---

478 Created in November 2011, the committee of private creditors of Greece was codirected by the General Director of the Institute of International Finance and a BNP Paribas advisor. See Zettelmeyer, et al., Economic Policy, (2013).

479 It was the EFSF payment obligations up to 15 % of the value of older bonds.

480 The final part was 97 %.

481 Financial and sovereign debt crises: Some lessons learned and those forgotten, (2013).

482 For example, in October 2006, Norway recognised that certain loans were granted to support its own industry in crisis. Subsequently, Norway cancelled $ 80 million of "illegitimate" debt affecting five developing countries. See Centre in-

However, no accountability procedure exists to seize sovereign property. In a restructuring procedure, it is crucial to benefit from a preferred creditor status, as we will now explain.

1.2.3. Absence of formal hierarchy of creditors

In a bankruptcy procedure, creditors' treatment depends on their securities. Secured creditors will have priority while unsecured creditors will be subordinated. In terms of sovereign debt, there is no supranational restructuring law. Thus, there is no formal hierarchy of creditors[483]. However, by positioning themselves as lenders of last resort, international financial institutions have *de facto* the benefits of a preferred creditor status, while no legal basis under international law supports this situation. Private creditors seem to accept the assertion of a preferred creditor status[484]. The IMF transformed this status in a condition of its financial assistance[485]. As debt restructuring within the Paris Club depends on the IMF approval, this provision has never been legally tested. The preferred creditor status of other international financial institutions, such as the World Bank, is based on a preferential access to foreign currency in case of exchange.

No debt restructuring mechanism at a European or global level exists. Similarly, no international law provides certain creditors with a privileged status. Consequently, the priority of a Member State over other creditors may be obtained either by agreement between the debtor and the creditor[486] or unilaterally granted by the debtor[487]. International law does not

ternational pour le développement et la solidarité, document de travail, juin 2007, p. 8.

483 Carreau & Shaw, La dette extérieure / The External Debt. 1995.

484 Rafael A. Morales, *Equality Of Treatment Of Creditors In The Restructuring Of Foreign Debt, in* La dette extérieure / The external debt (Martinus Nijhoff Publishers ed. 1995). Roubini & Setser, Bailouts or Bail-ins? Responding to Financial Crises in Emerging Economies, 2004, pp. 249-288.

485 Rutsel Silvestre J. Martha, *Preferred Creditor Status under International Law: The Case of the International Monetary Fund*, 39, The International and Comparative Law Quarterly (1990).

486 See Waibel, Sovereign Defaults Before International Courts and Tribunals, 2011, pp. 145 and foll.

487 Martha, The International and Comparative Law Quarterly, (1990).

prevent a State from agreeing with a creditor to get preferential treatment as long as there is no violation of a third party's rights.

The ESM Treaty includes in recitals 13 and 14 that bilateral loans have privileged status, *pari passu* with other creditors but a rank below the IMF[488]. States can create such unilateral obligations as stated by the International Law Commission[489] and recalled by the International Court of Justice in the *Nuclear Tests* case[490]. This provision is only affirmed as a preamble. It is necessary that the facility agreement expressly grants the preferred creditor status to the ESM, when the Treaty does not. *Vis-à-vis* third parties, this hierarchy is complex to implement, particularly for private creditors. Indeed, the applicable law to their bonds is domestic. Therefore, integrating the preferred creditor status may be a violation of these commitments to private creditors. The issue of whether the payment of certain creditors constitutes a violation of the *pari passu* principle has been considered in the case *NML Capital against Argentina*, as we will now examine.

---

488 Recital 13: "*Like the IMF, the ESM will provide stability support to an ESM Member when its regular access to market financing is impaired or is at risk of being impaired. Reflecting this, Heads of State or Government have stated that* the ESM loans will enjoy preferred creditor status in a similar fashion to those of the IMF, while accepting preferred creditor status of the IMF over the ESM. *This status will be effective as of the date of entry into force of this Treaty. In the event of ESM financial assistance in the form of ESM loans following a European financial assistance programme existing at the time of the signature of this Treaty, the ESM will enjoy the same seniority as all other loans and obligations of the beneficiary ESM Member, with the exception of the IMF loans*" (we emphasise).
Recital 14: "*The euro area Member States will support equivalent creditor status of the ESM and that of other States lending bilaterally in coordination with the ESM*".

489 See « Principes directeurs applicables aux déclarations unilatérales des États susceptibles de créer des obligations juridiques », *Annuaire de la Commission du droit international*, 2006, vol. II(2).

490 "46. *It is well recognized that declarations made by way of unilateral acts, concerning legal or factual situations, may have the effect of creating legal obligations. Declarations of this kind may be, and often are, very specific. When it is the intention of the State making the declaration that it should become bound according to its terms, that intention confers on the declaration the character of a legal undertaking, the State being thenceforth legally required to follow a course of conduct consistent with the declaration. An undertaking of this kind, if given publicly, and with an intent to be bound, even though not made within the context of inter- national negotiations, is binding*". Nuclear Tests (New Zealand v. France), Judgement, I.C.J. Report 1974, p. 457.

2. Contractual clauses and litigation

During a sovereign debt restructuring, private claims are governed by private law. In case of contractual violation, holdout creditors can decide to file a complaint with the courts (2.1.). To avoid restructuring plans in vain, it is necessary to limit vulture funds' activity through the integration of renegotiation clauses. The evolution of the contractual techniques used by the private sector to solve sovereign debt crises is focused on prevention of holdout. A market-based approach coupled with renegotiation clauses intends to facilitate future participation (2.2.).

2.1. Procedural issues of the Argentine Republic

Following existing procedural rules, vulture funds filed complaints with the courts that recognised the admissibility of their claims. This approach is not new. However, it was broadly successful amongst Argentine debt holders. Domestic courts and arbitral tribunals are a serious way to try to oblige a State to repay (2.1.1.). In particular, the controversial interpretation of the *pari passu* clause is central (2.1.2.).

2.1.1. Holdout creditors before courts

Following the 2001 default[491], Argentina has restructured most of its bond debt. However, creditors who did not participate in the restructuring, the so-called holdouts, seized national and arbitral tribunals. In 2007, Italian

491 *Abaclat and Others v. Argentine Republic*, ICSID Case No. ARB/07/5 (formerly *Giovanna a Beccara and Others v. The Argentine Republic*). See Julien Cazal, *L'arbitrage multipartite devant les tribunaux CIRDI*, 4, Les Cahiers de l'Arbitrage (2013). Sophie Lemaire, *Sur la compétence et la recevabilité : l'acquisition de titres d'État constitue un investissement. Une action de masse peut être tranchée par un tribunal CIRDI ; Note sous Centre international de règlement des différends sur l'investissement, décision sur la compétence et la recevabilité, 4 août 2011, Abaclat et autres contre République d'Argentine*, 2, Revue de l'arbitrage (2013). Bruno Poulin, *Restructuration des dettes souveraines et traités bilatéraux de promotion et de protection des investissements ; Note sous Abaclat and Others v. The Argentine Republic, affaire CIRDI number ARB/07/05, décision sur la compétence et la recevabilité en date du 4 août 2011*, Les Cahiers de l'Arbitrage (2011). Sébastien Manciaux, *Note sous CIRDI, Abaclat et autre con-*

holders of Argentine bonds filed a request for arbitration before the ICSID. The claim was based on the 1990 bilateral investment treaty between Italy and Argentina. *Abaclat and Others v. Argentine Republic* constitutes the first link between sovereign debt and investment law[492]. If the Argentine State were to be sentenced, the risk of contamination would be high for States affected by the financial crisis that granted bonds exchanges such as Greece[493].

The contagion was achieved with the case *NML Capital, Ltd. v. Republic of Argentina*. After several unsuccessful trials to circumvent the Argentine sovereign immunity by targeting companies located abroad, the fund NML Capital began to win its case in New York[494]. The interpretation of the *pari passu* clause is central in the dispute. There are various formulations of this clause. The traditional interpretation of the *pari passu* clause indicates that this is a simple provision aimed at preventing any subordination of creditors by law. In the case *NML Capital*, the clause is written as follows:

> "The Securities will constitute (except as provided in Section 11 below) direct, unconditional, unsecured and unsubordinated obligations of the Republic and shall at all times rank pari passu and without any preference among themselves. The payment obligations of the Republic under the Securities shall at all times rank at least equally with all its other present and future unsecured and unsubordinated External Indebtedness (as defined in this Agreement)".

Other versions of the clause include the notion that obligations "*will rank at least pari passu in priority of payment*". The interpretation of the clause depends on the writing. It is not accurate to consider that all versions of the clause will have the same legal effect, as we can ascertain below:

---

tre Argentine (ARB/07/5), décision sur la compétence et la recevabilité, 4 août 2011, 1, Journal du droit international (2012).

492 The Argentine bond debt reached $ 94 billion. The exchange offers in February 2005 and June 2010 modified the participation rate from 76.2 % to 92.6 %. Holdout creditors represented almost $ 6.2 billion of unexchanged bonds, most of them held by vulture funds.

493 Daniella Strik, *Investment Protection of Sovereign Debt and Its Implications on the Future of Investment Law in the EU*, Volume 29, Journal of International Arbitration (2012) ; Sophie Lemaire, *L'arbitrage d'investissement et la restructuration de dettes souveraines (de l'expérience argentine au cas grec)*, 2014, Revue de l'Arbitrage (2014).

494 See *NML Capital, Ltd. v. Republic of Argentina*, 699 F.3d 246, 258 (2d Cir. 2012).

> "If, in the future, parties intend to bar preferential payment, they may adopt language like that included in the [trust deed]. If they mean only that subsequently issued securities may not explicitly declare subordination of the earlier bonds, they are free to say so".

The issue before the District Court for the Southern District of New York related to the meaning of the second sentence. According to Argentina, the clause intended to provide protection against legal subordination or other discrimination by preventing the creation of a legal hierarchy in favour of holders of a particular category of debt. *NML Capital* argued that Argentina had in fact subordinated their creditor rank by repaying creditors who accepted the restructuring plans of 2005 and 2010, and by implementing a legislation that bans any repayment to holdout creditors (the Lock Law)[495].

Judge Griesa of the District Court for the Southern District of New York followed this new interpretation of the *pari passu* on 23 February 2012. He considered that the second sentence meant more than a formal protection, although it forbade Argentina:

> "as bond payer, from paying on other bonds without paying on the [defaulted] Bonds. Thus, the two sentences of the Pari Passu Clause protect against different forms of discrimination: the issuance of other superior debt (first sentence) and the giving of priority to other payment obligations (second sentence)".

The reasoning is based on the differences between sovereign debt and corporate debt in case of bankruptcy[496]. Argentina appealed this decision before the Court of Appeals of the Second Circuit, which confirmed the interpretation of the District Court on 26 October 2012 and 23 August 2013. However, the concept of rateable payment is not contained in the text and

---

495 Article 3: "*Prohíbese al Estado nacional efectuar cualquier tipo de transacción judicial, extrajudicial o privada, respecto de los bonos a que refiere el artículo 1° de la presente ley*" de la Ley 26.017 "*Deuda pública*", enacted February 10, 2005.

496 "*When sovereign default they do not enter bankruptcy proceedings where the legal rank of debt determines the order in which creditors will be paid. Instead, sovereigns can choose for themselves the order in which creditors will be paid. In this context, the Equal Treatment Provision prevents Argentina as payor form discriminating against the [defaulted] Bonds in favour of other unsubordinated, foreign bonds*".

results of an interpretation of Judge Griesa[497]. Nevertheless, the fact that Argentina voted the Lock Law induced a change in the creditor hierarchy. The US Supreme Court declined to review the case on 7 October 2013 and opposed the revision of the Court of Appeal decision on 16 June 2014.

Argentina's main legal problem was that New York State Law governed its bonds. Changing terms was therefore impossible since in this specific case no US court would give effect to Argentine legislation. So the country had to choose between fully repaying its creditors or refusing to enforce a claim obtained by holdout creditors in the United States[498]. Since a waiver of sovereign immunity was included in the bonds, US decisions may, in principle, be recognised and enforced elsewhere[499]. Argentina therefore risked the seizure of its assets in all jurisdictions where American judgments are recognised[500]. The interpretation of the *pari passu* clause in the sense that "everyone is paid or nobody receives anything" is problematic for all financial operators[501]. Indeed, clearing houses, resellers, holdings or trustees across the world may be prosecuted for assis-

497 There is no rateable payment clause, contrary to Italian bonds for example: "*The debt securities will be direct, unconditional, unsecured and general obligations of Italy. They will rank equally with all of our present and future unsecured and unsubordinated general borrowing. The full faith and credit of Italy will be pledged for the due and punctual payment of the debt securities and for the due and timely performance of all of our obligations under the debt securities. We will pay principal and interest on the debt securities out of the Ministry of Economy and Finance of Italy.* We will pay amounts due on the debt securities equally and rateably with all general loan obligations of Italy" (we emphasise). See Tolek Petch, Legal Implications of the Euro Zone Crisis. Debt Restructuring, Sovereign Default and Euro Zone Exit (Kluwer Law International. 2014), p. 113.

498 Id. at. 101-146.

499 Christoph G. Paulus, *Jüngste Entwicklungen im Resolvenzrecht*, 67, Zeitschrift für Wirtschafts- und Bankrecht (2013).

500 Unless domestic courts uphold a restrictive view of sovereign immunity as there is no consensus on the extent of the application of that concept.

501 « *Cette nouvelle interprétation de la clause dénature les règles actuelles en matière de recouvrement de la dette privée et de faillite. En dépit de son nom, la clause de pari passu ne parvient à assurer ni le respect uniforme des dispositions d'un contrat ni la distribution équitable des actifs rares. Elle ne fait que remplacer le système souverain fragile et morcelé de restructuration de la dette issu des années 1980 par un autre, plus risqué et plus morcelé encore, qui donne tous les pouvoirs à un seul créancier récalcitrant.* ». Anna Gelpern, in Paris, Rapport annuel d'activité, 2013.

tance to Argentina if the Argentine State repays through them the creditors that accepted the restructuring.

2.1.2. Alternative diplomatic methods

The situation in Argentina highlights sovereign debt management weaknesses and their global consequences[502]. The intrusive nature of this court decision prevents Argentina from repaying creditors that accepted the restructuring terms. This leads *de facto* to another default. One can consider that it is a scandalous treatment. However, it is also a call from the judiciary power to States to enact restructuring. The United States[503], Mexico, Brazil[504] and France[505] highlighted in *amicus curiae* written for legal proceedings that the NML case was a threat to all negotiated sovereign debt restructuring. Nevertheless, such *amicus curiae* remain a procedural right that is only intended to inform the court[506].

Within the French national courts, a demonstration of support from the French State to the Argentine Republic exists in three judgments of the Court of Cassation on 28 March 2013[507]. In those judgments, international

502 Sovereign risk: a world without risk-free assets? (2013).

503 The United States also sent an *amicus curiae* supporting Argentina in *BG Group Plc case. v. The Republic of Argentina*, UNCITRAL.

504 La Cour suprême des États-Unis et la dette souveraine de l'Argentine : l'examen des rapports d'amicus curiae de la France et du Brésil. (2014).

505 France decided on 26 July 2013, and on 24 March 2014 to submit an *amicus curiae* to the Supreme Court. This echoes an existing controversy against France in the 1930s: "*The revival of the debt controversy has led to unusual outbursts of sentiment against France which is partly due to the persistent anti-French campaign of some of our newspapers and popular magazines as well as to France's apparently complete misunderstanding of the American political scene*". See Gideonse, War Debts, 1933.

506 Séverine Menétrey, L'*amicus curiae*, vers un principe commun de droit procédural ? (Dalloz-Sirey, 2010).

507 Pierre Chevalier, *Dossier documentaire : immunités d'exécution des États. Cour de cassation (France), civ. 1, 28 mars 2013*, 117, Revue generale de droit international public (2013) ; Antoine Bolze, *Saisies sur les créances de l'État argentin : encore raté ! Note sous Cour de cassation, première Chambre civile, 28 mars 2013, pourvoi numéro 11-10.450 et Cour de cassation, première Chambre civile, 28 mars 2013, pourvoi numéro 10-25.938*, pp. 186-187, La Gazette du Palais (2013) ; Malik Laazouzi, *La neutralisation de la renonciation conventionnelle à l'immunité d'exécution de l'État étranger en France ; Note sous Cour de cassa-*

customary law guided the Court of Cassation to stop *NML Capital* seizures in the Argentine branches of French companies. The Court refers to the 2004 UN Convention on Jurisdictional Immunities of States and their Property[508]. This international convention ratified by France[509] is however not yet applicable. It is part of customary law. These alternative diplomatic methods were hardly criticised as they establishes a new formalism to waive sovereign immunity[510]. Confirmed in a decision on 5 March 2014[511], the French jurisprudence became more complex in a deci-

---

tion, première Chambre civile, 28 mars 2013, Société NML Capital contre République argentine et Total Austral, pourvoi numéro 10-25.938 ; contre République argentine, pourvoi numéro 11-13.323 ; contre République argentine et BNP Paribas, pourvoi numéro 11-10.450, 4, Revue des contrats (2013) ; Horatia Muir Watt, *Immunité d'exécution ; Note sous Cour de cassation, première Chambre civile, 28 mars 2013, société NML Capital contre République argentine, pourvoi numéro 10-25.938*, 3, Revue Critique de Droit International Privé (2013).

508 Laurence Usunier, *La coutume internationale invoquée pour anticiper l'entrée en vigueur d'une convention internationale ; Note sous Cour de cassation, première Chambre civile, 28 mars 2013, pourvoi numéro 10-25.938, Cour de cassation, première Chambre civile, 28 mars 2013, pourvoi numéro 11-10.450 et Cour de cassation, première Chambre civile, 28 mars 2013, pourvoi numéro 11-13.323*, 2, Revue Trimestrielle de Droit Civil (2014).

509 Law No. 2011-734 of 28 June 2011 authorising the ratification of the UN Convention on Jurisdictional Immunities of States and their Property, French Official Gazette No. 0149 of 29 June 2011, p. 10953.

510 The French Court of Cassation argued that « *selon le droit international coutumier, tel que reflété par la Convention des Nations-Unies, du 2 décembre 2004, sur l'immunité juridictionnelle des États et de leurs biens, si les États peuvent renoncer, par contrat écrit, à leur immunité d'exécution sur des biens ou des catégories de biens utilisés ou destinés à être utilisés à des fins publiques,* il ne peut y être renoncé que de manière expresse et spéciale, en mentionnant les biens ou la catégorie de biens pour lesquels la renonciation est consentie » (we emphasise). However, no special requirement is provided in Articles 18 and 19 of this Convention.

511 Cour de cassation, première Chambre civile, 5 mars 2014, pourvoi numéro 12-22.406. See Antoine Bolze, *Origine publique des fonds = immunité d'exécution ; Note sous Cour de cassation, première Chambre civile, 5 mars 2014, pourvoi numéro 12-22.406*, 203 La Gazette du Palais (2014). Baptiste Tranchant, *Jurisprudence française en matière de droit international public*, 1 Revue générale de droit international public (2015).

sion on 13 Mai 2015[512]. Previously, the French Court of Cassation considered that under international customary law, States could waive their immunity under an explicit and special provision. The special requirement disappeared with this last decision. Consequently, the seizure of sovereign assets may be facilitated if no further legal measure is taken.

As for Argentina, the Argentine government is organised both nationally and internationally to defend its position. In response to the US decision, the Argentine government adopted a new law on 11 September 2014, just before a repayment due on 30 September 2014, to reimburse the creditors that accepted the restructuring[513]. In August 2014, Argentina submitted, along with the G77 and China, a draft resolution to the General Assembly of the United Nations for the establishment of a multilateral legal framework for sovereign debt restructuring. The objective is to establish an international consensus based on the recognition that a minority of creditors cannot alter a debt restructuring agreed upon by a majority of creditors. The General Assembly and the Economic and Financial Com-

---

512 Cour de cassation, première Chambre civile, 13 mai 2015, *Société Commissions import-export (Commisimpex) contre République du Congo*, pourvoi numéro 13-17.751 : « *le droit international coutumier n'exige pas une renonciation autre qu'expresse à l'immunité d'exécution* ». See Laura Weiller, *Revirement : abandon de l'exigence du caractère spécial de la renonciation à l'immunité d'exécution*, 7, Procédures (2015). Claude Brenner, *Renonciation à l'immunité d'exécution étatique : vérité un jour, erreur le lendemain ; Note sous Cour de cassation, première Chambre civile, 13 mai 2015, pourvoi numéro 13-17.751*, p. 248, La Gazette du Palais (2015). Raphaël Kaminsky & Joseph Dalmasso, *Une révolution en marche dans le droit des immunités – La fin des régimes spéciaux pour les immunités diplomatiques et l'arbitrage international ?*, 38, La Semaine Juridique Entreprise et Affaires (2015).

513 See in particular Article 2 "*La presente ley tiene por objeto implementar instrumentos legales que permitan el cobro de los servicios correspondientes al cien por ciento de los Títulos emitidos en el marco de la Reestructuración de Deuda Soberana 2005-2010 […], en salvaguarda del orden público nacional y de los contratos celebrados en el marco de dicha Reestructuración, ante la ilegítima e ilegal obstrucción de los mecanismos de cobro de los fondos pagados por la República Argentina con fecha 26 de junio de 2014, dispuesta por órdenes judiciales dictadas por la Corte de Distrito Sur de la Ciudad de Nueva York en el marco de la causa NML Capital Ltd. et al v. Republic of Argentina que, tal como han sido dictadas, resultan de imposible cumplimiento, y violatorias tanto de la soberanía e inmunidades de la República Argentina como de los derechos de terceros.*" de la Ley 26.984 "*Pago Soberano. Reestructuración de Deuda*", promulgated on 11 September 2014.

mittee adopted this project on 9 September 2014[514]. On 5 December 2014, the Economic and Financial Committee also adopted a draft resolution entitled *Sustainability of external debt and development*.

The monopolisation of the international diplomatic scene was essential for Argentina to obtain a reaction from the international community[515]. For now, the consensus reached by States seems limited to the integration of modified contractual clauses in order to facilitate negotiations with private creditors. A global mechanism must be developed[516].

2.2. Legal technicality and privatisation of sovereign debt litigation

Sovereign debt restructuring implies reaching new agreements with creditors. In the absence of an international judicial entity specialised in sovereign debt restructuring, international private law has been particularly used to develop contractual tools. A proposition is based on the remodelling of existing clauses to be adapted to potential litigation (2.2.1.). In this matter, the collective action clause has been particularly debated (2.2.2.). However, these contractual techniques are limited and do not constitute a comprehensive sustainable solution (2.2.3.).

2.2.1. Clauses anticipating litigation

The purpose of the contractual approach is to facilitate negotiations between debtors and creditors through the integration of clauses. These contractual tools correspond to an *ex ante* management of sovereign debt as they are integrated in case of default. Governments have sought to renegotiate more carefully the legal tools used in their commercial and financial relations, in particular bilateral investment treaties and free trade agree-

514 It aims at improving the effectiveness, stability and predictability of the international financial system. Moreover, the purpose is to achieve a sustained and equitable economic growth, albeit with a sustainable development, based on the circumstances and priorities of each country. See Christoph G. Paulus, *Staatspleite, Anleihenprozess, UN-Vollversammlung*, 47, Zeitschrift für das gesamte Insolvenzrecht (2014).

515 See online the recent request of Argentina against the United States before the ICJ (rejected).

516 See Chapter 7.

ments, while facing litigation before arbitral tribunals. For example, since the Lisbon Treaty has come into effect, the European Union has exclusive competence to negotiate any new investment treaty and examine the way sovereign debt restructuring is treated[517].

In bond contracts, several provisions are also analysed to improve coordination in the event of restructuring and to discourage holdout creditors. For instance, the exit consent clause allows a group of creditors holding sovereign bonds to amend non-financial terms. Subsequently, holdout creditors are encouraged to accept an offer of restructuring[518]. Another example is the sharing clause that stipulates that any creditor receiving a disproportionate payment compared to the one received by other bondholders should share the amount. Another option is the insertion of collective representation clauses to delegate the power to represent debt creditors to a third party during negotiations.

In case of a change in the balance of the contract, parties can consider two types of restructuring clauses: maintenance of value and rehabilitation. The first clause allocates monetary risks between the parties of an international transaction (for instance indexation clauses or clauses referring to a currency). The second clause is used to apprehend different types of contractual changes[519]. However, even in the absence of any clause, investors often rely on the concept of *force majeure*. *Force majeure* aims to ensure the continuity of the contract and adapt it to a situation caused by

---

517 The North American Free Trade Agreement provides exceptions in this area in its Article 1410: "Nothing in this Part shall be construed to prevent a Party from adopting or maintaining reasonable measures for prudential reasons, such as: *[...] (c) ensuring the integrity and stability of a Party's financial system*". Moreover, the US-Uruguay bilateral investment treaty signed on 4 November 2005 expressly excludes on Appendix G entitled "*Sovereign Debt Restructuring*" the submission of debt restructuring to most treaty standards. See Lemaire, Revue de l'Arbitrage, (2014).

518 Lee C. Buchheit & Mitu G. Gulati, *Exit Consents in Sovereign Bond Exchanges*, 48, UCLA Law Review (2000).

519 There are many examples of such clause, such as the "government take clause" that passes on the cost of increasing oil prices on buyers, the "first refusal clause" that obliges the seller to match its prices with competitors, the "most favoured customer clause" or the "rising and falling clause" that is used to revise the financial terms of a contract.

an unforeseen event. Another more elaborated contractual provision[520] is the hardship clause[521]. The use of federal class action procedures in the United States has also been suggested since the restructuring of sovereign debt can satisfy the basic condition to initiate a class action[522]. Several cases have been presented to judicial courts. Nonetheless, they have failed due to procedural reasons, particularly as they were not a mandatory class action[523].

Another proposal is to insert in sovereign bonds a structure defining creditor hierarchy. Such clause in favour of a creditor hierarchy would be based on the issuance date and would give priority to the oldest holders. In addition, it may reduce excessive borrowing. In fact, the issue of over borrowing is hardly considered in regulatory proposals from market participants. However, we consider that over borrowing is the source of the problem[524]. The international credit control may be part of the banks responsibilities and included in their credit policies[525]. Nevertheless, since the crisis of the Eurozone States, the successful return of collective action clauses apparently constitutes the sole legal and political solution to sovereign debt crisis.

2.2.2. Integration of collective action clauses

Collective action clauses (CACs) are contractual provisions inserted in sovereign bond contracts between bond issuers, either public or private, and bond buyers. In case of a risk of default, CACs allow the debtor to modify debt repayment terms upon approval of a majority of creditors.

---

520 Klaus Peter Berger, *Renegotiation and Adaptation of International Investment Contracts: The Role of Contract Drafters and Arbitrators* 36, Vanderbilt Journal of Transnational Law 1347 (2003), pp. 1347-1380.

521 Bruno Oppetit, *L'adaptation des contrats internationaux aux changements de circonstances : la clause de hardship*, Journal de Droit International (1974).

522 Lee C. Buchheit, et al., *Sovereign Bonds and the Collective Will* Georgetown University Law Center.

523 See *Hirshon c. Bolivia* in 1995 and nine cases involving Argentina in 2004 and 2005.

524 See Forteau, Le défaut souverain en droit international public : les instruments de droit international public pour remédier à l'insolvabilité des États, 2011.

525 Jacques Attali calls for the creation of an international financial criminal court for the winners of the non-management of the crisis that are, according to him, banks. See "Pour un Tribunal financier international", L'Express, 16 March 2010.

The purpose is to facilitate future restructuring via for example an agreement on haircuts. The contract provides quorum and majority rules applicable to all creditors. CACs can provide an aggregation principle to be incorporated in the restructuring plan of all sovereign bonds. Thus, sovereign debt restructuring is organised. Litigation is blocked to holdout creditors[526].

Since the Rey Report adopted by the G10 in 1996[527], CACs are repeatedly recommended. The use of CACs is however not common in bonds. CACs were extensively discussed within the IMF after the failure of the Krueger Plan[528]. In November 2010, the inclusion of such clauses has been proposed, as part of the preparation of the ESM. A new model was released in 2012[529]. The ESM Treaty made CACs compulsory in all bonds contracts as of 1 January 2013[530]. The Greek law bonds were retroactively modified by decree to include these clauses and the Member States gradually integrated CACs[531].

---

526 Romain Bardy, *Le Mécanisme européen de stabilité et la BCE*, Revue des affaires européennes (2012).

527 The resolution of sovereign liquidity crisis (1996).

528 G10, "Report of the G-10 Working Group on Contractual Clauses", 26 September 2002; Collective Action Clauses in Sovereign Bond Contracts—Encouraging Greater Use, (2002).

529 The collective action clause of the European Union model developed by the Economic and Financial Committee (EFC) in 2011 is presented online. See Keegan S. Drake, *Disenfranchisement in Sovereign Bonds*, *in* A Debt Restructuring Mechanism for Sovereigns. Do we need a legal procedure? (Christoph G. Paulus ed. 2014).

530 Michael Bradley & Mitu Gulati, Collective Action Clauses for the Eurozone: An Empirical Analysis (2012); Mathias Audit, *Les clauses d'action collective comme remède à la crise souveraine de la zone euro*, *in* Quelle souveraineté budgétaire pour les États? (Jean-Marc Sorel & Régis Chemain eds., 2013); ICMA, ICMA Sovereign bond consultation paper. 2013. ICMA, ICMA Sovereign bond consultation paper supplement. 2014.

531 In the French case, Article 59 of the 2013 Finance Act requires the introduction of collective action clauses in government securities issuance: « *I. — Les titres d'État, d'une maturité supérieure à un an, ainsi que les titres issus de leur démembrement, comportent des clauses d'action collective autorisant l'État, s'il dispose de l'accord de la majorité des détenteurs de titres, à modifier les termes du contrat d'émission. Toute proposition en ce sens est soumise au vote des détenteurs de titres [...] L'État ne peut exercer les droits de vote attachés à ses propres titres d'État qu'il a acquis ou pris en pension. Il n'est pas tenu compte de ces titres pour le calcul du quorum et de la majorité* ». See also Decree No. 2012-1517 of 29 December 2012 on collective action clauses applicable to gov-

With the introduction of CACs, negotiations are facilitated. Such clauses contractually define a procedure that creditors follow in case of default. The model proposed by the ICMA in August 2014 concentrates the main market-based practices in the form of steps for the optimal course of restructuring. However, this instrument cannot constitute by itself a global solution[532].

2.2.3. Limits of contractual approach and ad hoc mechanisms

Despite the announcement effect, CACs are not new. Current contracts often include them. In 1995, these clauses were introduced during the Mexican debt restructuring by the IMF in Mexican bonds indexed in dollars[533]. CACs were presented as a harmful cure for debt crisis. We observe a link between their political and legal efficiency. Promoting their integration avoids returning to the debate on the establishment of a global restructuring system.

If the example of CACs illustrates the limitations of the contractual approach, by extension all *ad hoc* mechanisms may be criticised. Multiple treatments applied to different creditors and debtors lack legal certainty. Such mechanisms are not organised like domestic insolvency proceedings of private companies.

Meanwhile, domestic insolvency proceedings are often interpreted as serving three purposes. First, domestic insolvency proceedings enable the debtors to eliminate the problem of holdout creditors during and after restructuring negotiations. Second, domestic insolvency proceedings shall ensure companies' access to funding throughout restructuring. Third, such proceedings apply predetermined rules and procedures[534]. However, current bond contracts only address to some extent the first objective. Contractual innovations that may meet the first objective and begin to address

---

ernment bonds and the Ministerial Decree of the Minister of Economy and Finance of the same date which details the conditions of application and implementation of collective action clauses.

532 The Design and Effectiveness of Collective Action Clauses (2002).

533 Mitu Gulati & Anna Gelpern, A Modern Legal History of Sovereign Debt § 73 (Law and Contemporary Problems ed. 2010).

534 Toward a Statutory Approach to Sovereign Debt Restructuring: Lessons from Corporate Bankruptcy Practice around the World (2003).

the two other objectives are not inconceivable. Such innovations require a global consensus[535].

*

Sovereign debt restructuring has changed significantly since the 1980s due to the securitisation of debt contracts and the changing nature of sovereign creditors. In the 1970s and 1980s, creditors were mainly banks and States. Sovereign debt was constituted of syndicated loans or international agreements. Renegotiations were conducted under the auspices of banking advisory committees or the Paris Club. The bonds' proliferation however did not produce a unified representation. On the contrary, bonds froze the beginning of a structured process of negotiation. Debt restructuring were implemented with take-it or leave-it exchange offers, preceded by informal discussions amongst creditors.

Nowadays, *ad hoc* mechanisms are the only mechanisms used in the international financial system to restructure sovereign debts. The Paris Club stands out as the only organised entity, whereas the Greek crisis reminds us that the proliferation of creditors and the fragmentation of financing involve a strengthened coordination between creditors.

CHAPTER 6. International Financial Institutions and Rescheduling

There is a shift of paradigm in the management of sovereign debt by international financial institutions. Market-based appreciation and contractual logic are no longer at the centre of rescheduling. Debt and development are both analysed by international financial institutions. These institutions work to prevent another so-called lost decade[536]. Financial support is provided to States under certain conditions. Debt restructuring by public and private lenders result in the conclusion of new agreements governed by in-

535 Christoph G. Paulus, A Debt Restructuring Mechanism for Sovereigns: Do we need a legal procedure? (C. H. Beck, Hart Publishing, Oxford, Nomos. 2014).
536 Crises de la dette : prévention et résolution. (2003).

ternational law or by the internal law as defined in these institutions' Articles of Agreement[537].

In the following chapters, restructuring not only refers to the fact that the parties effectively reschedule or reduce debt, but also to all measures taken in this regard, *e.g.* conditionality, adjustment measures within the framework of arrears loans, overall relief instruments put in place when the financial situation of a State requires action. Restructuring and its implications in terms of policies concern both developed and developing countries.

Integrating the development dimension in the sovereign debt analysis enables to differentiate two fundamentally contradictory situations. While the financing is mostly accomplished through the market, conditionality and default treatment remain distinct for each State. Indebted States often lose flexibility and freedom, while over-indebted States are directly placed under their lenders' supervision. The International Monetary Fund (1.) and the World Bank (2.) are in charge in times of crisis of providing financial assistance and advice on economic policy in order to contain the crisis. This chapter focuses on palliative financing provided by multilateral public creditors.

1. The International Monetary Fund, an ad hoc rescheduling regulator

The International Monetary Fund is an essential institution for the international monetary and financial system. The IMF is involved in informal renegotiation not only as creditor, but also as monitoring institution. Appointed to fill a role of sheriff[538], the IMF ensures that sovereign debtors fulfill all conditions set by their creditors for the debt renegotiation. The

537 Sovereign debts are subjected to agreements between sovereign debtors and international financial institutions. The 1986 Vienna Convention on the Law of Treaties between States and International Organisations or between International Organisations applies to such agreements. However, IMF financial assistance, which enjoys immunity under Article IX, Section 3 of the IMF Articles of Agreement, is subjected to its internal rules.

538 According to the words of George Soros in the Davos Forum held in 2010. See Rosa M Lastra, *The role of the IMF as a global financial authority*, 2, European Yearbook of International Economic Law (2011).

IMF has a functional duality[539] due to the evolution of its function and its involvement in sovereign debt treatment. Indeed, the Fund is responsible for managing existing debts (1.1.) and structuring a comprehensive mechanism (1.2.).

1.1. Mediator of renegotiations

The IMF has a unique position as mediator in negotiations between sovereign debtors and creditors. The IMF institutes a stability and creditworthiness safeguard through the application of conditionality and monitoring, while also acting as a lender of last resort (1.1.1.), as the Greek example demonstrated it (1.1.2.).

1.1.1. A financial mediator and a lender of last resort

The IMF holds the role of financial mediator and lender of last resort. It has great influence on procedural matters and sovereign debt restructuring negotiations since its *ad hoc* intervention in the bank restructurings in the 1970s and 1980s. Commercial banks actually required sovereign debtors to conclude stand-by arrangements with the Fund before any disbursement or rescheduling[540]. Furthermore, the IMF participates in the London Club and is active in the Paris Club renegotiations with public creditors[541]. Thus, the IMF has profoundly influenced restructuring[542] by establishing lending into arrears, developing the notion of burden sharing and defending its preferred creditor status[543].

---

539 Georges Scelle, *Règles générales du droit de la paix*, *in* Recueil des cours de l'Académie de droit international de La Haye (Hague Academy of International Law ed. 1933). Hassane Cissé, *Le fonds monétaire international et l'endettement extérieur des États*, *in* La dette extérieure / The external debt (Martinus Nijhoff Publishers ed. 1995), pp. 277-313.

540 See Chapter 5.

541 The Emerging of a Multilateral Forum for Debt Restructuring: the Paris Club. (2008).

542 Rosa M. Lastra, *International Financial Architecture*, *in* Legal Foundations of International Monetary Stability (Rosa M. Lastra ed. 2006).

543 Recent developments in the euro area questioned the IMF preferred creditor status: "*It is increasingly likely that Greece will become the first sovereign ever to*

As a crisis manager, the Fund may help States to solve their balance of payments' problems, reconstitute their international reserves or stabilise their currency. To this end, lending into arrears provides fundings for sovereign debtors to reimburse private creditors during a debt restructuring. These resources are intended to rebalance the situation of indebted States and enable them to regain access to financial markets. This ultimately reduces costs associated with a default and supports the repayment ability of a sovereign debtor[544]. The mechanism of lending into arrears did not exist at the origin of the IMF. It was only in 1989 that the IMF agreed to change its policy, due to the difficulties of some Member States to reach agreements for their adjustment programmes[545]. This mechanism ensures a central role for the IMF in sovereign debt restructuring[546]. Legally, all agreements are subjected to its internal regulations[547] that safeguard its preferred creditor status[548].

If the conditions are not filled, the Fund does not follow this loan policy. In this case, negotiating with other creditors ensures that disbursements are not misappropriated. The purpose of the new funding is to support States in crisis. It is not to repay private creditors. The IMF seeks to avoid securing private creditors. If private creditors believe that the IMF refunding protects them in last resort, they will not change their risky invest-

---

choose to restructure debt owed to the IMF – putting in question for the first time the IMF's status as an unchallengeable preferred creditor when it comes to sovereign debt". See Christopher Spink & John Geddie, *IMF Set to be Dragged into Greek Official Sector Involvement*, International Financing Review (2013).

544 IMF., "How the IMF Helps to Resolve Balance of Payments Difficulties", Factsheet, October 2008.

545 To get a disbursement, three conditions must be cumulatively filled: 1) the aid must be essential for the success of the adjustment program; 2) negotiations between the debtor and private creditors should have begun; and 3) the agreement on a financial set must happen shortly. In 1998, due to several changes in debt composition with the spread of sovereign bonds, the third criterion has been changed: « *il existe deș indications claires que l'emprunteur souverain et ses créanciers privés négocient de bonne foi un plan de restructuration de la dette* ». See Fund Policy on Lending into Arrears to Private Creditors – Further Consideration of the Good Faith Criterion. (2002). IMF Policy on Lending into Arrears to Private Creditors. (1999).

546 Pierre-François Weber, *(Re)structuration des dettes souveraines – Où en est-on ?*, 7 Revue de la Stabilité Financière (2005).

547 Article XI, Section 3 of the Articles of Agreement of the International Monetary Fund.

548 See Chapter 5.

ments. Subsequently, the IMF intends to involve all creditors by advocating a debt burden sharing since the early 1970s[549]. Sharing information on each creditor's exposure to the indebted State is necessary and should be made in good faith[550]. Through its expertise and strategic positioning, the Fund plays a real role of mediator. The Fund may encourage States to restructure their debt by involving the private sector, which absorbs some of the restructuring costs. To convince private creditors, the IMF may use its position by arguing that a lack of private participation would lead to a suspension of the IMF support and thus to a higher probability of default[551].

The IMF approach is specific to each State. However, two principles remain constant[552]. First, the IMF provides States with assistance to solve their problems of balance of payments. The Fund is not usually responsible for managing unsustainable debt situations or problems of liquidity. Subsequently, any financial assistance must comply with the IMF Articles of Agreements[553]. Conditionality, policies and procedures adopted by the Fund to ensure its credibility are based on its Articles of Agreement. The Fund has innovated by creating various specific mechanisms of assistance

549 The IMF explained in a 1971 report that it is important to reach in the future « *un partage du fardeau équilibré entre les différents créanciers, afin d'éviter toute impression que les nouveaux apports de capitaux seraient largement compensés par les remboursements aux créanciers [antérieurs]* ». See IMF, "*Multilateral debt renegotiations – Experience of Fund member*", Staff Memorandum 1971, SM/71/204 quoted by Jérôme Sgard, *Restructurer les dettes souveraines : la méthode efficace du FMI*, 3 L'Économie politique (2012).

550 Since 2002, the IMF has published the principles relating to the criterion of good faith. A State demonstrates good faith by engaging in an early dialogue with its creditors until the end of its debt restructuring, by sharing all non-confidential information in real time, including in particular an explanation of its economic problems and financial circumstances justifying a restructuring, by providing creditors an opportunity to get back on their restructuring strategies.

551 The Problem that Wasn't: Coordination Failures in Sovereign Debt Restructurings. (2011). See in particular the description of debt swap techniques.

552 Javier Diaz-Cassou & Aitor Erce, *IMF Interventions in Sovereign Debt Restructurings*, *in* Sovereign Debt: From Safety to Default (Robert W. Kolb ed. 2011).

553 "*Fund resources are provided to members to assist them in resolving their balance of payments problems in a manner that is consistent with the Fund's Articles and that establishes adequate safeguards for the temporary use of the Fund's resources*". See Guidelines on Conditionality. (2002). IMF, "Operational Guidance to IMF Staff on the 2002 Conditionality Guidelines – revised January 25, 2010".

in accordance with its Articles of Agreement[554]. Originally, the IMF operated as a mutual bank or an inter-state cooperative, by collecting quota subscriptions from its members. Gradually, standing borrowing arrangements and new arrangements to borrow were introduced[555]. In addition, the Board of Directors approved a legal framework for the issuance of bonds to the public sector. Since 2009, the Fund issues bonds that can be subscribed by its Member States. Financing agreements have also been concluded to increase or collect resources[556]. Reinforcing the IMF diminishes its apparent decline in credibility as institution of financial assistance[557].

This trend was strengthened by the global financial crisis that has deeply reformed the Fund. The real challenge is global economic governance[558]. G20 members first increased the IMF resources. The Fund may provide a rapid assistance in case of financial shocks, natural disaster or other factors of fragility[559]. Thus, the IMF has taken advantage of the financial crisis. It has set up credit lines[560] and acted within its Articles of Agreement[561] to become the central operator of the coordination of international sovereign debt management initiatives. The IMF led the operations in Greece, Ireland and Portugal. In order to ensure multilateral sup-

---

554 Article V, Section 2 b) and Section 3 a) of the Articles of Agreement of the International Monetary Fund.

555 On 13 December 1961, the Standing Borrowing Arrangements were established to supplement $ 6 billion dollars to ten Member States. Following the Mexican crisis of 1995, the Board of Directors implemented in January 1997 the New Arrangements to Borrow (NAB) in order to provide supplementary resources to the IMF. These NAB were enlarged on 11 March 2011 and have been continuously activated since the crisis.

556 The financial agreement between France and the IMF was signed on 12 October 2012 and came into force on 13 February 2013. See the database « Base Pacte – Accords et Traités » of the French Ministry of Foreign Affairs.

557 Carreau & Julliard, Droit international économique, 2013, pp. 661-689.

558 John W. Head, *The Global Financial Crisis of 2008-2009 in Context – Reflections on International Legal and Institutional Failings, "Fixes", and Fundamentals*, 23, Global Business & Development Law Journal (2010).

559 IMF, "IMF Crisis Lending", Factsheet, 25 April 2014.

560 In 2009, the IMF introduced the Flexible Credit Line to complement the Rapid Financing Instrument and the Rapid Credit Facility. In 2010, the Fund introduced the Precautionary Credit Line replaced in 2011 by the Precautionary and Liquidity Line. See the list on the IMF website.

561 Article IV, Section II of the Articles of Agreement of the International Monetary Fund.

port of international lenders, the IMF worked closely with the European Commission and the ECB to monitor the implementation of debt restructuring programmes. These programmes took the form of bond exchanges supplemented by the granting of new lines of credit. Consequently, the existing Fund policy has been modified, particularly on conditionality and surveillance under Article IV. The Fund has intensively changed its activities of analysis and consulting[562].

However, one must keep in mind that the major concern of international capital market is to maintain creditors' confidence. These IMF conditional credit lines stigmatise the States that use them. Such financial assistance can become a funding palliative[563].

The IMF is not an international central bank. However, it acts as a lender of last resort[564] to fill an institutional gap of the international monetary system[565]. Proposals to assign this task of lender of last resort were discussed in 1995 during the Mexican crisis[566], when the emergency funding mechanism was created in response to a need of rapid assistance. Due to the crises in Thailand, Indonesia and South Korea, the debate was strengthened in 1997. These crises in Asia led to the creation of an additional facility and formalised the IMF's role of lender of last resort. The generalisation of financial crisis questions the Fund's action, in particular regarding the Argentine situation[567]. If the financial system needs a lender of last resort to prevent the escalation of panic, this role cannot be used to reassure private creditors. Finding a balance between rescuing the financial system to prevent deflation and leaving some doubt on this intervention is difficult[568].

---

562 Michael Breen, The politics of IMF lending (Palgrave Macmillan. 2013), pp. 161-175.

563 Tirole, Revue de la Stabilité Financière, (2012). He affirms that these measures « *étaient a priori une bonne idée, [mais] n'ont eu aucun succès et n'ont jamais été utilisées.* ».

564 Fischer, Journal of Economic Perspectives, (1999).

565 Joseph P. Joyce, The IMF and global financial crises: Phoenix rising? (Cambridge University Press. 2013), pp. 52-71.

566 Jeffrey Sachs, et al., *The Mexican Peso Crisis: Sudden Death or Death Foretold?*, 41 Journal of International Economics (1996).

567 Jan Joost Teunissen & Age Akkerman, The crisis that was not prevented: lessons for Argentina, the IMF, and globalisation (Fondad. 2003).

568 Charles Kindleberger & Z. Robert Aliber, Manias, panics and crashes: a history of financial crises, 6th ed (Palgrave Macmillan. 2011). Their approach to the crisis is narrative, while the one developped by Rogoff is more empirical.

The IMF is at the centre of the international financial architecture[569]. The Fund is a mediator between creditors and debtors, a lender of last resort and a manager of crisis. Developing countries benefit from the IMF expertise. Due to the crisis, the Fund had to adapt itself and increase its financial assistance.

1.1.2. IMF and debt restructuring

The IMF faced new types of debt restructuring. For half a century, the restructuring had mainly followed a North-South logic. The developed countries in the North were helping the developing countries in the South. It has now changed. In the case of Europe, the new South is located inside the North. The history of sovereign debt restructuring is characterised by the new chapter of the monetary union[570]. The IMF's support to the Eurozone began in 2008 and 2009 in Hungary, Latvia and Romania, before being extended to Greece in spring 2010[571]. In October 2009, the Greek government revealed the extent of its deficit. The situation has rapidly deteriorated due to a drop of market confidence, a fear of unsustainable debt and a deterioration of the Greek sovereign rating. In April 2010, Greece was excluded from the bond market, resulting in a unique restructuring often compared to the Brady Bonds for Latin American countries in the 1980s[572]. The governments of the Eurozone and the Institute of International Finance proposed a participation of the public sector to banks and institutional investors. This proposal was accompanied by an offer from the private sector. Most of the Greek bonds held by banks and institutional

---

569 It is no longer only "*an honest broker between debtor countries and their creditor banks [that] consists of serving as ultimate judge of the appropriate mix between the magnitude of a heavily indebted developing country's adjustment effort and the commitment to it of new external finance for its remaining balance of payments deficit*". E. Walter Robichek, *International Monetary Fund: An Arbiter in the Debt Restructuring Process*, 23, Columbia Journal of Transnational Law (1984).

570 Lastra, The Role of the International Monetary Fund. 2014. Antonio Sáinz de Vicuña, *Restructuring in a Monetary Union: Legal Aspects*, see id.

571 Bismuth, Revue des affaires européennes, (2012).

572 See Guier, La position du Gouvernement américain en matière d'endettement des États : du plan Baker à l'initiative Brady, 1995; Manuel Monteagudo, *The Debt Problem: The Baker Plan (1985) And The Brady Initiative (1989) – History, Experience, Practice And Prospects*, see id.

investors were subjected to national regulators and governments' pressure. A creditors' committee, similar to the 1980s London Club, supervised the operation[573]. In 2011, the private sector was oriented to accept a exchange of bonds to lengthen their maturity[574]. On 9 March 2012, bonds from private creditor were exchanged. However, the ISDA triggered the Greek CDS arguing that no real consensus existed. The bonds exchange was considered a credit event[575]. The public sector financed Greece through the European Financial Stability Facility (EFSF) and the European Financial Stabilisation Mechanism (EFSM), both replaced since 1 July 2013 by the European Stability Mechanism (ESM). Credit lines were open to Greece, in addition to the guarantees provided by the European Member States[576]. Greece, classified as a developed country, had to respect the traditional conditionality policy[577]. The IMF considered that the Greek debt crisis originated in internal policies. The financial assistance was therefore based on the implementation of restructuring programmes involving cuts in public spending and tax increases[578]. This intervention, motivated by political and economic issues, was aimed at restoring the credibility of the Greek bailout for financial markets. This resulted in funding the Greek deficit, contrary to the provisions of the IMF Articles of Associations.

---

573 Zettelmeyer, et al., Economic Policy (2013).

574 Bénédicte Serbini, *Les enjeux de la restructuration de la dette souveraine grecque pour le mécanisme européen de stabilité*, Cahiers du Laboratoire d'économie appliquée au développement (2011).

575 In fact, the Greek legislation (Greek Bondholder Act, 4050/12, 23 February 2012) included a restructuring with the consent of a qualified majority of creditors. This legislation established retroactive collective action clauses in Greek bond contracts governed by Greek law.

576 See the figures published on the website of the European Financial Stability Mechanism.

577 Carreau, La surveillance internationale des politiques budgétaires. 2013.

578 Greece had to decrease the number of public servants, privatise public services and public enterprises, reform the labour market, and reduce wages, benefits and pensions. In response, the Syriza party was elected on 25 January 2015 by promising to end the austerity. See in this respect Yánis Varoufákis, Le Minotaure planétaire : l'ogre américain, la désunion européenne et le chaos mondial (Éditions du Cercle. 2015).

Due to the crisis in Greece and Argentina and in response to vulture funds, the IMF deals with new challenges[579]. Indeed, the IMF considers that restructuring is often a *minima* and too late, resulting in a failure to restore debt sustainability and sustainable access to financial markets. The IMF analyses current contractual limits. The restructuring of Greek debt has benefited from the introduction of legal mechanisms to remedy the situation. Unlike former bonds, new bonds include standard clauses to protect creditors and are governed by English law. Public and private creditors are organised in co-financing agreements. Collective action clauses have been introduced to limit the holdout strategies. However, the current market-based approach of debt restructuring has become less effective to overcome the widespread problem of collective action. Therefore, the inclusion of strengthened clauses in sovereign debt bonds is necessary[580].

The IMF also listed techniques to prevent the use of its resources to repay private creditors. The IMF may jeopardise its own stability as it participated in one third of the bailout programmes since 2010. The majority of provided fundings are for private creditors[581]. In Greece, the IMF assistance was conventionalised in the ESM Treaty. Subsequently, the increase of official lenders requires strengthening the legal framework of the official sector involvement, particularly for creditors outside the Paris Club. The official sector involvement refers to the issue of risk sharing between official creditors. Indeed, the distribution between public and private sector must be negotiated. For now, no option clearly prevails.

The IMF is at the centre of a wider consultation on the establishment of a legal framework on sovereign debt restructuring[582]. Political initiatives

579 Sovereign Debt Restructuring – Recent Developments and Implications for the Fund's Legal and Policy Framework. (2013). The recitals of the ESM Treaty refers to the practice of the IMF, whose purpose is presented in Article I (v): "*to give confidence to members by making the general resources of the Fund temporarily available to them under adequate safeguards, thus providing them with opportunity to correct maladjustments in their balance of payments without resorting to measures destructive of national or international prosperity*".

580 "*There is merit in considering whether a more robust form of aggregation clause could be designed and successfully introduced into international sovereign bonds*". Id. at. See Staff Guidance Note for Public Debt Sustainability Analysis in Market-Access Countries. (2013).

581 You Never Give Me Your Money? Sovereign Debt Crises, Collective Action Problems, and IMF Lending. (2013).

582 Petch, Legal Implications of the Euro Zone Crisis. Debt Restructuring, Sovereign Default and Euro Zone Exit. 2014, pp. 50-54.

have focused on collective action clauses to fix various problems. However, the IMF has advocated for the creation of a new mechanism for sovereign debt restructuring.[583].

1.2. IMF proposals to manage restructuring

Various categories of stakeholders including international financial institutions, informal clubs, national authorities, and private financial institutions were involved in resolution of international debt crisis. Despite their involvement, the common crisis resolution was considered ineffective. For twenty years, the IMF studies the legal, institutional and procedural aspects of a statutory solution allowing a sovereign debtor and a qualified majority of creditors to reach an agreement binding to creditors (1.2.1.), and a contractual approach that involves debt restructuring clauses. While the statutory approach was abandoned (1.2.2.), the contractual approach prospered.

1.2.1. The sovereign debt restructuring mechanism

The sovereign debt restructuring mechanism refers to the IMF statutory proposal. The idea of such a mechanism is not new. Such mechanism is based on an international bankruptcy procedure adapted from Chapters 9 and 11 of the US Bankruptcy Code. The mechanism was first proposed after the Mexican crisis. The IMF would have been reorganised to act as debt tribunal rather than as lender of last resort[584]. This international debt tribunal echoed the 1986 and 1998 UNCTAD reports on Trade and Development that called for the establishment of an international insolvency framework for sovereign debtor[585]. The IMF was in charge of developing the project. In the 1990s, Michel Camdessus and Stanley Fischer suggest-

---

583 Panizza, et al., Journal of Economic Literature, (2009).

584 Sachs, Do We Need an International Lender of Last Resort?. 1995. Steven L. Schwarcz, *Sovereign Debt Restructuring: A Bankruptcy Reorganization Approach*, 85 Cornell Law Review (2000).

585 UNCTAD Trade and Development Report 1986, United Nations, New York and Geneva; UNCTAD Report on Trade and Development Report 1998, United Nations, New York and Geneva, p. 8.

ed that Article VIII Section 2 (b) of the IMF's Articles could be interpreted as a sovereign protection against litigation[586]. In 1995 and 1996, the IMF sought to adapt banking financing rules of developing countries[587]. The opportunity of a sovereign bankruptcy regime was strengthened with the failure of Argentina in 2001, which consolidated the commitment to an ambitious reform[588]. Since 2001, the IMF has named the project Sovereign Debt Restructuring Mechanism (SDRM) [589]and presented it as a solution to compensate the lack of international financial architecture[590].

The implementation of a negotiated legal framework to restructure sovereign debt must necessarily follow a graduated approach[591]. Supporters of the project consider that this mechanism may facilitate a solution through mediation and arbitration, and an equal treatment between States. The assumption is that ordered debt service suspensions are better than chaotic defaults[592]. Opponents of the project assert that the creation of such a mechanism increases the restructuring costs, as the introduction of CACs would increase the probability of default[593].

The IMF Executive Board discussed a detailed proposal in 2002 and 2003[594]. The SDRM, announced by Anne Krueger, has been amended sev-

586 This proposal remains a modest alternative to a comprehensive mechanism that would allow a broad interpretation of Article VIII Section 2 (b) to impose a temporary way of action for creditors. Nevertheless, the need of an authoritative interpretation of Article XXIX(a) would be necessary. See François Gianviti, *The Reform of the International Monetary Fund (Conditionality and Surveillance)*, 34, The International Lawyer (2000).

587 Jérôme Sgard, *The IMF meets commercial banks: sovereign debt restructurings between 1970 and 1989*, mimeo (2012).

588 Bankruptcy Procedures for Sovereigns: A History of Ideas, 1976-2001, (2002), pp. 470–507.

589 Anne Krueger, International Financial Architecture for 2002: A New Approach to Sovereign Debt Restructuring (International Monetary Fund ed., 2001).

590 A New Approach to Sovereign Debt Restructuring, (2002), p. 47.

591 Sean Hagan, *Designing a Legal Framework to Restructure Sovereign Debt*, 36, Georgetown Journal of International Law (2005).

592 Andrew G. Haldane, Mark Kruger, "The Resolution of the International Financial Crisis", *Banque of Canada Review*, *Banque of England*, 2001.

593 However, the Mexican crisis demonstrated that CACs do not affect the cost of financing. See Bond Restructuring and Moral Hazard: Are Collective Action Clauses Costly? (2001).

594 Proposed Features of a Sovereign Debt Restructuring Mechanism (2003).

eral times[595]. The final proposal includes four pillars. The first pillar is a majority restructuring:

> "the mechanism would allow a sovereign and a qualified majority of creditors to reach an agreement that would then be made binding on all creditors that are subject to the restructuring".

The second pillar is based on prevention of disruptive litigation by discouraging

> "creditors from seeking to enhance their position through litigation during the restructuring process".

The third pillar focuses on protecting creditor interests by including

> "safeguards that give creditors adequate assurances that their interests are being protected during the restructuring process".

The fourth pillar's priority is to guarantee financing[596].

Based on the fact that capital disintermediation obstructs sovereign debt restructuring, the IMF seeks to create a sovereign bankruptcy law associated with the establishment of a tribunal. One overall mechanism would enable fast and structured renegotiation. Such mechanism would provide moratorium and debt suspension. Restructuring arrangements adopted by a qualified majority of creditors would be imposed on minority creditors[597]. The establishment of such dispute resolution forum would implement an international judiciary system for sovereign debt resolution. The establishment of the SDRM is similar to the creation at an international level of a bankruptcy proceeding for States based on the provisions of Chapter 11 of the US Bankruptcy Code[598] An independent forum would separately analyse complaints. Proponents argue that this mechanism would fill a gap in the international financial system. Such mechanism would provide a framework to solve collective action problems and coordinate creditors

595 The two most important problems remain the design of a standstill on payments and the imposition of a stay on creditor litigation.

596 IMF, "Proposals for a Sovereign Debt Restructuring Mechanism (SDRM)", Factsheet, January 2003.

597 Rodrigo Olivares-Caminal, *Is there a need for an international insolvency regime in the context of sovereign debt? A case for the use of corporate debt restructuring techniques*, 24, Journal of International Banking Law and Regulation (2009).

598 Structuring and Restructuring Sovereign Debt: The Role of a Bankruptcy Regime, 2007, pp. 1-27.

while encouraging indebted States and their creditors to restructure their debt before defaulting[599].

1.2.2. Renunciation to the sovereign debt restructuring mechanism

The statutory approach of the sovereign debt restructuring mechanism project was abandoned in 2003[600] in favour of the contractual approach. Internal decision-making implies a consensus. The promoters of the SDRM project presented a series of technical papers. However, no agreement was reached to define a bankruptcy regime and its objectives[601]. The proposal did not receive the required political support[602]. Without the support of the qualified majority of IMF shareholders, no further action could be implemented[603].

The SDRM remain ineffective in the event of non-cooperation between States and private creditors of their territory. As for the legal difficulties, the determination of the applicable law in case of litigation inevitably refers to the absence of international regime. The SDRM proposal was revolutionary in that it would have created a supranational court that would have had the authority to approve and enforce a decision taken by a qualified majority. Nevertheless, some points were not discussed, such as the cooperation between domestic courts and the SDRM court. This multilateral court could have changed a contract governed by French or German law. The substitution to French or German judge may not be have been recognised by those States.

599 Anne O. Krueger & Sean Hagan, *Sovereign Workouts: An IMF Perspective*, Vol. 6, Chicago Journal of International Law (2005).

600 The debate on the SDRM was buried. See IMF needs to do far more to help countries learn from each other's success and failures: interview with Mark Allen. (2004); . IMF, Sovereign Debt Restructuring – Recent Developments and Implications for the Fund's Legal and Policy Framework. 2013.

601 Brad Setser, *The Political Economy of the SDRM, in* Overcoming Developing Country Debt Crises (Barry Herman, et al. eds., 2010).

602 Richard Euliss, *The Feasibility of the IMF's Sovereign Debt Restructuring Mechanism: An Alternative Statutory Approach to Mollify American Reservations*, 19, American University International Law Review (2003).

603 Jérôme Sgard, *Crise de la dette souveraine : l'action multilatérale après le rejet de la proposition Krueger*, 223, La lettre du Centre d'études prospectives et d'informations internationales (2003), pp. 1-4.

Moreover, the IMF is criticised for its conflict of interest due to its role as creditor and insolvency judge. Yet as an international financial institution, the IMF plays a crucial role on sovereign debt management[604]. Many opponents to international financial reforms, including sovereign debt restructuring, sought to weaken the foundations of the IMF. The renunciation to one of the most structured proposals in this area is due to the lack of an adequate institutional channel in spite of an innovative idea[605]. The German government has used this idea in 2010-2011 to provide a response to the Greek crisis.

Despite the abandon of the SDRM, the debate highlights an old problem to which no concrete answer has been given yet. The SDRM demonstrates the necessary reforms in this area[606]. Some private creditors feared that the introduction of the SDRM would favour the public sector. This fear was echoed by the exclusion from SDRM operations of the Paris Club debts[607].

Subsequently, the IMF supported the use of collective action clauses and continues its work on this contractual tool. The drafting of CACs and *pari passu* clauses proposed in August 2014 by the ICMA has been extensively reviewed in IMF publications. These clauses have been utilised since October 2014 for new bonds issued in Kazakhstan, Mexico, Vietnam, Ethiopia and Belize. Available on the ICMA website, the standard *pari passu* clause applicable to sovereign debt is the following:

> "The Notes are the direct, unconditional and unsecured obligations of the Issuer and rank and will rank *pari passu*, without preference among themselves, with all other unsecured External Indebtedness of the Issuer, from time to time outstanding, provided, however, that the Issuer shall have no obligation to effect equal or rateable payment(s) at any time with respect to any such other External Indebtedness and, in particular, shall have no obligation to pay other External Indebtedness at the same time or as a condition of paying sums due on the Notes and vice versa".

604 Daillier, et al., Droit international public, 2009, pp. 1192 and foll.

605 Daniel K. Tarullo, *The Role of the IMF in Sovereign Debt Restructuring*, Vol. 6 Chicago Journal of International Law (2005).

606 Sovereign Debt Structure for Crisis Prevention, (2004).

607 Josselin, Global Governance, (2009). The author refers to a gang of private sector associations and their joint action: the Emerging Markets Traders Association, the International Primary Market Association, the International Securities Markets Association, the Security Industry Authority and the Bond Market Association.

The collective action clause is widely developed to organise negotiations between creditors in the event of a restructuring[608].

2. International financial institutions and debt management

According to John Maynard Keynes, "Miss Bank" would deal with long-term loans for public sector projects in the framework of reconstruction and development, whereas "Master Fund" would lend for short periods to assist States and stabilise their finances[609]. Both activities should be distinct. No cooperation or regular consultation would be provided. However, the IMF began to lend for longer periods to solve structural problems, while the World Bank granted loans for specific projects. A closer collaboration became necessary[610].

In terms of sovereign debt, the World Bank and the IMF work together to implement a generic management (2.1.). These two financial institutions play a major role in the field of development. Their mission is based on programmes to stabilise the situation of indebted States (2.2.).

2.1. Sovereign indebtedness versus development

International financial institutions benefit from the principle of implied powers[611]. Subsequently, they adapted their activities to the needs of their members (2.1.1.). While the IMF rapidly assists in case of crisis, the World Bank has been oriented towards the management of sovereign access to finance. This set of functions is structured to facilitate sovereign debt management (2.1.2.).

---

608 See Annex 3.

609 Keynes described the IMF and the World Bank as twins in a speech made on March 1946 at the inaugural meeting of Governors in Savannah, Georgia, United States: see transcript Roy Harrod, *The Life of John Maynard Keynes*, London, Macmillan & Co. Ltd, 1951, pp. 631-632.

610 James M. Boughton, Tearing Down Walls: The International Monetary Fund 1990-1999 (International Monetary Fund. 2012), pp. 81-96.

611 Dominique Carreau & Fabrizio Marrella, Droit international, Onzième édition (Pedone. 2012), XV, N° 168 s.

2.1.1. Initiators of debt management

As discussed in the first chapter, the World Bank is the main provider of financing for economic development projects. Its Articles of Agreement take into account sovereign interest[612] in project financing[613]. In times of crisis, the World Bank redeploys its activity in the field of sovereign debt management[614]. According to its Articles of Agreement, the World Bank shall renegotiate its debt with defaulting States[615]. Similarly to the IMF, provisions on immunity from jurisdiction are included in the World Bank's Articles[616]. The assistance of the World Bank is limited to developing countries and most of its programmes are tailored for those countries[617]. Its public debt expertise dates back to the 1960s[618]. Despite the criticism and shortcomings of some of its programmes, the World Bank stands as the general coordinator of public creditors, including regional banks. In terms of available fundings, the World Bank products for States

---

612 Article III, Section 4 (v): "*In making or guaranteeing a loan, the Bank shall pay due regard to the prospects that the borrower, and, if the borrower is not a member, that the guarantor, will be in position to meet its obligations under the loan; and the Bank shall act prudently in the interests both of the particular member in whose territories the project is located and of the members as a whole*".

613 Article III, Section 4(vii): "*Loans made or guaranteed by the Bank shall, except in special circumstances, be for the purpose of specific projects of reconstruction or development*".

614 Sorel, Annuaire Français de Droit International (2006).

615 Article IV, Section 7: "*In cases of default on loans made, participated in, or guaranteed by the Bank: (a) The Bank shall make such arrangements as may be feasible to adjust the obligations under the loans, including arrangements under or analogous to those provided in Section 4 (c) of this Article*".

616 Article VII, Section 3: "*Actions may be brought against the Bank only in a court of competent jurisdiction in the territories of a member in which the Bank has an office, has appointed an agent for the purpose of accepting service or notice of process, or has issued or guaranteed securities. No actions shall, however, be brought by members or persons acting for or deriving claims from members. The property and assets of the Bank shall, wheresoever located and by whomsoever held, be immune from all forms of seizure, attachment or execution before the delivery of final judgment against the Bank*".

617 Dalvinder Singh, *The Role of the IMF and World Bank in Financial Sector Reform and Compliance*, *in* Redefining sovereignty in international economic law (Wenhua Shan & Penelope Simons eds., 2008).

618 Facing the increasing of indebtedness indicators, it launched the alert, arguing that the problems of developing countries were borrowing and reckless lending; see the annual report of IBRD 1964/1965, pp. 57-63.

are multiple[619]. Other financial institutions complement this action. Some IMF programmes are directed towards developing countries. Regional development banks complete the financing structuring[620].

The debt management programme is part of the official development assistance. The crisis of the 1980s raised the issue of debt sustainability. In 1989, official creditors decided to cancel debt of the poorest countries[621]. In the mid-1990s, the international community considered that the existing mechanisms of debt relief for the poorest countries were inadequate to solve their debt problems. Subsequently, in 1996, the World Bank President and the IMF Managing Director proposed a debt relief programme for heavily indebted poor countries (HIPC). This initiative HIPC is the first concerted effort to alleviate multilateral debt of a defined number of States. This programme has allowed the coordination of restructuring and refinancing to ensure debt viability. This initiative was unique and unified for the first time all official creditors to solve the debt issue in a common way. It has gradually been improved and adjusted.

In 2005, the HIPC initiative was complemented and reinforced by a multilateral debt relief initiative (MDRI). The MDRI provides a debt relief of debt owed to the International Development Association (IDA), the International Monetary Fund (IMF) and the African Development Bank (ADB)[622]. However, the final decision depends on each institution[623]. For example, the IMF grants a total and immediate debt cancellation for States

---

619 Manuel du service de la dette (2009).

620 See the example of the EBRD: Felicitas Chen, *The Correlation between Human Rights and the Loan Policies of the World Bank and the EBRD*, *in* Ethics and human rights in a globalized world: an interdisciplinary and international approach (Klaus Hoffmann-Holland ed. 2009).

621 Carreau, Journal du Droit International (1985).

622 "*The IMF, the International Development Association (IDA) of the World Bank, and the African Development Fund (AfDF) cancel 100 percent of their debt claims on countries that had reached, or would eventually reach, the completion point – the stage at which a country becomes eligible for full and irrevocable debt relief – under the joint IMF-World Bank enhanced Initiative for Heavily Indebted Poor Countries (HIPC Initiative)*". See IMF, "The Multilateral Debt Relief Initiative", Factsheet, 17 September 2015.

623 "*The IMF and the World Bank cooperated closely in the implementation and monitoring of the MDRI, particularly when assessing qualification for MDRI relief and monitoring MDG-related spending after debt relief had been provided. [...] Although the MDRI was an initiative common to several international financial institutions, the decision to grant debt relief was ultimately the separate re-*

that fulfill its requirements. The IDA provides for a gradual cancellation over a period of forty years. The ADB cancels all the unpaid debt by heavily indebted poor countries when they achieve a completion point. In 2007, the MDRI was extended to the Inter-American Development Bank (IADB) for Bolivia, the Co-operative Republic of Guyana, the Republic of Haiti, the Republic of Honduras and the Republic of Nicaragua. In practice, once a State reaches the completion point defined by the HIPC programme, all official creditors – and some private creditors – are required to amend their contracts to reduce the debt net value[624]. These contractual amendments ensure a debt rebalancing to consolidate HIPC public finances. In order to avoid a reduction of IMF and World Bank lending capacities, the G8 members undertook to cover the costs.

2.1.2. Debt renegotiation and debt relief

Debt relief decisions have occurred in the context of the UN Millennium Development Goals[625]. A strengthened debt management complements this debt relief. The sovereign debt management of developing countries has evolved over the past quarter of century in favour of a reduction of poverty. Debt management is complex because few concrete results in reducing poverty exist. The ability of HIPC to devote a larger part of public spending on social programmes is still limited. The theoretical justification of these programmes is that debt undermines economic growth[626]. The HIPC initiative and the MDRI have been successful because they reduced debts to sustainable levels.

However, these initiatives of debt relief have been severely criticised[627]. The selection procedures are complicated and demanding, whereas only a

---

sponsibility of each institution, and the approach to coverage and implementation varied". See IMF, "The Multilateral Debt Relief Initiative", Factsheet, 17 September 2015.

624 Guder, The Administration of Debt Relief by the International Financial Institutions: A Legal Reconstruction of the Hipc Initiative, 2010, pp.131-190.

625 Se World Bank website that focuses on the link between debt relief and Millennium Development Goals.

626 Nancy Birdsall, et al., Delivering on Debt Relief: From IMF Gold to a New Aid Architecture (Center for Global Development. 2002).

627 Rapport d'information sur les activités et le contrôle du Fonds monétaire international et de la Banque mondiale, (2000).

small number of States are concerned. Above all, the involvement of private creditors is limited. Financial assistance is derived from public and private bilateral creditors in form of a reduction of eighty percent of the debt stock. Private creditors are not all included. Therefore, a further development is expected[628]. Inconsistencies are denounced. In terms of method, apprehension and perception of development are questionable. Economic growth, financial, fiscal and macroeconomic management are envisaged without taking into consideration social and cultural rights or human rights development.

Legally, the debt relief process through the HIPC and MDRI is not determined by a binding contractual relationship, but rather by recognised principles of international law. Such principles as the obligation to cooperate with the IMF and the World Bank, along with other international institutions, are employed. The lack of legal commitments reveals the soft law. One can nevertheless consider that debt relief is the product of an institutional and decision-making framework. Debt relief is legally valid. For the World Bank, the HIPC initiative is an agreed international (but non-binding) framework. Progressively, this debt relief practice may become permanent. Therefore, the degree of normativity of these acts may in the long-term exceed their legal nature[629].

Finally, there is no recognition of the odious debt doctrine, nor a permanent questioning of the conditionality of international financial institutions. The concept of odious debt, theorised in 1927[630], was never formally adopted by any court or court decision[631]. According to this doctrine, *pacta sunt servanda* would be limited to debts contracted for the interest of the country[632]. However, repudiating a debt does not imply that citizens

---

628 Susan Park & Antje Vetterlein, Owning Development. Creating Policy Norms in the IMF and the World Bank (Cambridge University Press. 2010).

629 Guder, The Administration of Debt Relief by the International Financial Institutions: A Legal Reconstruction of the Hipc Initiative, 2010, pp. 131-194.

630 « *Si un pouvoir despotique contracte une dette non pas pour les besoins et dans les intérêts de l'État, mais pour fortifier son régime despotique, pour réprimer la population qui le combat, etc., cette dette est odieuse pour la population de l'État entier* », SACK, Les effets des transformations des États sur leurs dettes publiques et autres obligations financières, 1927. See Chapter 1.

631 Nehru & Thomas, The Concept of Odious Debt: Some Considerations, 2008, pp. 205-227; Ochoa, Harvard International Law Journal (2008).

632 Michalowski, Unconstitutional Regimes and the Validity of Sovereign Debt: A Legal Perspective, 2007, pp. 47-59.

can benefit from debt restructuring[633]. The debate on odious or illegitimate debt continues in the UNCTAD[634]. By expanding the scope of analysis to international law and to commercial insolvency, it is possible to articulate a narrow definition of odious or illegitimate debt that is legally enforceable[635]. Although the concept of odious debt is not recognised in international public law, it does not mean that indebted States have no possibilities. A defence based on other legal systems may be organised, in particular private law can help finding adequate measures while the decision is executed[636].

Beyond sovereign debt is the issue of poverty reduction. The poorest countries are unable to generate resources to repay their debts, while eliminating poverty requires huge expenses[637]. A highly indebted poor country seeking to stop its debt service may invoke the International Covenant on Civil and Political Rights signed in New York on 16 December 1966[638]. Thus, the impact of structural adjustment policies and economic reforms in sovereign debt management is considered by the United Nations. The twentieth session of the Council of Human Rights of 2 July 2012 underlined

> "the effects of foreign debt and other related international financial obligations of States on the full enjoyment of all human rights, particularly economic, social and cultural rights".

---

633 Feibelman, Journal of International Banking Law and Regulation (2010).

634 UNCTAD, Eighth Conference on Debt Management, Geneva, 14-16 November 2011. See Chapter 8.

635 A. Mechele Dickerson, *Insolvency Principles: The Missing Link in the Odious Debt Debate*, *in* Sovereign Debt: From Safety to Default (Robert W. Kolb ed. 2011).

636 Lee C. Buchheit, et al., *The Dilemma of Odious Debts*, 56, Duke Law Journal (2007); Friedrich Benjamin Schneider, Odious Debts. Status quo und Regelungsmodell unter besonderer Berücksichtigung internationaler Menschenrechts (Schriften zum Völkerrecht Band 212 ed., Duncker & Humblot. 2015).

637 Enrique Cosío-Pascal, *Paris Club: Intergovernmental Relations in Debt Restructuring*, *in* Overcoming Developing Country Debt Crisis (Barry Herman, et al. eds., 2010).

638 International Covenant on Civil and Political Rights, adopted and opened for signature, ratification and accession by General Assembly resolution 2200A (XXI) of 16 December 1966, entry into force 23 March 1976, in accordance with Article 49. See Noel G. Villaroman, *Debt Servicing and its Adverse Impact on Economic, Social and Cultural Rights in Developing Countries*, 9, Journal of Human Rights (2010).

The conclusion remains the same since this issue is debated. A comprehensive solution for the sovereign debt management is missing[639].

2.2. Monitoring sovereign debt levels

The World Bank and the IMF monitor the evolution of sovereign debt levels through a common assessment framework: the Joint World Bank-IMF Debt Sustainability Framework for Low-Income Countries, and the application of comparable legal categories when restructuring.

In addition to debt relief, the World Bank and the IMF adopted this Joint Word Bank-IMF Debt Sustainability Framework to track the debt evolution of States concerned by a risk of over-indebtedness[640]. New funding are granted in order to reduce the possibilities of new indebtedness. Based on this framework, the IMF analyses debt sustainability and determines access to its funding. The World Bank uses it to decide whether a loan or an IDA credit is applicable to a HIPC country. This joint framework aims at:

> "fostering coherent and responsible lending practices, identifying emerging debt-related vulnerabilities, and elaborating country-owned debt strategies"[641].

However, this only applies to a limited number of creditors.

In addition, this joint framework is not binding *vis-à-vis* public lenders and private creditors. The institutional framework is therefore limited, al-

---

639 "*11. Regrets the absence of mechanisms to find appropriate solutions to the unsustainable foreign debt burden of low- and middle-income heavily indebted countries, and that, to date, little headway has been made in redressing the unfairness of the current system of debt resolution, which continues to place the interests of the lenders above those of indebted countries and the poor in those countries, and therefore calls for an intensification of efforts to devise effective and equitable mechanisms to cancel or reduce substantially the foreign debt burden of all developing countries, in particular those severely affected by the devastation of natural disasters, such as tsunamis and hurricanes, and by armed conflicts*". Human Rights Council, General Assembly of the United Nations, 20th session, Agenda item 3, 2 July 2012, A/HRC/20/L.17.

640 Duvall, Debt Relief for Low-Income Countries. 2014.

641 Communiqué of the International Monetary and Financial Committee of the Board of Governors of the International Monetary Fund, No. 07/71, 14 April 2007, para. 14.

though principles are emerging. Indeed, the World Bank is focusing on the long-term sustainability of fiscal policy. Its work includes principles and guidelines incorporated in the Global Bank Insolvency Initiative. The World Bank and UNCITRAL, supported by the IMF, have also developed standards for bankruptcy based on the Principles for Effective Creditor Rights Systems, as well as the UNCITRAL Legislative Guide on Insolvency Law[642].

In terms of transparency, the IMF encourages States to create more rigorous reports on debt sustainability. For instance, the IMF country report on Greece highlights errors in the analysis of debt sustainability and calls for a greater vigilance regarding data provided by States. It is in this context that Argentina was censored in February 2013[643] for reporting manifestly false statistics on inflation and economic growth[644]. Analyses and reports permit a better implementation of the programmes. Such analyses are conducted under the bilateral consultations of Article IV and are fundamental to macroeconomic knowledge and policymaking expertise. Nonetheless, this control remains legally insufficient. Even if false reports are punishable, there is no power to censure or oppose economic, monetary or fiscal policies contradicting the stability objectives. Paradoxically, such control remains a recommendation, while the IMF monitoring converts into a financial supervision when its assistance is needed.

In case of restructuring, legal changes are implemented. Depending on the performed economic operation, legal impacts differ. If there is a debt reduction or a debt cancellation, a part or the entire amount of the debt is cancelled[645]. In case of a rescheduling, contractual maturities are postponed or debt bonds are replaced by new bonds that include other contractual terms[646]. If the creditors and the borrower agreed on a restructuring or a rescheduling, there is a novation or a suspension of the initial contracts. Creditors can choose to maintain the existing agreements or modified

642 See Chapter 8.

643 Statement by the IMF Executive Board on Argentina, Press Release No. 13/33, 1 February 2013.

644 Subsequently, the IMF continues to monitor data. See Statement by the IMF Executive Board on Argentina, Press Release No. 14/577, 15 December 2014.

645 Soren Ambrose, *Social Movements and the Politics of Debt Cancellation*, 6, Chicago Journal of International Law (2005).

646 Vinod K. Aggarwal, Debt Games: Strategic Interaction in International Debt Rescheduling (Cambridge University Press. 1996). See in particular the study of game theory applied to sovereign debt renegotiation pp. 15-98.

them. Subsequently, if the second agreement is not respected, it is possible to refer to the initial conditions. This conditional innovation is used as soon as the State defaults *vis-a-vis* the rescheduling agreement[647].

Concerning debt buy backs, this technique allows the sovereign debtor to purchase its debt with a haircut[648]. Swaps are considered as a technical restructuring and as a method of speculation on the secondary market. The list of swap possibilities is numerous: debt for debt swap, debt for equity swap, debt for bond swaps. Other arrangements exist, for example in terms of debt swap into investments[649].

The World Bank and the IMF monitor the sovereign debt evolution through their joint framework and similar legal categories in case of restructuring. We consider such common tools a preliminary to the implementation of a normative system of sovereign debt management.

*

When considering sovereign debt management, we demonstrated that there is a political preference for *ad hoc* mechanisms. Flexibility and informality are not considered as problems *per se* for sovereign debt management. However, they become problematic when cooperation stops. In the field of sovereign debt, not only are the Paris and London Clubs informal, but the entire restructuring mechanism is in itself informal. No international agreement has ever materialised a set of simple rules. The rules of international law, the contractual clauses and the internal rules of international institutions are systematically suspended or circumvented.

International public indebtedness is characterised by continuous imbalances. In such situations, financial markets provide no solution. Consequently, multilateral or bilateral programmes monitor States. Commitments are rescheduled and financial products restructured. Such operations have informally brought together the international public system and the international private system of sovereign financing. Through this joint work on debt consolidation, the idea of a formal sovereign debt mechanism has re-emerged. Such mechanism is a comprehensive response to the

---

647 Carreau & Shaw, La dette extérieure / The External Debt. 1995, pp. 33 and foll.

648 A Primer on Sovereign Debt Buybacks and Swaps. (2007). Jeremy Bulow & Kenneth Rogoff, *The Buyback Boondoggle*, 2, Brookings Papers on Economic Activity (1988).

649 These debt swaps for assets can reduce the amount of debt while stimulating investment to encourage economic growth.

endemic problem of permanent indebtedness. Even if we may relativise the idea that the latest crisis has reached the magnitude of the 1929 financial crisis, the current instability has the merit of questioning new reforms instead of considering a global collapse.

When a State is unable to repay its financial obligations, which procedure shall apply? International financial institutions have adopted the HIPC initiative and reinforced by the multilateral debt cancellation initiative. However, such programmes only offer general guidance to State governments that borrow mainly from private creditors to solve their debt crisis.

Title III. CONCLUSION

In this title, we analysed the contractual approach privileged in *ad hoc* mechanisms. Informal clubs like the Paris Club or the London Club enforces such approach. In general, private creditors value pragmatic solutions to resolve debt instability over an organised debt rescheduling mechanism. Due to the current absence of international insolvency law managed by public entities under the auspices of international financial institutions, the sovereign debt management problem remains opportunistic.

The measures taken to address the crisis are mainly domestic. Even the initiatives within the European Union are focused on the coordination of national rescue plans compatible with the rules of European law, especially in regards to competition law.

The financial crisis did not lead to the creation of a supranational auditor of public finances. The G20 only call the international community to strengthen supervision and financial regulation. However, the efforts of policy coordination to implement structural adjustments have increased. States seek to influence economic and political costs induced by the international financial integration. Abandoning economic diktat to discuss legal regulation is not yet achieved. Nevertheless, the current financial crisis confirmed that adaptations are indispensable to the proper functioning of sovereign financing. We will address this imperative management in the following title and will refer to propositions as well as legal principles.

Title IV. SOVEREIGN DEBT MANAGEMENT, AN INTERNATIONAL PRIORITY FOR STATES

Since the crisis in 2008, the overall level of sovereign debt remains too high and continues to increase. The perspectives of short-term reduction are unstable[650]. Thus, it is crucial to develop an understanding of this environment, its implications and consequences for the international financial system. Sovereign debt management is a major problem for developed economies. Consequently, States seek to use existing tools – such as monetary policy, fiscal austerity – to provide an answer to a critical situation. As previously examined, the main difficulty of debt management is the *sui generis* character of sovereign debt.

These issues of general interest should not be addressed at a national level because of the interdependence in this field[651]. Although no general mechanism has been established, States presently share the imperative of managing sovereign debt. They recognise the necessity to implement a policy towards a stabilisation of sovereign debt. Such policy constitutes the *sine qua non* foundation of growth and development[652].

This imperative of sovereign debt management takes two forms. First, it seeks to prevent, mitigate or restore the confidence of private creditors when a State defaults by integrating new standards. Second, its purpose is to help States to return to an economic, social and political sustainable situation by implementing concrete rules (Chapter 7). Legally, this requirement results in the emergence of an international law of sovereign debt that may be strengthened by the formal adoption of standards (Chapter 8).

650 Debt: the view from Basel (2015).

651 Frédéric Allemand, *Le développement de la coordination des politiques budgétaires dans l'UE, in* Quelle souveraineté budgétaire pour les États ? (Jean-Marc Sorel & Régis Chemain eds., 2013).

652 84e Rapport annuel de la BRI. IV. Dette et cycle financier : perspectives nationales et mondiales. (2014).

CHAPTER 7. Global Debt Management and Framework Proposals

The international environment of the last crisis has imposed the idea that solutions cannot be limited to a domestic context. A global solution, imposed or accepted, would allow the implementation of an effective sovereign debt management. Ideally, a transnational mechanism, based on domestic bankruptcy procedures, offers a comprehensive solution. In 1939, the League of Nations unsuccessfully tried to launch an international tribunal for sovereign debt based on a litigation approach[653].

However, as we demonstrated, sovereign insolvency cannot be treated through legal action. Negotiation should be prioritised. Moreover, the purpose is not to find a forum where disputes may be settled in accordance with a chosen applicable law. The legal framework of sovereign debt management implies to consider the whole sovereign funding in order to answer current instabilities.

Thus, we first consider global indebtedness level where the priority is to restore financial multilateralism (1.). Second, we analyse the development of legal frameworks under international institutional leadership (2.).

1. Institutional action to restore financial multilateralism

Institutional capacities have been strengthened to implement international cooperation (1.1.) oriented towards a coordination of standards, a minimum harmonisation of national rules and implementation of supervision (1.2.).

---

653 The League of Nations proposal took place in a difficult context. The Committee considered that the conclusion of an international convention to establish an international debt tribunal would be unrealistic due to the current international situation. The report was indeed published a few months before the invasion of Poland by Germany. Therefore, the Committee did not analyse in detail the project annexed to the report. See « Rapport du Comité pour l'étude des contrats d'emprunts internationaux », *Publications de la SDN*, Questions économiques et financières, 1939, II.A.10.

1.1. Strengthening international cooperation

Due to the inability to obtain an international consensus on a general mechanism for managing sovereign debt (1.1.1.), the stated objective of States and international institutions is to tackle the decline of financial multilateralism (1.1.2.).

1.1.1. Status quo of the international consensus

The international community is from reaching a consensus on the costs and benefits of a global mechanism for sovereign debt restructuring. Among the most ambitious proposals is the idea that an international recognised institution would formulate a draft framework and set up a schedule to implement an international treaty. Such an international convention would require States to include specific clauses in their financing and international contracts and to incorporate a mechanism for the application of creditors' seniority[654]. However, apart from the IMF regular economic assessments and budgetary policies, no coercive decision is imposed on States[655]. Regarding private creditors' treatment, international regulators such as the Basel Committee are only in charge of regulating relations. Consequently, as it stands, the use of the International Law Commission is not possible in this area.

Political difficulties explain the failure of previous initiatives in creating a sovereign debt restructuring mechanism. Collective action difficulties are problematic for both private investors and sovereign debtors. Private investors are constantly opposing the creation of a mechanism. This opposition is due to the fact that private creditors defend their own interests outside of the scope of formal institutions. However, private creditors' defence is not always effective and their losses can be significant. The Argentine example demonstrated it. A mechanism may then facilitate negotiations by accelerating them and minimizing the impact of the crisis. A lack of investors' interest in such a mechanism underlies the reason for private creditors' refusal. The rejection of private creditors and public

654 Patrick Bolton & Jr. David A. Skeel, *Inside the Black Box: How Should a Sovereign Bankruptcy Framework Be Structured*, 53, Emory Law Journal (2004).

655 See the IMF decision of 27 September 2009 to make mandatory assessment programs in the financial sector for 25 countries.

debtors is explained by the perception of a shift in the balance of costs and benefits of restructuring. Even if all agree on the importance of such mechanism, negotiations may fail because of the opposition to redistribution. Whatever the reason, the impossibility to encourage the creation of a mechanism is the central cause of the continued failure of initiatives to fill the void of international financial governance.

However, it is widely accepted that sovereign debt management should be brought to the centre of international debate. The UN General Assembly mentioned it repeatedly in its resolutions in the aftermath of the crisis[656]. These resolutions discuss the lessons learnt from debt crises and to assess ongoing work on sovereign debt resolution mechanisms to guide the agendas of policymakers[657]. Calls for structured approaches to solve this question have been included in the United Nations resolutions since 2009[658] and particularly in September 2014 and 2015.

Pleading for a statutory approach to sovereign default is not new within the United Nations. This plea echoes all previous initiatives in sovereign debt restructuring intended to:

> "increasing the efficiency, stability and predictability of the international financial system and achieving sustained, inclusive and equitable economic growth and sustainable development"[659].

International organisations, the IMF, UNCTAD, NGOs, think tanks, universities, and other international fora have been organising consultations and conducting research for several years to explore the feasibility and the

656 General Assembly of the United Nations, "*External debt sustainability and development*", 21 December 2009, A/RES/64/191; General Assembly of the United Nations, "*External debt sustainability and development*", 20 December 2010, A/RES/65/144; 22 December 2011, A/RES/66/189; 21 December 2012, A/RES/67/198; 20 December 2013, A/RES/68/202.

657 UNCTAD, Sovereign debt crises and restructurings: Lessons learnt and proposals for debt resolution mechanisms (United Nations ed., Special event of the Second Committee of the General Assembly 2012).

658 General Assembly of the United Nations, "*Towards the establishment of a multilateral legal framework for sovereign debt restructuring processes*", 9 September 2014, A/RES/68/304.

659 General Assembly of the United Nations, "*Modalities for the implementation of resolution 68/304, entitled "Towards the establishment of a multilateral legal framework for sovereign debt restructuring processes"*", 28 November 2014, A/C.2/69/L.4/Rev. 1.

configuration of a potential debt restructuring mechanism[660]. The Institute for International Finance published its Principles for Stable Capital Flows and Fair Debt Restructuring due to the restructuring of Greek debt. The IMF updated its 2003 proposal in 2014, positioning itself this time in favour of a market-based approach to debt contracts[661]. Discussions on this subject are important both for democracy and for the legitimacy of a settlement on the question of sovereign debt. Such debates are the basic prerequisites to establish rules for debtors and creditors. Subsequently, the General Assembly of the United Nations intends to join the debate on the development of a tool for the prevention and resolution of debt crisis.

Until now, the *status quo* is based on the contrast between the way internationally integrated sovereign financing is functioning and the way purely national disputes are conducted. Ultimately, the current situation lies in politicians and experts' hands[662]. During the last financial crisis, solutions were improvised, *ad hoc* and decentralised. The IMF moderately contributed and was openly influenced by private operators. This management reveals a decline of financial multilateralism. International financial institutions and regulators would prefer to avoid such decline in the future[663]. According to these institutions and regulators, introducing simple amendments in bond contracts cannot resolve the system deficiencies. Different laws from various jurisdictions govern a large number of debt products. Subsequently, a simple formula that collects creditors' votes would not alleviate the difficulties of negotiation. However, this formula is the highest judicial level reached by current political leaders. Efforts to further improve debt contracts and ways to assist indebted States are continuous. If some recommendations are implemented, a substantial progress may be observed without negotiating an international treaty.

660 IMF, Sovereign Debt Restructuring – Recent Developments and Implications for the Fund's Legal and Policy Framework. 2013.

661 The Fund's Lending Framework and Sovereign Debt – Preliminary Considerations (2014).

662 Christoph G. Paulus, *Sovereign Defaults to be Solved by Politicians or by a Legal Proceeding?*, 1, Law and Economics Yearly Review (2012).

663 Sgard, L'Économie politique (2012).

1.1.2. Promoting financial multilateralism

Even in the absence of a concrete progress towards a multilateral legal framework for restructuring sovereign debt, discussions have significantly improved. The first contribution is the acceptance of a restructuring. This acceptance is only part of a broader process concerning economic and political issues, both national and international. However, as we demonstrated, each stakeholder involved in restructuring is positioned according to his own interests. Some seek to maintain international links in short and long-term. Other can vote against a significant restructuring in order to benefit from budget cuts or bonds exchange. Those stakeholders consider that any restructuring leads to the exclusion of financial markets or to a disproportionate increase in borrowing costs[664]. Such consideration in a deeply interconnected world may discourage a beneficial restructuring by creating a disproportionate fear of limited access to capital markets, of serious trade disruptions or of foreign investment reduction. Emphasizing the high costs and risks of restructuring is hazardous. Neglecting to adequately elaborate on the severity or duration of these costs understates the effect of any restructuring. Such behaviour encourages more intensive austerity measures. Therefore, the discourse of researchers is fundamental to understand the potential implications of each decision[665].

Nowadays, a selective presentation of information distorts the comprehension of sovereign debt. Over the past decade, the discourse on sovereign debt has dramatically changed. The renewed efforts of the United Nations[666] as well as the opposition to the US judicial decisions[667] are pertinent examples. While some courts consider that restructuring has a critical importance for sovereign economic health[668], the transition to the acceptance of this reality has taken time, especially due to partisanship judgments.

---

664 Borensztein & Panizza, The Costs of Sovereign Default 2009; Juan J. Cruces & Christoph Trebesch, *Sovereign Defaults: The Price of Haircuts*, 5, American Economic Journal: Macroeconomics (2013).

665 Lienau, The longer-term consequences of sovereign debt restructuring, 2014.

666 See Chapter 8.

667 See the case *NML v. Argentina* in Chapter 5. See also Joseph E. Stiglitz & Martin Guzman, *A Fair Hearing for Sovereign Debt*, Project Syndicate (2015).

668 *NML Ltd v. Republic of Argentina*, 131 F. Appendix 745, 747 (2nd Cir. 2005).

In the area of sovereign debt restructuring, it is impossible to ignore the political factor[669]. The actions of indebted States generate resistance especially in case of social programme cuts that ultimately have an impact on the ability to repay financial commitments. The financial support that sovereign debtors receive from other governments is also a leading political factor. Such financial support is more oriented by foreign policy objectives than by economic and financial analyses[670]. Since the introduction of the Brady Plan, a debt strategy appeared and has been conducted with the support of international organisations for operations on debt reduction[671]. Thus, different methods of debt crises treatment were established in the international financial community. Governments merely provide support for measures adopted by other international financial officers, or act more directly by leading the search for a solution. The range of possibilities is based on the acceptance of the detrimental consequences of the absence of restructuring.

The debate remains the same in terms of costs' distribution between international financial agents. Some argue that the more a State receives funding from official creditors, the more its ability to repay private creditors increases. Since the 1980s, international operators' strategy has aimed at ensuring debt service and safeguarding the system as a whole, through adjustments and new loans. When this solvency has required debt reduction, adjustment programmes have been implemented under the supervision of the IMF. Financial contributions from commercial banks and multilateral financial institutions are then provided.

All stakeholders co-exist – States, international institutions, NGOs or business operators – and are bound by different norms, standards of soft and hard law. Private operators are more concerned by a less restrictive liberalism, while public stakeholders call for more financial stability. However, the interaction between all of them is directed towards the construction of stability[672].

---

669 Rieffel, Restructuring Sovereign Debt: The Case for Ad Hoc Machinery, 2003, pp. 111 and foll.

670 See Chapter 1.

671 See Chapter 2. Guier, La position du Gouvernement américain en matière d'endettement des États : du plan Baker à l'initiative Brady. 1995.

672 Régis Bismuth, *Le système international de prévention des crises financières – Réflexions autour de la structure en réseau du Forum de stabilité financière*, 1, Journal du droit international (2007).

1.2. Sharing good management practices

The legal no man's land does not prevent sharing good management practices. States seek to impose discipline by establishing rules and internationally shared principles (1.2.1.). Given the absence of a comprehensive mechanism, preventing debt crisis consists of harmonising good management and governance practices for a sustainable financing (1.2.2.).

1.2.1. International audits

To manage indebtedness levels, States shall consider the *ex ante* situation, considering that management begins with debt accounting. Identifying and measuring debt problems implies considering multiple factors, including sovereign off-balance sheet commitments. Indeed, sovereign debt includes the State budget and a range of other commitments. The role assigned to any court of auditors is precisely one that requires considerable knowledge of public debt. This includes knowledge of analytical management tools and a review of debt management policies[673]. Due to the absence of an international court of auditors[674], such knowledge is complicated. This is primarily because the identification of these off-balance sheet commitments is necessary, inasmuch as accounting strategies and final information provided to policymakers[675]. For instance, if a State's budget is not mainly spent for public expenditure, reducing such expenses is artificial.

---

673 Bouvier, Revue française de finances publiques, (2013), pp. 151 and foll.

674 There is one non-governmental international institution, the International Organisation of Supreme Audit Public Finance Institutions (INCOSAI), but its role is rather confined to the exchange of good practices by its motto "*Experientia mutua omnibus prodest*". It has published a *Code de déontologie de l'INTOSAI à l'intention des contrôleurs du secteur public*.

675 For example, the defined benefit pension schemes for civil servants are off-balance sheet because they are considered contingent liabilities. See Tirole, Revue de la Stabilité Financière (2012).

The possibilities are residual[676]. Inevitably, the real goal is the search for efficiency and savings[677].

The difficulty to measure debt is a central aspect of managing sovereign debt. Debt management is complex and accounting devices require technical expertise. In addition to IMF formal audits, the evaluation of sovereign risks may be improved by the creation of independent institutions that would bring together professional experts. Surveys and audits demonstrate a growing ascendancy of law on fiscal policies. Considering a unified and centralised regulation in this field is impossible. If we consider a State, with an internal organisation more or less centralised, the political control over finance is already complex. How could a central political control exist over international finances?

Since 2008, the International Organisation of Supreme Audit Institutions (INTOSAI) established a working group on global financial crisis. It became in 2012 the Working Group on Financial Modernisation and Regulatory Reform. The primary objective of this group is to develop standards, professional rules and good practice guidelines for public sector auditors, as stated below:

> "Reinforcing public debt audits, considering direct commitments as well as other liabilities and financial contingencies, with the objective to identify issues and risks in the management and expected developments of sovereign debt and financial deficits"[678].

The INTOSAI underlines the role of maintaining the viability of financial policies held by the audit institutions of public finances.

---

676 In France for example, the State guarantees loans to the departments that get indebted to pay their investments or to pay subsidies to municipalities and their associations, or regions that borrow to build schools or to provide economic aid. All public entities are supported in different levels via the financing of environmental protection, of economic action, culture, education.

677 Hertzog, A la recherche d'une théorie du système financier public complexe, 2005. Since 1975, France has generated structural deficits, both in budget presentation and execution.

678 INCOSAI, "Beijing Declaration on Promotion of Good Governance by Supreme Audit Institutions", Congress Secretariat, XXI INCOSAI, 2013. INTOSAI, *Numéro spécial sur le XXIe INCOSAI*, 41, Revue internationale de la vérification des comptes publics (2014).

1.2.2. Towards an accounting of the overall debt level

In order to establish an accounting of the overall debt level, international institutions cooperate to promote transparency for a better regulation. In the field of statistics, transparency was progressively introduced in the international banking market thanks to an international cooperation[679]. Promoting formal rules without fiscal coordination is not new. Initially, the purpose was to discipline lenders' behaviour without providing any further assistance. Additional efforts are currently implemented to reduce the overall debt level. The IMF acts as a permanent sovereign auditor[680]. Public finances transparency is promoted in the name of good governance. Since 1998, the IMF has established a code of good practices for public finances[681]. It is based on four pillars: a clear definition of roles and responsibilities (primarily of the legal and institutional framework), the transparency of budgetary procedures, public information, and respect of integrity. The overall system is then evaluated in reports on the observance of standards and codes[682]. This optional procedure may be mandatory as part of the conditions of IMF assistance. Subsequently, IMF conditionality indirectly enforces these measures[683]. In the end, the issue is no longer the creation of a series of commitments for disbursement, but rather the international stability. The IMF[684] and the World Bank[685] promote these princi-

679 Kenneth Rogoff, *International Institutions for Reducing Global Financial Instability*, 13, Journal of Economic Perspectives (1999).

680 The IMF is "*the permanent auditor of countries, which should voluntarily submit themselves to examination in order to lower their borrowing costs. Annual Article IV consultations could be supplemented by quarterly reviews that would enhance the credibility of the data released under the [Special Data Dissemination Standard] and thus help to reduce the costs of adjustment programs*" in Arminio Fraga, *Crisis Prevention and Management: Lessons from Mexico*, *in* From Halifax to Lyons: What Has Been Done About Crisis Management? (Peter Kenen ed. 1996).

681 IMF, "Code of Good Practices on Fiscal Transparency", 2007.

682 The IMF and the World Bank have developed the Reports on the Observance of Standards and Codes (ROSCs) and the Financial Sector Assessment Program (FSAP).

683 The central criterion for determining whether or not the IMF provides assistance is the debt sustainability analysis. See Sean Hagan, *Debt Restructuring and Economic Recovery*, *in* Sovereign Debt Management (Rosa M. Lastra & Lee Buchheit eds., 2014).

684 FMI, Manuel sur la transparence des finances publiques (International Monetary Fund 2007).

685 Banque Mondiale, Manuel du service de la dette, 2009.

ples and guidelines, as well as the OECD[686]. These initiatives provide comprehensive public information. Fiscal transparency is fundamental to improve government priorities. At the end, price stability and financial balance depend on the maintenance of a measured budget[687].

Financial globalisation collides with limited territorial legal framework. The approach taken by States interlaces legal basis, procedural elements and institutional mechanisms. The interdependence of States cannot escape the political will of governments. This interdependence implies cooperation for successful economic growth and financial crisis containment. The implementation of such cooperation may be considered as an international solidarity through the application of international law to enable sustainable development[688]. Thus, UNCTAD experience and work in this area aims at ensuring a proper debt management or renegotiation[689]. These standards are fundamental instruments of solidarity. The objective is to equitably safeguard debtors and creditors interests among international economic cooperation[690]. However, such standards are still confined to soft law or a paralegal level. Close to the rules of law, their informality removes them from the legal system. Standards are nevertheless at the centre of today's international law discourse.

Since the 2014 resolution of the General Assembly of the United Nations, the consensus on the need to include all stakeholders in a construc-

---

686 Transparence budgétaire : les meilleurs pratiques de l'OCDE, (2002). OCDE, *Améliorer la viabilité des finances publiques*, *in* Études économiques de l'OCDE : Grèce 2009 (2010).

687 Tomas Hellebrandt, et al., *La clé d'un assainissement budgétaire réussi : coopération ou confrontation avec la politique monétaire?*, 16, Revue de la Stabilité Financière (2012).

688 International solidarity can be defined as « *la cohésion sociale qui se crée et se développe au sein de la société internationale et qui aboutit à l'établissement d'une communauté sociale rassemblée autour d'intérêts et d'objectifs communs ; fondée sur l'interdépendance des États et d'autres acteurs internationaux, elle vise à maintenir l'ordre et assurer la survie même de la société internationale et à réaliser les objectifs collectifs, qui nécessitent la coopération internationale et l'action commune* ». See the report « Droits de l'homme et solidarité internationale », United Nations High Commissionner for Refugees quoted by Marie Bouriche, Les instruments de solidarité en droit international public (Connaissances et savoirs. 2012).

689 UNCTAD Resolution 165 (S-IX) of 11 March 1978, "Debt and Development Problems of the Developing Countries".

690 Bouriche, Les instruments de solidarité en droit international public, 2012, pp. 11-62.

tive debate on sovereign debt management is strengthened. The legitimacy and economic efficiency of the proposed measures depend on a collective and intelligible debate. In 2013, UNCTAD initiated consultations with legal and economic experts on a project of a model mechanism. This mechanism is structured and organised around a unifying set of general principles and internationally accepted procedures. The formulation process developed from such a general approach provides it with greater legitimacy. The objective is to achieve a coordination at an international level through procedures to deal with sovereign debt crises, sovereign default and disputes arising therefrom[691].

2. *Defining rules to ensure stability*

The issue of a proper legal framework on sovereign debt management has recently been a focus of international discussion. The multidimensional nature of financial stability encompasses various aspects of the economic functioning, all of which are sensitive to market failures or externalities, and motivate State intervention[692]. Regardless of the defined goals, whether economic, social, structural or developmental, suggesting rules would be beneficial for international cooperation. The common objective of all discussions is to develop a more efficient and equitable international system in economic and social terms. This objective implies a consensus on the reforms regarding financial innovations (2.1.). In terms of sovereign debt, this process only reached the stage of debating it (2.2.).

2.1. Financial innovation for collective interest

The dramatic increase of sovereign debt in advanced economies calls for regulation. Among the many initiatives is the reform of the over-the-counter (OTC) derivatives markets. Supported by the G20, this reform was designed to secure the financial system by limiting risk and enhancing transparency. However, such dispersed reforms remain insufficient. Coordination is essential since many regulatory changes are engaged simulta-

---

691 External debt sustainability and development (2014).

692 Objectifs et dispositifs de stabilité financière : dernières évolutions, (2014), pp. 51-64.

neously on different market practices (2.1.1.). Agreeing on new standards is not sufficient. It is also imperative that States introduce such agreements in their national regulations in order for these agreements to be effective and efficient[693] (2.1.2.).

2.1.1. Modifying global finance

The evolution of international bank regulation is characterised by responses to crises[694]. Previously, banking regulation was treated as a domestic case. Banking market changed due to mergers and acquisition, resulting in a system of global banks. An international economic integration has been developed without addressing its risk and impact[695]. National regulatory authorities have become increasingly interdependent. Their tools and mandate to protect financial stability are still limited to their national territory. This limitation has to be reconsidered. The development of a banking system through international cooperation, based on the rules of communication of national authorities, has greatly benefited from crisis, especially in the European Union[696].

The transition to a new banking and financial model implies disintermediated crisis management methods that pave the way for innovative approaches. One of these methods considers that financial innovation should serve collective interest. Researchers have studied this possibility at a European level. This idea involves developing instruments based on the mutualisation of sovereign risk. Solidarity would emerge from coordination and discipline imposed to national policies. The Eurozone crisis, characterised by high sovereign debt levels and high borrowing costs for certain Member States, had an unprecedented impact. It impacted not only peripheral States, but also States without sovereign debt problems. These States were economically, politically and financially affected. The causes

693 Banque de France, Les produits dérivés de gré-à-gré : nouvelles règles, nouveaux acteurs, nouveaux risques, § 17, (Banque de France. 2013).

694 Duncan Wood, Governing global banking. The Basel Committee and the Politics of Financial Globalization (Ashgate. 2005).

695 Ethan B. Kapstein, *Resolving the Regulator's Dilemma: International Coordination of Banking Regulations*, 43, International Organization (1989).

696 Zdenek Kudrna, *Cross-Border Bank Resolution of Failed Banks in the European Union After the Crisis: Business as Usual*, Vol. 50, Journal of Common Market Studies (2012). See Chapter 7.

and consequences of the European sovereign debt crisis are shared. To avoid the considerable political obstacles that hinder the emergence of solidarity between politically divided States, new instruments must be proposed.

2.1.2. Towards a regulation of European debt bonds

In order to implement a regulation of European debt bonds, various proposals have been analysed: Blue Bonds[697], Redemption Bonds[698], Eurobills[699], European Safe Bonds[700]. The European Commission itself has proposed the introduction of Stability Bonds jointly issued by Member States and accompanied by a budgetary supervision[701]. Each proposal is based on a particular solidarity. Some instruments mutualise interest rate levels between Member States by creating an *ex ante* solidarity. Others provide support to States in difficulty in the event of losses and offer an *ex post* solution. The introduction of such instrument would change the status of sovereign bonds and affect investors' assets reserve.

These reforms remain subjected to the will of Member States to accept the sharing of budgetary resources, a concept which until now has been systematically denied. Since the crisis, the sovereignty of States is affected in the name of economic control policies. It is particularly the case for budgetary policy. This budgetary policy is an instrument of sovereignty to change a situation. For example, public spending may support consumption, investment, and may indeed promote economic recovery. However,

697 The Blue Bond Proposal (2010).

698 Annual report (2011).

699 Eurobills, not Eurobonds (2011). The safe part of the debt would be issued in the form of a mutual debt with a maturity of less than one year. These Eurobills would benefit from a joint and several guarantees such as the blue obligations.

700 European Safe Bonds: ESBies (2011).

701 Livre vert sur la faisabilité de l'introduction d'obligations de stabilité (2011). Different forms are examined, from the absence of joint liability (each Member State is responsible for its debts obligations) to a joint and several liability (each Member State is responsible not only for its own debts, but for the debts of other States in case of default), through an intermediate device combining an absence of joint responsibility and a degree of superiority and enhancement through guarantees (senior bonds stability, partial guarantee by means of gold reserves or other assets, assignment of specific revenue). See Merler & Pisani-Ferry, Revue de la Stabilité Financière (2012).

these financial products potentially provide a solution to the problem of transmitting credit risk from sovereign debtors to banks. Large banks supervision may even be extended at a European level to mutualise losses. Nevertheless, any coordination is restrictive since it assumes to build a complex and expensive political discipline.

2.2. A unique way to multilateral dispute settlement

A single mode of dispute resolution would mutualise benefits (2.2.1.) to solve international crises, as demonstrated by the situation in the European Union (2.2.2.).

2.2.1. A mutualisation of benefits

Most sovereign debt experts have a fixed position about the need of an international financial architecture reform. The establishment of a structured mechanism is still hardly debated. Proponents of such reform suggest that the lack of an organised mechanism constitutes a void of international financial architecture. Such void leads to a slow debt restructuring and arbitrary results. These disputes result in distrust of debtors and creditors. They consider that the *ad hoc* treatment is overall negative: palliative implementations take too much time and give rise to future defaults.

Reformers believe that the current situation based on the market is disorganised, inefficient and expensive. The central question turns around the issue of creditors' collective actions, in particular those of holdout creditors and vulture funds. The inadequacy of the current situation severely damages debtors' reputation and prompts unnecessary delays to restructuring negotiations. A statutory system may reduce these problems, increase transparency, reduce moral hazard, minimise the need for a formal sector bailout, and combat the externalities of a default at an international level. It might also explicitly integrate third-party States that would provide financial contributions and protect their financial systems[702].

702 Resolution of Cross-Border Banks: A Proposed Framework for Enhanced Coordination (2010); UNCTAD, Sovereign debt crises and restructurings: Lessons learnt and proposals for debt resolution mechanisms, 2012.

Opponents argue that the current system has all necessary contractual instruments to manage sovereign defaults and that the creation of new institutions or mechanisms is useless at best and dangerous at worst. A universal settlement system is a chimera as the IMF advocates using the example of banking coordination[703]. States' insolvency would not be able to follow a unique litigation model on bankruptcy proceeding, since the ideal one is to encourage negotiation[704].

Sceptics consider that it is difficult to establish a better system through a statutory mechanism[705]. A formalised legal framework on sovereign debt would over-institutionalise the situation, while the current system would just need to be developed *per se*. The argument supporting contractual approach recognises that changing bond contracts documentation may be enough to regulate more effectively the restructuring process. This has led to the integration of CACs. Recent proposals suggest the inclusion of dispute resolution clauses referring to arbitration[706].

Both creditors and debtors are opposed to the establishment of a global mechanism. Two propositions to create a sovereign debt restructuring mechanism were promoted by States. The first one dates back to 1933 at the Pan American Conference of Montevideo. The second was advised at the UNCITRAL in the 1970s. In both cases, sovereign debtors were divided on the issue of establishing a mechanism, fearing an increase of their borrowing costs, while creditor States were opposed to all initiatives. Two other attempts failed due to the resistance of creditor States, specifically the US government. Harry Dexter White suggested a mechanism in what eventually became the Bretton Woods agreement of 1944. In 2001, the IMF proposed a sovereign debt restructuring mechanism. The international financial community rejected this SDRM because they refused to promote a right to default[707].

The ideal starting point for a discussion on the desirability of a sovereign debt restructuring mechanism is an analysis of the problems that

---

703 Hagan & Viñals, Resolution of Cross-Border Banks: A Proposed Framework for Enhanced Coordination, 2010.

704 Mathias Audit, Insolvabilité des États et dettes souveraines, L.G.D.J, 2011, p. 21.

705 Bolton & David A. Skeel, Emory Law Journal (2004); Sgard, L'Économie politique (2012).

706 IMF, The Fund's Lending Framework and Sovereign Debt – Preliminary Considerations, 2014.

707 IMF, Sovereign Debt Restructuring – Recent Developments and Implications for the Fund's Legal and Policy Framework, 2013.

such a mechanism aims to solve. One can mention a few. Long renegotiations often fail to restore debt sustainability. Additionally, there is a need for coordination between the creditors seeking their interests and holdout bondholders that refuse restructuring offers. Two other problems are the lack of access to private financing during the restructuring process and the excessive indebtedness caused by debt dilution. In particular, no rules effectively manage the collective action problems. As we will now notice, statutory proposals[708] and theoretical discussions[709] are numerous.

First, a current proposal for a legal framework includes reference to Chapter 11 of the US Bankruptcy Code. Chapter 11 applies to companies and is often presented as a model for debt restructuring proceedings[710]. This US proceeding idea was imitated and completed with provisions of the Chapter 9 that applies to municipalities.

Second, another proposal refers to an international tribunal or a debt restructuring court. Such independent entity would implement an internationally agreed debt restructuring mechanism[711]. Debt can be categorised as public, state guaranteed or private debt acquired by States. Such codification provides more transparency as to the real obligations of a State. Thus, it would be possible to determine which debts may be considered odious and would thus require potential involvement of public or private creditors.

Such debt restructuring court would have the authority to require creditors to provide new loans. These loans would be prioritised in case of default. National courts would be obliged to recognise the legitimacy of this international court. Therefore, creditors and debtors would be urged to respect rules. The court would be part of an arbitration and debt mediation mechanism, created under the auspices of the United Nations and with the

---

708 Barry C. Barnett, et al., *On Third World Debt*, 83 Harvard International Law Journal (1984); Steven L. Schwarcz, *Looking Forward: 2005-2010 – A Sovereign Debt Restructuring Reverie*, 6 Chicago Journal of International Law (2005).

709 Bolton & Jeanne, Structuring and Restructuring Sovereign Debt: The Role of a Bankruptcy Regime, 2007.

710 Christopher G. Oechsli, *Procedural Guidelines for Renegotiating LDC Debt: An Analogy to Chapter 11 of the U.S. Bankruptcy Reform Act*, 21, Virginia Journal of International Law (1981).

711 Recommendations of the Commission of Experts of the President of the United Nations General Assembly on Reforms of the International Monetary and Financial System (2009).

support of the Bretton Woods institutions. However, it would remain independent from these institutions.

Another conception would be the inclusion of a legal framework in contractual instruments. This inclusion would create a gradual institutionalisation of an *ad hoc* arbitral context. Once established, these procedures may create a ripple effect for the legal treatment of other sovereign bonds that do not necessarily contain such a clause. A sovereign debt court should be implemented to manage the current cases of imminent sovereign default in an effective and equitable way[712]. This proposal brings together a contractual clause, a debt court and resolution procedures[713]. The court would be composed of a panel of arbitrators according to clauses inserted in sovereign debt contracts.

According to this proposal, the procedure is divided into several stages. First, State creditors accept the resolution plan. Then, the sovereign debt court confirms that the procedure has been respected. Finally, the sovereign debtor would be required to follow the measures of the plan. This may entail reducing wages or privatising companies. However, at a national level, problems can arise, as the Greek legal experience illustrated it[714]. This proposal has been studied in the academic[715] and institutional[716] worlds. A similar and uninstitutionalised draft of arbitral proceedings con-

712 Christoph G. Paulus, *A Resolvency Proceeding for Defaulting Sovereigns*, International Insolvency Law Review (2012); Christoph G. Paulus, *A Standing Arbitral Tribunal as a Procedural Solution for Sovereign Debt Restructurings*, *in* Sovereign Debt and the Financial Crisis: Will This Time Be Different? (Gallina A. Vincelette & Carlos A. Primo Braga eds., 2010); Reforming the Process of Sovereign Debt Restructuring: A proposal for a Sovereign Debt Tribunal. (2008). See also Marcus H. Miller & Dania Thomas, *Sovereign Debt Restructuring: The Judge, the Vultures, and Creditor Rights*, *in* Sovereign Debt: From Safety to Default (Robert W. Kolb ed. 2011); A. Mechele Dickerson, *Insolvency Principles: The Missing Link in the Odious Debt Debate*, see id. Anna Gelpern, *A Skeptic's Case for Sovereign Bankruptcy*, *in* A Debt Restructuring Mechanism for Sovereigns: Do we need a legal procedure? (Christoph G. Paulus ed. 2014).

713 Christoph G. Paulus, *Should Politics be Replaced by a Legal Proceeding?*, id.

714 Aristides P. Chiotellis, *Sovereign Debt Restructuring and the Internal Legal Framwork: the Greek Experience*, *in* A Debt Restructuring Mechanism for Sovereigns. Do we need a legal procedure? (Christoph G. Paulus ed. 2014).

715 Mathias Audit, *A Debt Restructuring Mechanism for European Sovereigns: An Emerging Idea*, *in* A Debt Restructuring Mechanism for Sovereigns: Do we need a legal procedure? (Christoph G. Paulus ed. 2014).

716 Das, et al., Sovereign Debt Restructurings 1950-2010: Literature Survey, Data, and Stylized Facts, 2012.

sists of an *ad hoc* arbitration mechanism on a case-by-case basis. Creditors and debtors would propose two arbitrators for each party. A fifth arbitrator would be then chosen to head the panel[717].

Another approach empowers an international financial institution to act as an impartial advisor to foster negotiations between creditors and debtors. Necessary additional funding would be more easily released. Nevertheless, the IMF is not considered neutral due to its governance. The IMF could therefore not hold this function. However, the IMF is expert in the field of sovereign debt. Similarly to the Dispute Settlement Body of the WTO, the IMF could offer panels of independent experts. The panel would be responsible for mediation between debtors and creditors, assisting in finding an acceptable solution, while following the international guidelines that have been signed by the parties.

A mixture of the two solutions also exists. For example, the IMF or the expert panel may first act to facilitate negotiations. In case of blocking, the international debt court would then take over[718].

Other proposals also exist, that are neither statutory nor institutional, such as the sovereign debt forum[719]. Composed of a neutral expert body established by an informal consensus, the forum would bring together creditors, debtors and international institutions. Discrete consultations would be provided in advance to both sovereign debtors and their creditors. Such consultations would accelerate the process of restoring economic stability. Consultations would aim at reaching a consensus on macroeconomic adjustments and debt treatment, while also protecting legal precedent. This idea is similar to the system proposed by the Paris and London Clubs.

The introduction of a method of settlement should prevail multilateralism over bilateralism. Legal options and proposals are numerous, such as the establishment of fora, the creation of a dispute settlement mechanism resulting from multilateral conventional instruments. However, the inability to achieve a consensus reflects the essence of the rule of law[720], which

---

717 Kunibert Raffer, *Considerations for Designing Sovereign Insolvency Procedures*, 1, Law, Social Justice & Global Development Journal (2005).

718 Secretary-General, External debt sustainability and development, 2014.

719 Gitlin & House, A blueprint for a Sovereign Debt Forum, 2014.

720 According to Guy Carcassonne : « *une bonne règle est celle qui diminue le niveau de volonté et de courage exigé des acteurs. [Les règles] ont été choisies*

is designing a single mode of dispute settlement in international economic law.

We consider that it is possible to implement a mechanism through a progressive integration of clauses. Such clauses, included in bonds, would refer to the applicable law and jurisdiction. The European framework could constitute a first step to test the effectivity of such clauses.

2.2.2. Towards a European crisis resolution framework

At European level, the idea of a structured mechanism has already materialised. Since the Greek crisis, the need to ensure an organised restructuring has become essential and such conditions are currently under consideration. Debt relief, implementation of obligations and exchange of securities created legal precedent. An upcoming restructuring in Europe would be complex, thus a systematic approach is envisaged. The proposal for a European crisis resolution mechanism would use the existing EU institutions[721].

The mechanism would be established by an international treaty or a directive and would be divided into three areas. The financial dimension would be insured by an interim financing of the ESM. The economic outline would measure debt sustainability and analyse the economic adjustments. The ECB or the European Commission would complete this task. Finally, the legal discussions would be submitted before the Court of Justice of the European Union. Inspired by the sovereign debt restructuring mechanism proposed by the IMF, a sovereign debtor could initiate the mechanism. The sovereign debtor would choose the place of dispute resolution. Following this procedure would enable the mechanism to gather a majority of bondholders and eliminate holdout creditors.

Another proposal considers an amendment of the Treaty establishing the ESM to address the issue of recalcitrant creditors by minimising litiga-

---

par des gouvernements, au terme de négociations, au terme de discussions. Elles ont été fixées d'une manière qui étaı̆t peut être exagérément influencée par les marchés, par les agences de notation [...] mais ces règles ont été établies théoriquement par une volonté politique. ». See Sorel & Chemain, Quelle souveraineté budgétaire pour les États ? 2013, pp.65-77.

721 François Gianviti, et al., *A European Mechanism for Sovereign Debt Crisis Resolution: A Proposal*, Bruegel Blueprint Series (2010).

tion risks[722]. The treaty would be modified to immunise the assets of sovereign debtors from seizure by creditors. Such immunity would reduce the propensity for court proceedings and encourage negotiation and restructuring[723].

Any change in this direction would enhance the economy of the European Union and represent a step forward in the financial structure to prevent and minimise the effects of crises. We remain convinced that a sovereign debt restructuring mechanism would contribute to the improvement of a crisis resolution framework. It would strengthen the contractual elements by providing incentives to the integration of collective action clauses in sovereign bonds. As a statutory component, it could also incorporate features to improve crises resolution that can only be used under a contractual approach.

Inside the monetary union, different possibilities are considered to implement a framework for European crisis resolution. The success is moderated as evidenced by the proposed adoption of an amended budget disciplinary [724]. Such amendment should have limited legal effect[725] and would defend the adoption of a restrictive rule and automatic sanctions, while simultaneously involving the European Court of Justice. This represents a step towards the development of a legal framework on sovereign debt

---

722 Lee C. Buchheit & G. Mitu Gulati, *The Problem of Holdout Creditors in Eurozone Sovereign Debt Restructurings*, 28, Butterworths Journal of International Banking and Financial Law (2013).

723 A similar approach was adopted by the UN Security Council in 2003 to support Iraq's efforts to restructure its debt. This resolution provides that: "*petroleum, petroleum products, and natural gas originating in Iraq shall be immune, until title passes to the initial purchaser from legal proceedings against them and not be subject to any form of attachment, garnishment, or execution, and that all States shall take any steps that may be necessary under their respective domestic legal systems to assure this protection, and that proceeds and obligations arising from sales thereof, as well as the Development Fund for Iraq, shall enjoy privileges and immunities equivalent to those enjoyed by the United Nations*". Resolution 1483 (2003) adopted by the Security Council at its 4761st meeting on 22 May 2003.

724 Arnaud Sée, *Une nouvelle "discipline" budgétaire? Les sanctions des politiques budgétaires "indisciplinées" dans l'Union européenne*, *in* Quelle souveraineté budgétaire pour les États ? (Jean-Marc Sorel & Régis Chemain eds., 2013).

725 Sorel & Chemain, Quelle souveraineté budgétaire pour les États?, 2013, pp. 177-180.

management. Many criticisms to such amended budget disciplinary[726] refer to the essence of debt.

*

As previously stated, there are neither preventive measures nor control procedures to regulate or limit States' indebtedness. No rule of international law limits this sovereign action. Instead, there are rules on the balance of public finances. Budget disciplinary rules in the framework of European treaties are soft law instruments. There is no international institution able to intervene in situations of crisis, such as a global central bank acting unilaterally as lender of last resort. In addition, there is a lack of *ex post* regulation that would centralise and administrate States' financial difficulties, such as a supra bankruptcy procedure. As such, proposals are numerous.

As the crisis continues, the ambition of reforms is reinforced. The dilemma is reformulated. The main issue is no longer how debt affects sovereignty. States should choose how they would concede a part of their sovereignty. Will this concession be to financial markets or to a system based on international public law?

Legal tools have been widely explored, presented and discussed in recent years. It now lacks a political momentum. The absence of such political determination blocks the establishment of a legal framework to the extent that law results in a consensus dictated by economic or political discourses[727].

CHAPTER 8. Elaboration of an International Economic Law of Sovereign Indebtedness

Debt management is part of the particular international economic law. Non-binding commitments are part of this area in which soft law is fundamental. Both international law and international debt law are products of

726 Tirole, Revue de la Stabilité Financière (2012).

727 Jean-Marc Sorel, Le droit international économique à l'aube du XXIème siècle. En hommage aux Professeurs Dominique Carreau et Patrick Juillard (Pedone. 2009), pp.141-152. Jean-Marc Sorel, *Conclusions. Une fable moderne : l'État, l'Union européenne, les marchés financiers et l'aléa moral*, *in* Quelle souveraineté budgétaire pour les États? (Jean-Marc Sorel & Régis Chemain, 2013).

the reunion between political and economic powers. When there is no formal legal requirement, a State can escape its commitments and be opportunistic in its claims.

International economic law cannot be an autonomous branch of international law because it is intrinsically a legal instrument of economic policy. Whether for development or for investment, debt management is part of the long term and remains legally undecided. If there is an absence of rules of international law, several options are possible to develop a legal framework.

The first option refers to a voluntary contractual regime based on collective action clauses. The second one is based on a limited statutory model with an international treaty or an amendment of the IMF Articles of Agreement. The third option is the establishment of a comprehensive statutory scheme, as has occurred with the sovereign debt resolution mechanism proposed by the IMF. A fourth option is a less protective tool that supports creditors' positions and attenuates protections for defaulting States.

Beyond the lack of consensus on a preferred option, the goal is to develop a law to complete sovereign obligations and resolve default cases. Under these proposals, the prerequisite is to define the rights and obligations of the parties and identify institutional and contractual measures that will legally handle the negotiations. The debates on legal gaps, on the lack of definition, on the rights and obligations of each stakeholder, lead to the characterisation of requirements and basic principles applicable to debt. These characteristics may result in the outline of an international law of sovereign debt[728] composed of general principles (1.). Such general principles form the basis of *lex imperfecta* of sovereign debt management (2.).

1. General principles for comprehensive operations

We are now considering an international economic law of sovereign debt. This legal concept implies a global functioning. Soft law governs this functioning. This is the nature of international financing regulation (1.1.).

728 Milan J. N. Meetarbhan, *Vers un droit international de la dette exterieure?*, *in* La dette extérieure / The external debt (Martinus Nijhoff Publishers ed. 1995).

Informal sources such as soft law establish a set of practical rules for sovereign debt management (1.2.).

1.1. Soft law and international financing law

The sources of international sovereign debt law are informal (1.1.1.). Soft law is essentially understood as quasi-legal instruments without legal binding force. Soft law is valuable in international relations due to its dimension of compromise. In particular, international law is based on the power of persuasion of soft law (1.1.2.).

1.1.1. Codes of good conduct, reports and information sharing

Soft law is not a formal and binding source of international law but rather an intermediate legal instrument that assists the development and application of general international law in various ways[729]. The soft law character of an instrument does not necessarily establish *ex ante* its normative effects *ex post*. We determined in this dissertation the predominance of soft law instruments in financial law regarding sovereign debt. This predominance is atypical compared to the role of treaties in the field of international trade law[730].

Modern international financial law also lacks a stand-alone institution and is fragmented. There is no equivalent to the WTO in finance. These differences emphasise the lack of public character of the rule of law, both for the procedure and its legitimacy. However, this does not diminish the important role of soft law as a mechanism of coordination in international financial law. Many reasons justify its application and even its necessity. Soft law is notably faster and more flexible. Soft law is often more effective to be used by operators on the ever-changing financial markets.

We assume that general principles are necessary. On one hand, there is no international treaty regulating sovereign financing. On the other, the

---

729 Jean d'Aspremont, Formalism and the Sources of International Law. A Theory of the Ascertainment of Legal Rules (Oxford Monographs in International Law ed., Oxford University Press. 2011).

730 Chris Brummer, *Why Soft Law Dominates International Finance — and not Trade*, 13 Journal of International Economic Law (2010).

sources of law in this field are not part of international custom. Therefore, other rules or principles, formal or informal, should now be used to manage sovereign debt.

Soft law is composed of best practices, regulatory reporting, information sharing and cooperation strengthening. Promoting best practices consists of supporting the ones generally accepted, particularly in the areas of transparency, information sharing, and due diligence. International fora[731], professional associations such as the IASB and market regulators such as the Basel Committee create such practices. Regulatory and supervisory practices are gathered in codes of good conduct for operators. In parallel, databases are developed to allow regulators to understand the phenomenon of indebtedness. Reports record facts, as well as institutional opinions, financial perspectives and their implications for the global economy. Economists used these data to better analyse debt and project prudential rules.

These reports are fundamental for politics and often generate comparisons. Thresholds are based on such comparisons. These reports can also be used to encourage operators to stop adopting unwanted practices, or to identify alternative policies that regulators may follow. Therefore, these instruments are carefully discussed and negotiated. In addition, many international funding agreements are at first Memoranda of Understanding. Through these memoranda, banking authorities and financial markets share risk information and practices at regional and international levels.

1.1.2. Towards a standardised debt management

Principles are often based on an observation of domestic law. Legitimacy, impartiality, due diligence, good faith, transparency, respect of *pacta sunt servanda*, sustainability, have the status of shared principles that have emerged as general principles[732]. This reasoning under domestic law has continuously been applied to grant rules for sovereign debt restructur-

731 IMF, "A Guide to Committees, Groups, and Clubs", Factsheet, 17 April 2015.
732 Responsible Sovereign Lending and Borrowing: The View from Domestic Jurisdictions (2012).

ing[733]. The trend to systematise these domestic law principles peaked with the IMF proposal in 2003, based on Chapters 9 and 11 of the US Bankruptcy Code. Even alternative proposals, such as the Fair and Transparent Arbitration Procedure proposed by Jubilee 2000[734] is based on judicial rules and domestic procedural law[735]. To become general principles, such principles also need to exist at an international level in the relations between States. For instance, these principles are mentioned in resolutions of the General Assembly of the United Nations[736], in publications of the IMF[737] and other international institutions representing a substantial majority in the international community. The whole system is precisely based on proposals set forth by these international entities.

Most of sovereign debt regulation proposals are in line with the implementation of international standards, while failing to assemble the needed political support for their implementation. This failure does not mean that there is no need for regulation, contrary to what *status quo* proponents argue. Whether it is a politically unrealistic normative approach or not, the problem is that these proposals have been developed by inadequate procedures. The necessity for general principles to promote responsible sovereign financing exists. The lack of transparency, the imperfect information and the poor sovereign debt management are all reasons explaining indebtedness. Considering that, the impact on human life is incalculable[738].

It is impossible to know how to avoid a crisis or how a crisis may evolve in the absence of international financial standards. Some rules appear to worsen the crisis or exacerbate its systemic effect[739]. The global

---

733 Holger Schier, Towards A Reorganisation System For Sovereign Debt : An International Law Perspective (Martinus Nijhoff Publishers. 2007); UNCITRAL, Legislative Guide on Insolvency Law, United Nations, 2005.

734 Fair and Transparent Arbitration Process.

735 Jürgen Kaiser, *Taking Stock of Proposals for More Ordered Workouts*, *in* Overcoming Developing Country Debt Crises (Barry Herman, et al. eds., 2010).

736 See Chapter 7.

737 See Article 5 § 3.b on the situation of the sovereign borrower before disbursement. Article 6 § 1.a and § 1.b.ii is related to the restrictions for the use of borrowed funds.

738 Raffer, Debt Management for Development. Protection of the Poor and the Millennium Development Goals. 2010, pp. 132-148.

739 Giovanoli, N.Y.U. International Law and Politics (2009).

regulation of financial services cannot prevent a crisis[740], but the implementation of regulatory policies can moderate its effects. After establishing a consensus at a European and international level, sovereign debt can be regulated. Obviously the development of such tools remains insufficient to cover everything. The goal is not a change of law, but a change of the conduct of stakeholders.

1.2. Soft law regulation of sovereign financing

Adopting principles to be integrated into a code of good conduct for the purpose of guiding negotiations between creditors and sovereign debtors has been discussed in several fora. Soft law discussions are held in different fora. The Bretton Woods institutions considered soft law solutions (1.2.1.), as well as market professionals (1.2.2.) and the UNCTAD (1.2.3.). In these initiatives, there is an acknowledgement of the asymmetry between a hard law of international trade regulation and a soft law on sovereign funding[741].

1.2.1. Soft law and international financial institutions

One of the essential problems of the functioning of the international financial system is the difficulty of cooperation. The establishment of rules of conduct to be followed by market participants, both before and during a debt crisis, would be beneficial. In the early 2000s, proposals were numerous when the IMF recommended the SDRM. Informal guidelines could be developed to reduce the uncertainty of creditors' collective actions before and during debt restructuring. Such guidelines could be gathered in a code of good conduct that debtors and creditors would endorse. The first proposition in that sense is attributed to Jean-Claude Trichet in 2001, when he was President of the Bank of France[742]. The idea of a voluntary code of

740 Larosière, The High-Level Group Report on Financial Supervision in the EU. 2009.

741 Chris Brummer, Soft Law and the Global Financial System: Rule Making in the 21st Century (Cambridge University Press. 2012).

742 Vers un Code de bonne conduite volontaire pour restructurer la dette souveraine (2003).

good conduct completes the whole procedure. Such code would complement the contractual solution and standardise the use of CACs in sovereign bonds.

The development of a code of good conduct resulting from a flexible formula is a more precise framework to resolve several issues regarding sovereign debt management, especially if it is sufficiently observed. Such code would define responsibility of creditors in sovereign financing. It would provide guidelines for rescheduling periods and specify the standards applicable to the treatment of principal and interest. Such code would even endorse the minimal conditions under which a proportion of export revenues or project income could be attributed to a creditor to repay a debt. Such code could also remind the principles linking reimbursement to ability to pay. We can consider a code of good conduct that would include the scope of negative covenants, the principles concerning exchange rates and interest rates policy based on a more equitable allocation of risks. Criteria to defend human rights and development could also be included[743].

The IMF developed a criterion of good conduct in the modified version of the conditionality for loans in arrears. Far from being the only source of production of such tools[744], the IMF remains the only institution that verifies their application. States receiving funding from the IMF in a debt crisis must act in good faith to reach a stand-by agreement with their creditors[745]. Specifically, States should act in good faith during the negotiations with their creditors. Such approach should continue until the restructuring is completed. States are required to provide early feedback to creditors on the design of the restructuring and on the proposed measures. In addition, States should share pertinent non-confidential information with all creditors[746].

Concerning this general surveillance, the main functions of the IMF are monitoring States (Article IV, Section 3 of the Articles of Agreement)[747],

743 Meetarbhan, Vers un droit international de la dette exterieure? 1995.

744 The Financial Stability Board, the Basel Committee and the International Organisation of Securities Commissions also produce standards.

745 They must demonstrate a "*good faith effort to reach a collaborative agreement with its creditors*".

746 Das, et al., Sovereign Debt Restructurings 1950-2010: Literature Survey, Data, and Stylized Facts, 2012.

747 Article IV, Section 3. Surveillance over exchange arrangements.

providing financial assistance (Article V, Section 3 of the Articles of Agreement)[748] and technical assistance (Article V, Section 2 (b) of the Articles of Agreement)[749]. The Fund uses these three missions as instruments to meet the objectives defined in Article I of the Articles of Agreement[750]. For the surveillance of fiscal policies, States should send necessary information to enable the Fund to exercise its general mission control (Article VIII, Section 5)[751]. Other financial system surveillance measures, in partnership with the World Bank, have been implemented since the crises of the 1990s: the Financial Sector Assessment Program (FSAP) and the Reports on the Observance of Standards and Codes (ROSCs). In 2001, guidelines for public debt management were published in cooperation with debt managers worldwide. These guidelines provide a set of voluntary principles to improve debt management practices and reduce financial vulnerability. Such guidelines cover both domestic and external public debt and focus on the principles applicable to a wide range of States with different institutional structures.

---

748 Article V, Section 3. Conditions governing use of the Fund's general resources.

749 Article V, Section 2. Limitation on the Fund's operations and transactions.

750 Article I. Purposes: "*The purposes of the International Monetary Fund are:*

(i) To promote international monetary cooperation through a permanent institution which provides the machinery for consultation and collaboration on international monetary problems.

(ii) To facilitate the expansion and balanced growth of international trade, and to contribute thereby to the promotion and maintenance of high levels of employment and real income and to the development of the productive resources of all members as primary objectives of economic policy.

(iii) To promote exchange stability, to maintain orderly exchange arrangements among members, and to avoid competitive exchange depreciation.

(iv) To assist in the establishment of a multilateral system of payments in respect of current transactions between members and in the elimination of foreign exchange restrictions which hamper the growth of world trade.

(v) To give confidence to members by making the general resources of the Fund temporarily available to them under adequate safeguards, thus providing them with opportunity to correct maladjustments in their balance of payments without resorting to measures destructive of national or international prosperity.

(vi) In accordance with the above, to shorten the duration and lessen the degree of disequilibrium in the international balances of payments of members.

The Fund shall be guided in all its policies and decisions by the purposes set forth in this Article".

751 Article VIII, Section 5. Furnishing of information.

In 2013, the IMF and the World Bank reviewed these guidelines in light of regulatory changes in the financial sector. After the financial crisis, such changes took into consideration the evolution of macroeconomic policies. Through a collaborative process with the Member States of the World Bank, the proposed revisions reflect the experiences accumulated over the last decade by States and debt management councils. On the one hand, these revisions include additional guidance to achieve a balance between flexibility, transparency and accountability. On the other, risk assessment, CACs use and the development and maintenance of sovereign securities market are also prevalent. These reviews should ensure that sufficient support is provided to debt managers. The purpose is to improve debt management practices and reduce vulnerability to financial shocks.

1.2.2. Soft law and market professionals

Political resistance towards the SDRM has created self-regulatory dynamics. The promotion of a code of good conduct for fair debt restructuring has been discussed since the failure of the SDRM. Commercial banks gathered all proposals through professional associations. Amongst these professional associations are the international association of legal practitioners from bankruptcy (INSOL International)[752] and the International Capital Market Association (ICMA)[753]. These professional associations comprise leading banks, investors and issuers of sovereign debt. All of them focused on new *ex post* management rules. Subsequently, the Institute of International Finance (IIF) focused on the elements of a code of good conduct.

In 2004, a final text was proposed: the Principles for Stable Capital Flows and Fair Debt Restructuring[754]. The G20 and the IMF examined this proposal. Since then, a group of senior financial managers of major banks and global financial institutions have been advocating for its adoption. These market-based principles are voluntary and constitute a flexible framework. They are intended to be applied to all sovereign debtors in or-

752 Giovanoli, N.Y.U. International Law and Politics (2009).

753 ICMA was particularly interested in models of CACs to be included in sovereign debt bond contracts.

754 IIF, "*Principles for Stable Capital Flows and Fair Debt Restructuring in Emerging Markets*", 2004.

der to promote cooperation between debtors and creditors[755]. In October 2012, the Institute completed these principles with the lessons learnt from the Greek restructuring experience[756].

The Principles for Stable Capital Flows and Fair Debt Restructuring constitute a response of market professionals to this regulatory need. Larger issuers and creditors are concerned by the prospect of a bankruptcy system of sovereign debtors. Therefore, they accept to follow a code of good conduct, especially if such an adoption undermines any sovereign bankruptcy court proposal[757].

These IIF principles are based on six pillars: transparency, information, dialogue, cooperation, good faith and fair treatment. A restructuring process is defined as equitable if sovereign debtors respect these six pillars. Sovereign debtors should cooperate closely with their creditors and agree to exchange information. They should avoid unwarranted capital controls and resume partial or full payments as soon as possible. Gathered in a code of good practice, these principles have the advantage of fostering a better organisation or reducing costs, while also ensuring flexibility. The stated objectives are prevention and reduction of sovereign debt crises by establishing voluntary practices. The need for better data transparency is recurring. Indeed, differences between States are based on data transparency and investor relations[758]. The ultimate purpose is that such a code, compatible with other mechanisms but not substitutable, becomes a market standard.

This self-regulatory stakeholder's approach may be beneficial. On the one hand, States want a return to the financial market. On the other, uncertainty is reduced for creditors. However, the underlying debate on self-regulation refers to the lack of accountability among stakeholders[759]. This code of good conduct is an example of soft law and new governance. Such

---

755 Initially, the IIF principles were applicable only to emerging markets. But in 2010, it was agreed to expand the application to all States to include voluntary sovereign issuers.

756 Principles for Stable Capital Flows and Fair Debt Restructuring & Addendum. (2012).

757 Eric Helleiner, *Filling a Hole in Global Financial Governance? The Politics of Regulating Sovereign Debt Restructuring*, *in* The politics of global regulation (Walter Mattli and Ngaire Woods ed. 2009).

758 Costs of sovereign default. (2006).

759 Marie-Anne Frison-Roche, Responsabilité et régulations économiques, Vol. 5 (Dalloz. 2007).

code is not binding, but flexible and designed to secure the commitments of borrowers and creditors. It applies only to a subset of debt instruments and therefore has a limited scope. Yet this soft governance can have a strong effect if the rules are respected and followed by stakeholders. Indeed, the impact on State's reputation is important as such impact constitutes a clear signal for financial markets.

The major inconvenient remains that such a code would not solve creditors' problems. Self-fulfilling conduct, individual actions and minority blocking would continue[760]. The code of good conduct has not succeeded. One motive for this failure is that it is not equitable as it is in favour of creditors[761]. Furthermore, there is no mechanism to oblige States and creditors to respect it. This is the major critic against such non-binding codes. Non-compliant conducts are not sanctioned. To obtain a binding outcome, some consider using a state insolvency management system modelled by the experience of domestic laws on commercial bankruptcy[762].

These principles need to be examined and complemented. Expectations *vis-à-vis* sovereign debtors are numerous, while requirements *vis-à-vis* creditors are more laconic. Creditors also need a clearer code to guide their conduct. However, the 2012 addendum written by the IIF is still not sufficient. Fairness is addressed in the addendum that states that sovereign debtors shall treat fairly all creditors. No creditor or group of creditors should therefore be excluded from an *ex ante* restructuring. The addendum also underlines the formation of a committee of creditors. Such committee would organise negotiations from the beginning of the restructuring. It repeats the structure and procedure of the Club of London.

While these principles are broadly consistent with IMF policies, there are still differences. First, these principles were initially adopted by large financial institutions and supported by borrowers from emerging markets. The G20 and the IMF International Monetary and Financial Committee welcomed these principles, but have been reluctant thereafter. The 2012 addendum encourages private creditors' participation to create macroeco-

---

760 Involving Private Creditors in the Prevention and Resolution of International Debt Crises (2003).

761 Barry Herman, *Why the Code of Conduct for Resolving Sovereign Debt Crises Falls Short, in* Overcoming Developing Country Debt Crises (Barry Herman, et al. eds., 2010).

762 R.M. Auerback, *Sovereign debt – default and restructuring of debts owed to private creditors*, 18, Journal of International Banking Law and Regulation (2003).

nomic parameters that support the debt sustainability analysis of IMF programmes. This addendum considers that negotiations should be left to creditors and debtors. Differentiated treatments would be made accordingly. Nevertheless, a formal participation would oppose IMF's independence. Such formal participation may even reduce the IMF credibility by incorporating private creditors' objectives and interests. For these reasons, the IMF did not approve these IIF principles.

The United Nations has been advocating for reforms of the international financial architecture. The UN is actively engaged in the debate. The UN Charter serves as a normative frame since international cooperation objectives are reflected in the resolution of economic problems, while also promoting solutions (Articles 1 (3) and 55)[763].

The restructuring of Iraq's debt demonstrated that the UN Security Council can prevent creditors from temporarily seizing its assets[764]. Barely two months after abandoning the IMF's proposal, an *ad hoc* restructuring mechanism of sovereign debt was adopted by the UN Security Council in Resolution No. 1483-1403 of 22 May 2003. This measure to freeze assets was confirmed in 2004[765]. Although creditors can obtain final judgments, they are not able to seize oil reserves or central bank assets[766].

763 Article 1(3): "*To achieve international co-operation in solving international problems of an economic, social, cultural, or humanitarian character, and in promoting and encouraging respect for human rights and for fundamental freedoms for all without distinction as to race, sex, language, or religion*".
Article 55: "*With a view to the creation of conditions of stability and well-being which are necessary for peaceful and friendly relations among nations based on respect for the principle of equal rights and self-determination of peoples, the United Nations shall promote: b. solutions of international economic, social, health, and related problems; and international cultural and educational cooperation*".

764 Resolution 1483 (2003) adopted by the Security Council at its 4761st meeting on 22 May 2003, § 22.

765 Resolution 1546 (2004) adopted by the Security Council at its 4987th meeting on 8 June 2004: "*Further decides that the provisions of paragraph 22 of resolution 1483 (2003) shall continue to apply, except that the privileges and immunities provided in that paragraph shall not apply with respect to any final judgement arising out of a contractual obligation entered into by Iraq after 30 June 2004*".

766 Rodrigo Olivares-Caminal, *Statutory Sovereign Debt Resolution Mechanisms*, *in* Sovereign Debt Management (Rosa M. Lastra & Lee Buchheit eds., 2014).

In 2011, the UN General Assembly called for a debt resolution[767]. In 2012, the Guiding Principles on foreign debt and human rights were presented to the Human Rights Council[768].

1.2.3. Soft law and the United Nations Conference on Trade and Development

The principles developed by the UNCTAD are not a new foray into the debt world. In 1964, UNCTAD had already worked on proposals for reduction, guidelines for restructuring and reforms of the international monetary system and finance development[769]. UNCTAD provides technical support to the Bureau of the *ad hoc* Committee[770] on a multilateral legal framework for the sovereign debt restructuring process established by the UN General Assembly.

In May 1976, the Fourth Conference instructed the Secretary General to convene a new intergovernmental group of experts on debt and development problems. The purpose was to advance the initiated work concerning a code of good practice. The first initiative can be identified in 1977, when an UNCTAD Trade and Development Report called for the establishment of explicit principles of debt rescheduling[771]. In 1980, the UNCTAD ap-

767 Resolution adopted by the General Assembly of the United Nations on 20 December 2010 on the report of the Second Committee (A/RES/65/144): "*Also calls for the consideration of enhanced approaches to sovereign debt restructuring and debt resolution mechanisms, based on existing frameworks and principles, with the broad participation of creditors and debtors, the comparable treatment of all creditors and an important role for the Bretton Woods institutions and other relevant organizations within the United Nations system, and, in this regard, calls upon all countries to promote and contribute to the discussions, including within the United Nations and other appropriate forums, on the need for and feasibility of a more structured framework for international cooperation in this area*".

768 Report of the Independent Expert on the effects of foreign debt and other related international financial obligations of States on the full enjoyment of all human rights, particularly economic, social and cultural rights, Cephas Lumina, "*Guiding principles on foreign debt and human rights*", A/HRC/20/23, 10 April 2012.

769 UNCTAD, The History of UNCTAD: 1964-1984 (United Nations. 1985), pp. 75-99.

770 *Bureau of the Ad Hoc Committee on a Multilateral Legal Framework for Sovereign Debt Restructuring Processes.*

771 Selected Issues Relating to the Establishment of Common Norms in Future Debt Reorganizations. (1977), TD/AC 2/9.

proved a set of detailed features for future operations relating to the debt problems of interested developing countries[772], which affirms the need to find a way to resolve debt service difficulties[773]. In 1986, an UNCTAD report included a detailed proposal to establish a sovereign debt restructuring proceedings under Chapter 11 of the US Bankruptcy Code[774]. The annual reports on trade and development regularly emphasise the need for a procedure, especially in 1998[775], 2001[776], 2009[777] and 2014[778].

UNCTAD reached a legal and institutional diagnosis in 2009 when it launched the initiative Promoting Responsible Sovereign Lending and Borrowing[779]. Domestic rules on sovereign debt managing do not solve two fundamental characteristics of modern finance. First, States use their sovereignty to manage debt problem. Second, debt crises have global and profound implications on economic growth and financial stability. Debt crisis has led State to use domestic decisions. Domestic rules have therefore an international impact. However, globalised financial problems can-

772 See Marilyn J. Seiber, International Borrowing by Developing Countries, 1st Edition (Pergamon Press. 1982), pp. 165-167.

773 It is emphasised that "*finding a means through which debt-servicing difficulty could be avoided was one of the most important tasks facing the international community [...] In the multilateral forum agreed upon by the debtor and creditors, the Chairman would conduct the debt operation in a fair impartial manner, in accordance with the agreed objectives, so as to lead to equitable results in the context of international economic cooperation*".

774 Trade and Development Report, (1986), pp. 119-146.

775 Trade and Development Report. Financial Instability. Growth in Africa, 1998, pp. 83-107.

776 Trade and Development Report. Global Trends and Prospects, Financial Architecture. (2001), pp. 61-76. "*One way out of this dilemma would be recourse to the principles of orderly debt workouts*".

777 Trade and Development Report. Responding to the Global Crisis. Climate Change Mitigation (2009), pp. 113-129. "*In view of the potential impact of the global financial and economic crisis on developing countries, a multilaterally agreed mechanism for a temporary standstill on debt repayments would greatly help orderly debt workouts*".

778 Trade and Development Report. Global Governance and Policy Space for Development (2014), pp. 3-4. "*Establishing a multilateral structure for dealing with sovereign debt restructuring that would take into consideration general interests, and not just the private ones – a proposal made by UNCTAD two decades ago – appears more pertinent and urgent than ever*".

779 The purpose is "*to develop a set of principles to establish internationally recognized principles that promote and reinforce responsible sovereign lending and borrowing practices*".

not be treated by unilateral strategies. Coordinated and widespread actions shall be implemented. It is in this context that international law is important[780].

UNCTAD created a forum for discussion between stakeholders in order for them to develop a text. This freedom strengthens the legitimacy of the process, which seeks to establish a unified set of principles that are both balanced in their design and widely approved. Published by UNCTAD in 2012, these principles received limited feedback from private stakeholders that continue to fill the current institutional and legal void with *ad hoc* mechanisms.

By identifying common standards among stakeholders, the objective is to promote shared responsibility of lenders and borrowers at international level. To do so, the group of experts systematised sovereign debt practices to offer a unified regulatory framework. These principles are a starting point for a debate on responsible sovereign financing. The aim is not to impose rules, but rather to strengthen practices so that these practices become general principles with concrete impact on the conduct of borrowers and creditors. Experts systematise and consistently generalise best international practices while also offering a holistic approach to debt regulation. These principles can be used in disputes but also in negotiations.

Those principles bring together existing rules of international law relating to debt problem and recent experiences. Written in the spirit of a code of good conduct for debtors and creditors, the principles consider the nature of debt and the economic problems under a restructuring. They reflect best practices in contract law and bankruptcy proceeding, as well as financial, constitutional and administrative practices. The preamble underlines the subsidiarity of these principles regarding existing rules[781]. Indeed, such principles are intended to be applied by States and their bilateral,

780 Juan Pablo Bohoslavsky & Yuefen Li, *UNCTAD Principles on Responsible Sovereign Financing*, *in* Sovereign Debt Management (Lee Buchheit & Rosa Lastra eds., 2014).

781 According to the Preamble: "*The normative contribution of these Principles lies not in the creation of new rights nor obligations in international law but in identifying, harmonizing and systematizing the basic principles and best practices applied to sovereign lending and borrowing and in elaborating the implications of these standards and practices for lenders and borrowers at the international level. This set of principles should apply without prejudice of other international rules concerning the action of lenders or borrowers*".

multilateral or private lenders. These principles are *ex ante* rules to be applied before starting negotiations.

The practices identified are vast: shared responsibility, transparency, debt monitoring, due diligence. Five principles are constantly solicited: legitimacy, impartiality, transparency, good faith and sustainability. These principles do not create anything new, but refer to existing practices. Legal changes exceptionally derived from an original creation and mainly result in an adaptation[782]. Thus, this mimic of a bankruptcy rule and the imitation of the rule of lender of last resort attract most attention. These principles also refer to best practices by suggesting the establishment of a debt management office (Principle 13), and recognizing the active role of the legislative branch for sovereign borrowing (Principle 1)[783].

2. *An imperfect law for sovereign debt management*

The soft law instruments used by financial international law are essential. Such instruments allow reaching an agreement through contractual ways. Soft law encourages international community to solve global problems. Even though some States are opposed to these solutions, the latter are indirectly implemented. In the absence of a disciplinary mechanism in the international financial field, it is crucial that creditors and sovereign borrowers understand the benefits of soft law commitments. There is an imperfect law managing sovereign borrowing (2.1.). This imperfect law should go beyond the shadows of informality[784] (2.2.).

---

782 Bouriche, Les instruments de solidarité en droit international public, 2012, pp. 235-266.

783 Juan Pablo Bohoslavsky & Carlos Espósito, *Principles Matter. The Legal Status of the Principles on Responsible Sovereign Financing*, *in* Sovereign Financing and International Law. The UNCTAD Principles on Responsible Sovereign Lending and Borrowing (Carlos Espósito, et al. eds., 2013).

784 Armin von Bogdandy & Matthias Goldmann, *Die Restrukturierung von Staatsschulden als Ausübung internationaler öffentlicher Gewalt: Zur Möglichkeit der inkrementellen Entwicklung eines Staateninsolvenzrechts*, 73, Zeitschrift für ausländisches öffentliches Recht und Völkerrecht (2013). Bogdandy & Goldmann, Sovereign Debt Restructurings as Exercises of International Public Authority: Towards a Decentralized Sovereign Insolvency Law, 2013.

2.1. De-formalisation of international law

Prima facie, UNCTAD principles rise from soft law. However, they have the theoretical intention of being persuasive enough to influence the interpretation, application and development of other rules, and to become a hard law internationally applicable. The principles refer to responsibilities of lenders and sovereign borrowers. Such phenomenon of de-formalisation of international law[785] is particular to financial matters. By examining practices of debt management *ex ante* and *ex post*, UNCTAD principles provide a framework and an overall debt management plan that aims at improving financial stability. By focusing on due diligence and transparency, principles can contribute to crisis prevention.

Most of the principles set out by UNCTAD may be regarded as general principles of law. The legal basis of general principles of law is found in Article 38 of the Statute of the International Court of Justice[786], which states that the primary sources of international law are international conventions, international customs and the general principles of law. Secondary sources are judicial decisions and doctrine[787].

Nevertheless, some rules are undoubtedly sustained by international law. Lenders and borrowers cannot violate UN sanctions, as recalled by Article 25 of the UN Charter[788]. Moreover, corruption in matters of sovereign financing is illegal; transparency and accountability are required

---

785 Jean d'Aspremont, *The Politics of Deformalization in International Law*, 3, Goettingen Journal of International Law (2011).

786 Article 38 (1): "*The Court, whose function is to decide in accordance with international law such disputes as are submitted to it, shall apply: a. international conventions, whether general or particular, establishing rules expressly recognized by the contesting states; b. international custom, as evidence of a general practice accepted as law; c. the general principles of law recognized by civilized nations; d. subject to the provisions of Article 59, judicial decisions and the teachings of the most highly qualified publicists of the various nations, as subsidiary means for the determination of rules of law*".

787 Alain Pellet, *Article 38*, *in* The Statute of the International Court of Justice: a Commentary (Christian Tams, et al. eds., 2012).

788 Article 25 of the UN Charter: "*The Members of the United Nations agree to accept and carry out the decisions of the Security Council in accordance with the present Charter*".

in contracts with States, as underlined by Articles 9 and 34 of the UN Convention against Corruption[789].

International custom in the field of State financing is laconic. *Pacta sunt servanda* is often alleged. However, it may be limited by the concept of necessity based on political and economic circumstances that make impossible the total or partial repayment of debts. According to the Paris Club, equality among creditors should be on based on debt burden sharing. Each creditor applies to get a discount proportional to its exposure to the sovereign debtor. The sovereign debtor would benefit from a debt relief from private sector. These elements are presented in UNCTAD principles 7, 9 and 15. It is also possible to argue that financial assistance in violation of a *jus cogens* norm is contrary to law, following Article 53 of the 1969 Vienna Convention on the Law of Treaties[790]. The link between the debt instrument and the violation of *jus cogens* should be examined case by case.

UNCTAD has systematised general principles, but the question that remains unanswered is how far these principles are already required. It is difficult to identify the precise moment when domestic legal instruments are no longer soft law and become norms of international law. From the practical perspective, general principles are established when courts and tribunals recognise them. From a theoretical point of view, general principles exist before this recognition and are the basis for coming decisions.

---

789 Article 9 of the UN Convention against Corruption. Public procurement and management of public finances
Article 34 of the UN Convention against Corruption. Consequences of act of corruption: "*With due regard to the rights of third parties acquired in good faith, each State Party shall take measures, in accordance with the fundamental principles of its domestic law, to address consequences of corruption. In this context, States Parties may consider corruption a relevant factor in legal proceedings to annul or rescind a contract, withdraw a concession or other similar instrument or take any other remedial action*".

790 Article 53 of the 1969 Vienna Convention on the Law of Treaties. Treaties conflicting with a peremptory norm of general international law ("*jus cogens*"): "*A treaty is void if, at the time of its conclusion, it conflicts with a peremptory norm of general international law. For the purposes of the present Convention, a peremptory norm of general international law is a norm accepted and recognized by the international community of States as a whole as a norm from which no derogation is permitted and which can be modified only by a subsequent norm of general international law having the same character*".

Their fragmentation and application have been examined[791]. The interaction of different legal sources with the persuasiveness of economic and political principles may enhance their overall degree of normativity.

Insofar as common principles emerge, one can even call them standards. Debt management tools are techniques[792] for adapting legal solutions to the evolution of society[793]. Defining a standard is complex because of its empirical dimension[794]. However, we can agree on the fact that this soft law reflects a commitment of the parties. Although this commitment may be minor, it nevertheless reveals the beginnings of a more elaborate plan or a limited consensus among regulators concerning debt causes. We can consider them as negative covenants. In other circumstances, the specific actions that the parties intend to implement are identified as affirmative covenants.

Even if these agreements are not binding, their solemnity and impact on the parties are such that they inherently become essential. This is particularly so in the event of a lender's sanction, because sovereign reputation on financial markets is important. In order to prevent increasing debt costs, compliance with loan conditions is essential to allow international institutions to continue to provide assistance. The UN uses an equivalent technique called name and shame, particularly used on sovereign debt issues.

Obviously, a proposal based on soft law is indeterminate. Its success entirely depends on participants' commitment. The successful implementation of principles requires general commitment to refine, interpret or revise them and to reflect the political and economic changing environment.

---

791 Carlos Espósito, et al., Sovereign Financing and International Law. The UNCTAD Principles on Responsible Sovereign Lending and Borrowing (Oxford University Press. 2013).

792 « *Le standard est une technique de formulation de la règle de droit qui a pour effet une certaine indétermination de celle-ci. [Il] vise à permettre la mesure de comportement et de situation en termes de normalité.* » in Stéphane Rials, Le juge administratif français et la technique du standard. Essai sur le traitement juridictionnel de l'idée de normalité (LGDJ. 1980).

793 Yannick Radi, La standardisation et le droit international. Contours d'une théorie dialectique de la formation du droit (Bruylant. 2013).

794 « *Aujourd'hui encore, le standard demeure une notion que l'on redoute devoir définir tant elle est susceptible d'acceptions différentes. Ne fournissant pas de solution précise et fixe, le standard fait prédominer le fait sur le droit.* » in Céline Bloud-Rey, *Standard, in* Dictionnaire de la culture juridique (Denis Alland & Stéphane Rials eds., 2003).

No hard law solutions can ensure this implementation. However, we consider that such international reflection is more liable to change conduct in terms of borrowing and lending, while also targeting development results and financial stability.

2.2. Enhancing general principles

Several strategies can be developed to implement these principles, such as establishing legal bases for their institutionalisation or building sustainable measures for their application[795]. Seeking to negotiate formal treaty-based principles is both impractical and undesirable at this time. The negotiation of a treaty and its ratification would take too long[796]. In addition, an international treaty does not directly bind private creditors. There are no formal engagement tools able to create obligations between public and private operators in international law at the moment. Meanwhile, political tensions are important, and a consensus on what constitutes compliance to these principles is beginning to emerge.

Since 2012, a first strategy has been implemented with the support of different public stakeholders: States, civil society groups, market operators. This step does not change the nature of soft law of these principles. It allows consolidating and broadening the support. Without such broader support, these principles are likely to be portrayed as ineffective or as non-neutral. A diversification of supports reinforces their ambition and calls for regulation. We consider that the legalisation process of international financial law has started[797]. In that sense, the Norwegian Department of International Development led an audit of loans to developing countries us-

---

795 Anna Gelpern, *Hard, Soft, and Embedded. Implementing Principles on Promoting Responsible Sovereign Lending and Borrowing*, *in* Sovereign Financing and International Law. The UNCTAD Principles on Responsible Sovereign Lending and Borrowing (Carlos Espósito, et al. eds., 2013).

796 See for example the Vienna Convention on Succession of States in respect of property, State archives and debts. This work began in 1967. The Convention was adopted in 7 April 1983 and opened for signature the next day. It has not yet been executed. See the UN database, UN Treaty Collection.

797 In 2015, twelve States had approved the Principles according to the UNCTAD website.

ing these principles[798]. These principles are also discussed within the International Organisation of Supreme Audit Institutions of Public Finances[799]. They have even been included in an arbitral final award[800].

The second part of the implementation strategy consists of using this support to start an institutionalisation, as evidenced by the first set of amendments. The focus should be on the conception of institutions that provide an open and responsible regulatory process and mobilise groups to require disclosure, monitoring and evaluation. Releasing information on sovereign borrowing would strengthen democratic responsibility and market discipline. The creation of institutions to monitor information and promote competition can help developing expertise, consolidating best practices and creating improved conditions. In other words, the successful implementation of these principles implies disseminating information on sovereign debt. It involves specialists to collect, publicise and interpret this information.

The answer to the current situation could be an instrument that is not necessarily an international treaty. Such instrument cannot result from a formal procedure negotiated between traditional diplomatic stakeholders. Indeed:

> "true institutionalisation will appear with technical and restricted topics unlikely to question the sovereignty of States. In other words, the less the idea is ambitious, the more it is permitted to accept a completed form of institutionalisation"[801].

---

798 UNCTAD News, "*First debt audit based on UNCTAD principles*", 20 August 2013.

799 UNCTAD, "*UNCTAD Principles to be incorporated in auditing standards for sovereign debts – A major step forward*", 21 June 2013. Carlos Espósito, et al., *Introduction: The Search for Common Principles*, *in* Sovereign Financing and International Law. The UNCTAD Principles on Responsible Sovereign Lending and Borrowing (Carlos Espósito, et al. eds., 2013).

800 *Ambiente Ufficio S.p.A. and others v Argentine Republic, ICSID Case No ARB/08/9 (formerly Giordano Alpi and others v Argentine Republic), dissenting opinion of Santiago Torres Bernárdez*, 2 May 2013.

801 Translated from Jean-Marc Sorel, *L'institutionnalisation des relations internationales*, *in* Droit des organisations internationales (Evelyne Lagrange & Jean-Marc Sorel eds., 2013). « *La véritable institutionnalisation va apparaître avec des sujets techniques et restreints peu susceptibles de heurter la souveraineté des États. Autrement dit, moins l'idée est ambitieuse et plus il est permis d'accepter une forme achevée d'institutionnalisation* ».

Soft law can sometimes have bigger effects than hard law[802]

Discussions are at stake within existing fora, including the IMF, the Financial Stability Board, the Bank for International Settlements and the Paris Club. Some of them continue to explore the incorporation of these principles into surveillance and technical assistance. Professional associations may be consulted in parallel to analyse the possible connections with their own mechanisms of best practices. National debt management organisations can be used to incorporate the principles into debt contracts and operational practices. The debt restructuring process follows a hierarchical procedure well known by States and by financial entities involved in sovereign debt market.

Integrating the principles to guide interpretation during negotiations in arbitration fora offers a logical solution without being systematic[803]. The doctrine and experience with soft law suggest that non-binding and informal mechanisms can improve regulation and compliance in certain circumstances. However, they must be properly designed to minimise the risk of error and illegitimacy. The objective is to achieve legal compliance. If it is irrelevant to transform these principles into a treaty, incorporating them to the preambles of debt contracts is a solution. We consider that such integration would reinforce compliance by a phenomenon of convergence. The drafting of financing contracts already changes in the light of existing conducts on markets. This is a potential entry for soft law in sovereign debt management.

The current alternative to soft law is a legal void. Leaving unelected private operators in charge of risk regulation leads to a regulatory capture. This undermines democracy and constitutes a government failure. However, adopting principles is not *per se* enough. These principles must be effectively integrated into debt instruments in a gradual manner. The soft law paradox lies in its long-term legitimacy.

We welcome the adoption of the Basic Principles on Sovereign Debt Restructuring Processes by the UN General Assembly in September 2015 to the extent that an open debate continues. However, it is regrettable that

---

802 Robert Howse & Ruti Teitel, *Beyond Compliance: Rethinking Why International Law Really Matters*, 1, Global Policy (2010).

803 While soft law agreements are in place among the parties, promoted by the informality of rules, the asymmetric effects may damage the sustainability of these informal agreements. Similarly, *ex ante* principles can be impractical *ex post.*

the instruments taken into considerable are too general to be incorporated into debt contracts.

*

The legal framework of sovereign debt management lacks regulation. This is the whole point for sovereign debt management. What we stand for is the use of principles such as due diligence, good faith and transparency as universal standards in international economic law. In this dissertation, the plea for State intervention and regulation seeks to re-establish legal mechanisms in the political dimension. A need of financial stability has already been identified. Defined rules are expected. However, the political implementation is delayed. The sovereign debt restructuring mechanism proposed by the IMF did not emerged. This failure does not lesser the importance and necessity of such mechanism. Currently, two dynamics conduct the evolution of *ad hoc* mechanisms: an institutional dimension complemented by a normative dimension.

Implementing a comprehension mechanism can only be realised through government action. States can act and propose a model of regulation to be included in form of clauses. As we recognised in this dissertation, the biggest problem is not technical but political. The current system of global governance is inadequate due to lacks of knowledge, rules, policies, institutions and compliance.

Title IV. CONCLUSION

Financial deregulation in a world of financial innovation has changed the composition of sovereign debt from syndicated loans to bonds. The interconnection between finance and modern communications, notwithstanding clear benefits and opportunities, provides a ground for excessive risk. This risk is at the origin of the increase of financial market volatility and the subsequent economic and social losses.

The failure of the mechanism proposed by the IMF serves as a lesson. Alternatively, collective action clauses have been implemented. Such clauses are useful but cannot be a substitute of a comprehensive debt mechanism. Court decisions in this field are still limited and sometimes contradictory[804].

So far, efforts to incorporate rules of international law to sovereign debt operation have been made under the pressure of national regulators in an *ad hoc* way. Nonetheless, no contract used on the financial market refers to the application of international law. The role of national courts, even more than that of arbitration, is to extend the accountability of these debt products. The integration of standards will influence stakeholders' conduct.

A credible proposal should identify the most persistent problems, provide tools to solve these problems and explain how these tools will improve the *status quo*. This is what we defend with the integration of clauses into sovereign debt contracts, based on the UNCTAD principles.

804 Waibel, Sovereign Defaults Before International Courts and Tribunals, 2011.

PART II. CONCLUSION

The second part of this dissertation aims to demonstrate the growing role of the public sector in sovereign debt management after the 2008 crisis. Legal instruments are primarily governed by private law. Subsequently, debt restructuring is held within informal fora. After the negotiation between creditors and sovereign debtors, exchanged offers are integrated as amendments of the initial contracts. However, for an effective restructuring, all relevant creditors should be involved. This is not the business plan of vulture funds. Such funds focus on litigation to recover debt. Their claims are based on contractual clauses. To prevent such holdout creditors from deteriorating any attempt of negotiation, collective action clauses have been included in bond contracts. These clauses have become mandatory in European bonds and constitute the first legal response to the sovereign debt crisis.

To provide legal tools for sovereign debt management, the International Monetary Fund and the World Bank have supported many intentions of reform – including the introduction of CACs – and highlighted the benefits of a strong system of international financial crises prevention. Debt relief under the HIPC initiative and the MDRI has been developed since the mid-1990s. The SDRM was proposed in 2001 by the IMF. In 2005, the Joint World Bank-IMF Debt Sustainability Framework for Low-Income Countries was introduced. All these legal instruments internationally respond to sovereign debt problem. We demonstrated that tools exist, even if they require further implementation.

Achieving a comprehensive management implies that the imperative of sovereign debt management should include cooperation, best practices sharing, transparent accounting and rules applied by all. Within the Eurozone, a European crisis resolution framework has been organised. A European economic law of sovereign debt is currently been established. Progressively, the evolution is reaching an international level.

GENERAL CONCLUSION

This dissertation started by questioning the lack of legal framework to manage sovereign debt. We determined that the problem of sovereign debt is not new. The history of sovereign financing is composed of spectacular debt excesses, crises, defaults, and restructuring[805].

The initial hypothesis was based on the demonstration of the existence of a legal framework. In the first part of this study, we considered the structure of states indebtedness. As a subject of international law, the State can choose bilateral or multilateral creditors to borrow through international financial agreements. This type of debt is quantitatively less usual, while commercial banks have taken over with syndicated loans governed by private law. To meet an ever-increasing demand for capital, financial markets have quickly proven to be the preeminent intermediaries between investors and sovereign borrowers. Traded bonds are submitted to private law. However, these sovereign bonds are ambivalent, between private contracts and sovereign borrowers, as reflected in their specific clauses.

Subsequently, sovereign debt structure is more privatised. This privatisation refers both to the use of private law and to the transfer of debt management to the private sector. While sovereign debt should originally be ruled by a sovereign authority, legal instruments and operators are almost exclusively dominated by private law. This feature prevents any comprehensive legal regime. At the end of the first part of this dissertation, we demonstrated how this privatisation of sovereign debt constitutes a strengthening factor of crisis.

The second part of this study focused on responses to crises. We highlighted the attempts and legal solutions provided by each stakeholder. Informal clubs offer a privileged place to negotiate a restructuring. When negotiations are not foreseen and disputes arise, creditors use arbitration based on contractual terms inserted in sovereign bonds, as the mitigated success of vulture funds illustrates.

---

805 Ernst-Moritz Lipp, *Why the Debt Crisis Led to a Systemic Crisis and How to Escape from it*, *in* A Debt Restructuring Mechanism for Sovereigns. Do we need a legal procedure? (Christoph G. Paulus ed. 2014).

Internationally, the World Bank and the International Monetary Fund are developing tools to globally manage debt levels. The two institutions propose tools and concrete solutions to manage indebtedness. From this analysis, we identified the emergence of an international economic law of sovereign debt.

What is striking in this emergence is that no significant changes have taken place for over a decade. Currently, the *status quo* is based on the contrast between an internationally integrated way to finance States and a purely national litigation structure. One may expect that the crisis or *Krise* becomes a turning point or *Wendepunkt*, as its etymology implies. However, such turning point finally remains confined to an announcement. Regulatory changes are implemented but remains insufficient. No original solution more or less appropriate to the circumstances has emerged. Technically, old tools and legal insufficiencies have been tirelessly recycled to build new solutions. For instance, the European Union is using the conditionality of the IMF. The previous collective action clauses were modernised and added to the latest sovereign bonds. A new version of the sovereign debt restructuring mechanism abandoned by the IMF is currently debated in the UN.

Since the outbreak of the sovereign debt crisis, there has been a modest transformation of a sovereign debt paradigm towards more governance, democracy and human rights' consideration. The crisis is not yet finished and the ambition of reforms is more and more reinforced. Even if repayments are always foreseen, new interactions between creditors and debtors are organised. It gradually returns to the original idea of Article XIV of the Declaration of the Rights of Man and of the Citizen of 1789:

> "All the citizens have a right to decide, either personally or by their representatives, as to the necessity of the public contribution; to grant this freely; to know to what uses it is put; and to fix the proportion, the mode of assessment and of collection and the duration of the taxes".

In that sense, important questions can be formulated. How should sovereign debt be repaid? Which interests can be defended while imposing a reimbursement? Ethical and legal arguments are open to debate. Ethical arguments are particularly interesting when one considers that the moral concept of fault primarily refers to the idea of debt. In this sense, the German word *Schuld* refers both to guilt and debt as an obligation[806].

The current central question remains – how do we want to manage sovereign debt? The dilemma must be reformulated. Knowing how debt affects sovereignty is no longer the main issue. States must now choose how they will cede a part of their sovereignty. This cession can either be in favour of financial markets, or to a system based on international public law.

No international system of sovereign defaults treatment is in place or liable to be introduced. However, it is not due to a lack of knowledge or techniques. This type of crisis has been recurrent for several centuries and the benefits of international restructuring proceedings have already been identified. There is obviously no simple or universally applicable answer to the problems posed by debt accumulation or permanent deficit. Sovereign debt crises are often strengthened by crises of confidence. Therefore, the international legitimisation of a moratorium would be useful to sovereign debtors and both public and private creditors. A sovereign debt restructuring mechanism may make this process more effective for all parties concerned by defining a clear set of rules and procedures[807]. The resolution of such crises is also a long and complicated issue affecting all interests, as the situation in Greece illustrated it.

The theoretical, empirical and historical analysis of interactions between creditors and debtors proves that there is an intrinsic political dimension of the issue of sovereign debt. We noticed that in sovereign debt management, it is impossible to separate finance from politics. We determined that there is a political preference for *ad hoc* mechanisms. The establishment of a global mechanism is still missing. Flexibility and informality are not problematic *per se*. Nevertheless, they become problematic when there is no cooperation anymore.

---

806 See Friedrich Nietzsche, Zur Genealogie der Moral. Eine Streitschrift, (Verlag von C. G. Neumann. 1887). Zweite Abhandlung: „Schuld“, „schlechtes Gewissen“ und „Verwandtes“: *„Der Verbrecher ist ein Schuldner, der die ihm erwiesenen Vorteile und Vorschüsse nicht nur nicht zurückzahlt, sondern sich sogar an seinem Gläubiger vergreift: daher geht er von nun an, wie billig, nicht nur aller dieser Güter und Vorteile verlustig, – er wird vielmehr jetzt daran erinnert, was es mit diesen Gütern auf sich hat*“.

807 Eric Helleiner, *The Mystery of the Missing Sovereign Debt Restructuring Mechanism*, 27 Contributions to Political Economy (2008).

Sovereign debt is a highly interdisciplinary topic. Through economic analysis, the likely consequences of the decisions made by governments and regulators at national and international levels can be modelled. Jean Tirole, awarded the Nobel Memorial Prize in Economic Sciences in 2014 for his "*analysis of market power and regulation*"[808], supports the creation of supranational structures of control. He calls for a strong political intervention to reform and strengthen institutions to avoid another crisis[809]. He highlights the same issue arose by jurists, mainly deciding who regulates implies determining who monitors[810].

Legal sciences follow economic sciences[811]. Legal contributions may be positive and constructive by forging new perspectives[812]. Debts are also legal arrangements whose effects depend on their applicable law. Debt may be reimbursed under the terms of a contract or rescheduled following a novation or a contractual amendment. Debt may be prescribed or become insignificant due to inflation[813]. The pragmatism of international economic law implies that the function of the *instrumentum* prevails over its form.

It is not possible to simply acknowledge that the State's possibilities deteriorate as the sustainability of public finances declines. It is obvious that in case of financial assistance, sovereignty appears to vanish. However, it is impossible to conclude that markets have simply overthrown the financing system. If it were true, only the sanction of markets would be important. There is room for manoeuvre.

---

808 Bittermann, The Refunding of international debt, 1973, pp. 212-243.

809 Jean Tirole, *Lessons from the Crisis*, *in* Balancing the Banks. Global Lessons from the Financial Crisis (Mathias Dewatripont, et al. eds., 2010).

810 « *Décider qui règle l'addition revient aussi à décider qui surveille* »: Tirole, Revue de la Stabilité Financière (2012).

811 « *Le droit accompagne la réalité, il ne la précède guère. À rechercher une vaine perfection dans la société internationale, on en oublie que cette apparente 'imperfection' est aussi la marque d'un système juridique qu'il faut envisager différemment, comme un autre paradigme possible du droit, et non comme un droit inachevé dont l'aboutissement serait le modèle étatique.* ». Jean-Marc Sorel, Le droit international au début du XXIe siècle : un salutaire chaos permanent mêlant humanisme et réalisme, 2008.

812 Mathias Audit, *Legal Engineering for the Creation of an International Centre for the Financial Safeguard of States*, ICSID Review (2017) 32 (1), pp. 227-257.

813 Sir William Blair, *Odious Debt*, *in* Sovereign Debt Management (Lee Buchheit & Rosa Lastra eds., 2014).

The confidence seeking by investors and creditors is guaranteed by legal rules. Therefore, we consider that the integration of contractual clauses based on UNCTAD principles could restore a part of sovereignty while ensuring a framework for sovereign debt management. We demonstrated that the source of many anomalies is found both in the drafting of contracts and in the crisis management. The profound and irreversible influence of the indebtedness structure on States requires both containing the lack of control and implementing legal accountability. By modifying contracts to provide a crisis procedure, we would achieve the objective of preserving flexibility, while enhancing cooperation.

The lacks of control and legal accountability should be stopped due to the profound and irreversible influence of debt structure on States. Such clauses fit in the spirit of the new governance. They could be adapted over time and designed to secure borrowers and creditors' commitments. They would gradually apply to a subset of debt instruments. This soft governance would have a hard law effect if those rules are followed by all stakeholders[814].

814 Michel Foucault, « Nietzsche, la généalogie, l'histoire », in Hommage à Jean Hyppolite, Paris, P.U.F., 1971, pp. 145-172 : « *En elles-mêmes, les règles sont vides, violentes, non finalisées ; elles sont faites pour servir à ceci ou à cela ; elles peuvent être ployées au gré de tel ou tel. Le grand jeu de l'histoire, c'est à qui s'emparera des règles, qui prendra la place de ceux qui les utilisent, qui se déguisera pour les pervertir, les utiliser à contresens et les retourner contre ceux qui les avaient imposées ; qui, s'introduisant dans le complexe appareil, le fera fonctionner de telle sorte que les dominateurs se trouveront dominés par leurs propres règles.* ».

Bibliography

ABI-SAAB Georges, « Éloge du "droit assourdi" : quelques réflexions sur le rôle de la Soft Law en droit international contemporain », in *Nouveaux itinéraires en droit : hommage à François Rigaux*, Bruxelles, Bruylant, 1993, pp. pp. 59-68

ACHARYA Viral, DRECHSLER Itamar, SCHNABL Philipp, “A Pyrrhic Victory? Bank Bailouts and Sovereign Credit Risk”, *The Journal of Finance*, 2013

AFFAKI Georges, « Du sens des mots et du bon sens : de la bonne interprétation de la clause pari passu », in *Mélanges en l'honneur de Philippe le Tourneau*, Paris, Dalloz, 2007

AFT, « Charte Spécialistes en valeurs du Trésor (SVT) », Paris, Agence France Trésor, 2012

AGGARWAL Vinod K., GRANVILLE Brigitte, *Sovereign debt: origins, crises and restructuring*, Royal Institute of International Affairs, 2003

AGGARWAL Vinod K., *Debt Games: Strategic Interaction in International Debt Rescheduling*, Cambridge, Cambridge University Press, 1996

AGLIETTA Michel, DENISE Caroline, « Les dilemmes du prêteur en dernier ressort international », *Revue française d'économie*, 1999, 14, pp. 35-85

AHMED Faisal Z., ALFARO Laura, MAURER Noel, “Lawsuits and Empire: on the Enforcement of Sovereign Debt in Latin America”, *Law and Contemporary Problems*, 2010, 73, pp. 39-46

ALLEMAND Frédéric, « Le développement de la coordination des politiques budgétaires dans l'UE », in *Quelle souveraineté budgétaire pour les États?*, Jean-Marc SOREL and Régis CHEMAIN, Paris, Pedone, 2013, pp. 31-63

———, « La faisabilité juridique des projets d'euro-obligations », *Revue trimestrielle de droit européen*, 2012, Vol. 48, pp. 553-594

ALLEN Mark, LEIPZIGER Danny, “Enhancing Collaboration: Joint Management Action Plan (JMAP)”, Washington D.C., International Monetary Fund and the World Bank, 2007

ALTAMURA Carlo Edoardo, « La banque dans la tourmente : les banques françaises, la Banque de France et le marché de l'eurodollar », *Histoire@Politique*, 2013, 19, pp. 101-113

AMBROSE Soren, “Social Movements and the Politics of Debt Cancellation”, *Chicago Journal of International Law*, 2005, 6, pp. 267-285

AMSELEK Paul, LAVIGNE Pierre, *Le budget de l'État sous la Ve République*, Paris, L.G.D.J., 1966

ANDREADES André, « Les contrôles financiers internationaux », in *Recueil des cours de l'Académie de droit international de La Haye*, 1924, pp. 5-108

ANDREAU Jean, BEAUR Gérard, GRENIER Jean-Yves, *La dette publique dans l'histoire,* Paris, Comité pour l'histoire économique et financière, 2006

ANDRITZKY Jochen, *Sovereign Default Risk Valuation: Implications of Debt Crises and Bond Restructurings*, Berlin Heidelberg, Springer, 2006

ARACHTINGI Thierry, « Les contrats de crédit syndiqué à l'épreuve de la crise », *Revue Lamy Droit Civil*, 2009, 62, pp. 61-67

D'ARGENT Pierre, « La Commission des réclamations Erythrée/Ethiopie : suite et fin », *Annuaire Français de Droit International*, 2009, 55, pp. 279-297

ARNER Douglas W., *Financial Stability, Economic Growth, and the Role of Law*, Cambridge, Cambridge University Press, 2007

ARNER Douglas W., BUCKLEY Ross P., "Redesigning the Architecture of the Global Financial System", *Melbourne Journal of International Law*, 2010, 11, pp. 185-239

ARTAUD Denise, *La question des dettes interalliées et la reconstruction de l'Europe (1917-1929)*, Paris, Librairie Honoré Champion, 1978

ARTETA Carlos, HALE Galina, "Sovereign Debt Crises and Credit to the Private Sector", *Journal of International Economics*, 2008, 74, pp. 53-69

ARTUS Patrick, BETBEZE Jean-Paul, de BOISSIEU Christian, CAPELLE-BLANCARD Gunther, « La crise des subprimes », Paris, La Documentation française, 2008

D'ASPREMONT Jean, *Formalism and the Sources of International Law. A Theory of the Ascertainment of Legal Rules*, Oxford, Oxford University Press, 2011

———, "The Politics of Deformalization in International Law", *Goettingen Journal of International Law*, 2011, 3, pp. 503-550

ATWOOD Margaret, *Comptes et légendes : La dette et la face cachée de la richesse*, Paris, Boréal, 2009

AUDIT Mathias, *Insolvabilité des États et dettes souveraines*, Paris, L.G.D.J., 2011

———, "A Debt Restructuring Mechanism for European Sovereigns: An Emerging Idea", in *A Debt Restructuring Mechanism for Sovereigns: Do we need a legal procedure?*, Christoph G. PAULUS, Oxford, Nomos, C. H. Beck, Hart Publishing, 2014, pp. 213-222

———, « Les clauses d'action collective comme remède à la crise souveraine de la zone euro », in *Quelle souveraineté budgétaire pour les États ?*, Jean-Marc SOREL and Régis CHEMAIN, Paris, Pedone, 2013, pp. 123-142

———, "Legal Engineering for the Creation of an International Centre for the Financial Safeguard of States", *ICSID Review* 2017, 32 (1), pp. 227-257

AUERBACK R. M., "Sovereign debt – default and restructuring of debts owed to private creditors", *Journal of International Banking Law and Regulation*, 2003, 18, pp. 440-452

BADEL Laurence, *Diplomatie et grands contrats. L'État français et les marchés extérieurs au XXe siècle*, Paris, Publications de la Sorbonne, 2010

———, « Pour une histoire de la diplomatie économique de la France », *Vingtième Siècle. Revue d'histoire*, 2006, 2, pp. 169-185

Banque de France, *Les produits dérivés de gré-à-gré : nouvelles règles, nouveaux acteurs, nouveaux risques*, Paris, Banque de France, 2013

———, « Dette publique, politique monétaire et stabilité financière », *Revue de la Stabilité Financière*, 2012, 16

———, « La crise de la dette souveraine », *Documents et débats*, 2012, 4

———, « De la crise financière à la crise économique », *Documents et débats*, 2010, 3

———, « La crise financière », *Documents et débats*, 2009, 2

BARDY Romain, « Le Mécanisme européen de stabilité et la BCE », *Revue des affaires européennes*, 2012., pp. 33-746

BARNETT Barry C., GALVIS Sergio J., GOURAIGE Ghislain Jr., "On Third World Debt", *Harvard International Law Journal*, 1984, 83, pp. 83-151

BASTID-BURDEAU Geneviève, « L'exercice des compétences monétaires par les États », in *Recueil des cours de l'Académie de droit international de La Haye*, 1989, pp. 211-369

BASTID-BURDEAU Geneviève, « Les eurocrédits. L'apparition des contrôles étatiques », in *Les euro-crédits, un instrument du système bancaire pour le financement international*, Jean-Bernard BLAISE, Philippe FOUCHARD and Philippe KAHN, Paris, Librairies techniques, 1981, pp. 369-393

BECKER Torbjörn, RICHARDS Anthony, THAICHAROEN Yungyong, "Bond Restructuring and Moral Hazard: Are Collective Action Clauses Costly?", Washington D.C., International Monetary Fund, 2001

BERENSMANN Kathrin, "Involving Private Creditors in the Prevention and Resolution of International Debt Crises", Bonn, German Development Institute, 2003

BERGER Klaus Peter, *The creeping codification of the lex mercatoria*, The Hague, Kluwer Law International, 1999

———, "Renegotiation and Adaptation of International Investment Contracts: The Role of Contract Drafters and Arbitrators", *Vanderbilt Journal of Transnational Law*, 2003, 36

BI Ran, CHAMON Marcos, ZETTELMEYER Jeromin, "The Problem that Wasn't: Coordination Failures in Sovereign Debt Restructurings", Washington D.C., IMF, 2011

BINDER Christina, "Changed Circumstances in Investment Law: Interfaces between the Law of Treaties and the Law of State Responsibility with a Special Focus on the Argentine Crisis", in *International Investment Law for the 21st Century*, Christina BINDER, Ursula KRIEBAUM, August REINISCH and Stephan WITTICH, Oxford, Oxford University Press, 2009, pp. 608-630

BIRDAL Murat, *The political economy of Ottoman public debt: insolvency and European financial control in the late nineteenth century*, Tauris Academic Studies, 2010

BIRDSALL Nancy, WILLIAMSON John, DEESE Brian, *Delivering on Debt Relief: From IMF Gold to a New Aid Architecture*, Washington D.C., Center for Global Development, 2002

BIS, « 84e Rapport annuel de la BRI. IV. Dette et cycle financier : perspectives nationales et mondiales », Basel, Bank for International Settlements, 2014

———, “Sovereign risk: a world without risk-free assets?”, Basel, Bank for International Settlements, 2013

———, “Guide to the international financial statistics”, Basel, Bank for International Settlements, 2009

———, « Deuxième rapport annuel », Bâle, Banque des règlements internationaux, 1932

BISMUTH Régis, « La privatisation des organisations internationales », in *Traité de droit des organisations internationales*, Évelyne LAGRANGE and Jean-Marc SOREL, Paris, LGDJ, 2013, pp. 192-198

———, « NML c. Argentine – Commentaire joint des arrêts : 1ère Ch. civ., 28 septembre 2011, N° 09-72.057 (NML c/ Argentine) et 1ère Ch. civ., 28 mars 2013, N° 10-25.938 (NML c/ Argentine et Total Austral), N° 11-10.450 (NML c/ Argentine), N° 11-13.323 (NML c/ Argentine et Air France) », in *Les grandes décisions de la jurisprudence française de droit international public*, Alain PELLET and Alina MIRON, Paris, Dalloz, 2015, pp. 633-651

———, « Dette des États et emprunts toxiques des collectivités locales : Destins croisés », *Revue Internationale des Services Financiers*, 2014, 2, pp. 7-10

———, « L'assistance financière du FMI aux États membres de la zone euro : de l'inconcevable au conventionnel (ou comment "conventionnaliser" l'inconcevable) », *Revue des affaires européennes*, 2012, 4, pp. 747-758

———, « L'émergence d'un "ordre public de la dette souveraine" pour et par le contrat d'emprunt souverain? Quelques réflexions inspirées par une actualité très mouvementée », *Annuaire Français de Droit International*, 2012, LVIII, pp. 489-513

———, « Les fonds souverains face au droit international. Panorama des problèmes juridiques posés par des investisseurs peu ordinaires », *Annuaire Français de Droit International*, 2010.pp. 567-606

———, « Le système international de prévention des crises financières – Réflexions autour de la structure en réseau du Forum de stabilité financière », *Journal du Droit International*, 2007, 1, pp. 57-83

BITTERMANN Henry J., *The refunding of international debt*, Durham N.C., Duke University Press, 1973

BLAIR Sir William, “Odious Debt”, in *Sovereign Debt Management*, Lee BUCHHEIT and Rosa LASTRA, Oxford University Press, 2014, pp. 233-239

BLAISE Jean-Bernard, FOUCHARD Philippe, KAHN Philippe, *Les euro-crédits, un instrument du système bancaire pour le financement international*, Paris, Librairies techniques, 1981

BLAISE Jean-Bernard, FOUCHARD Philippe, « La valeur juridique de la syndication », in *Les euro-crédits, un instrument du système bancaire pour le financement international*, Jean-Bernard BLAISE, Philippe FOUCHARD and Philippe KAHN, Paris, Librairies techniques, 1981

von BOGDANDY Armin, GOLDMANN Matthias, "Sovereign Debt Restructurings as Exercises of International Public Authority: Towards a Decentralized Sovereign Insolvency Law", in *Sovereign Financing and International Law. The UNCTAD Principles on Responsible Sovereign Lending and Borrowing*, Carlos ESPOSITO, Yuefen LI and Juan Pablo BOHOSLAVSKY, New York, Oxford University Press, 2013, pp. 39-70

———, „Die Restrukturierung von Staatsschulden als Ausübung internationaler öffentlicher Gewalt: Zur Möglichkeit der inkrementellen Entwicklung eines Staateninsolvenzrechts", *Zeitschrift für ausländisches öffentliches Recht und Völkerrecht*, 2013, 73, pp. 61-104

BOHOSLAVSKY Juan Pablo, ESPOSITO Carlos, "Principles Matter. The Legal Status of the Principles on Responsible Sovereign Financing", in *Sovereign Financing and International Law. The UNCTAD Principles on Responsible Sovereign Lending and Borrowing*, Carlos ESPOSITO, Yuefen LI and Juan Pablo BOHOSLAVSKY, New York, Oxford University Press, 2013, pp. 73-86

BOHOSLAVSKY Juan Pablo, LI Yuefen, "UNCTAD Principles on Responsible Sovereign Financing", in *Sovereign Debt Management*, Lee BUCHHEIT and Rosa LASTRA, Oxford University Press, 2014, pp. 443-461

De BOISSIEU Christian, COUPPEYSOUBEYRAN Jézabel, *Les systèmes financiers. Mutations, crises et régulation*, Paris, Economica, 2013

BOLTON Patrick, JEANNE Olivier, "Structuring and Restructuring Sovereign Debt: The Role of a Bankruptcy Regime", Washington D.C., International Monetary Fund, 2007

BOLTON Patrick, SKEEL Jr. David A., "Inside the Black Box: How Should a Sovereign Bankruptcy Framework Be Structured", *Emory Law Journal*, 2004, 53, pp. 763-822

BOLTON Patrick, "Toward a Statutory Approach to Sovereign Debt Restructuring: Lessons from Corporate Bankruptcy Practice around the World", Washington D.C., International Monetary Fund, 2003

BOLZE Antoine, « Origine publique des fonds = immunité d'exécution; Note sous Cour de cassation, première Chambre civile, 5 mars 2014, pourvoi numéro 12-22.406 », *La Gazette du Palais*, 2014, 203, pp. 29-31

———, « Saisies sur les créances de l'État argentin : encore raté ! Note sous Cour de cassation, première Chambre civile, 28 mars 2013, pourvoi numéro 11-10.450 et Cour de cassation, première Chambre civile, 28 mars 2013, pourvoi numéro 10-25.938 », *La Gazette du Palais*, 2013, 186-187, pp. 23-24

BORCHARD Edwin, *State Insolvency and Foreign Bondholders: General Principles* New Haven, Yale University Press, 1951

BORENSZTEIN Eduardo, PANIZZA Ugo, "The Costs of Sovereign Default", Washington D.C., International Monetary Fund, 2009

BORENSZTEIN Eduardo, CHAMON Marcos, JEANNE Olivier, MAURO Paolo, ZETTELMEYER Jeromin, "Sovereign Debt Structure for Crisis Prevention", Washington D.C., International Monetary Fund, 2004

BOUCHER Julien, « Le juge administratif et la combinaison des conventions internationales – Conseil d'État, assemblée, 23 décembre 2011, M. Eduardo José Kandyrine de Brito Paiva, n° 303678 », *Revue française de droit administratif*, 2012, 28, pp. 1-18

BOUCHET Michel, GHOSE Amit, "Co-Financing Transactions between Multilateral Institutions and International Banks", Paris, OECD, 1992

BOUGHTON James M., *Tearing Down Walls: The International Monetary Fund 1990-1999*, Washington, D.C., International Monetary Fund, 2012

BOUGHTON James M., LOMBARDI Domenico, *Finance, Development, and the IMF*, New York, Oxford University Press, 2009

BOURGUINAT Henri, *Finance internationale*, Paris, Presses Universitaires de France, 1999

BOURICHE Marie, *Les instruments de solidarité en droit international public*, Connaissances et savoirs, 2012

BOUVIER Michel, « La dette publique », *Revue française de Finances Publiques*, 2013, 123

BRADLEY Michael, GULATI Mitu, "Collective Action Clauses for the Eurozone: An Empirical Analysis", in *Third Draft* (2012)

BRATTON William W., "Pari Passu and a Distressed Sovereign's Rational Choices", *Emory Law Journal*, 2004, Vol. 53, pp. 823

BREEN Michael, *The politics of IMF lending*, Palgrave Macmillan, 2013

BRENDER Anton, PISANI Florence, GAGNA Emile, *The Sovereign Debt Crisis: Placing a Curb on Growth* Paris, Editions La Découverte, 2012

BRENNER Claude, « Renonciation à l'immunité d'exécution étatique : vérité un jour, erreur le lendemain ; Note sous Cour de cassation, première Chambre civile, 13 mai 2015, pourvoi numéro 13-17.751 », *La Gazette du Palais*, 2015, 248, pp. 11-12

BRETON Régis, PINTO Caroline, WEBER Pierre-François, « Les banques, l'aléa moral et la dette publique », *Revue de la Stabilité Financière*, 2012, 16, pp. 63-78

BROCHES Aron, "International Legal Aspects of the Operations of the World Bank", *Recueil des cours de l'Académie de droit international de La Haye*, 1959, 98, pp. 297-409

De BROUWER Frédéric, « EMIR : état des lieux de la mise en oeuvre et défis majeurs à venir », *Bulletin Joly Bourse*, 2014, 4

BRUMMER Chris, *Soft Law and the Global Financial System: Rule Making in the 21st Century*, Cambridge University Press, 2012

———, "Why Soft Law Dominates International Finance — and not Trade", *Journal of International Economic Law*, 2010, 13, pp. 623-643

BRUNNERMEIER Markus K., GARICANO Luis, LANE Philip R., PAGANO Marco, REIS Ricardo, SANTOS Tano, THESMAR David, van NIEUWERBURGH Stijn, VAYANOS Dimitri, "European Safe Bonds: ESBies", 2011

BUCHHEIT Lee C., "A Quarter Century of Sovereign Debt Management: An Overview", *Georgetown Journal of International Law*, 2004, Vol. 35, pp. pp. 637-640

———, "The Sharing Clause as a Litigation Shield", *International Financial Law Review*, 1990, 9, pp. 15-16

BUCHHEIT Lee C., GULATI Mitu G., "The Problem of Holdout Creditors in Eurozone Sovereign Debt Restructurings", *Butterworths Journal of International Banking and Financial Law*, 2013, 28, pp.191-194

———, "Responsible Sovereign Lending and Borrowing", *Law and Contemporary Problems*, 2010, 73, pp. 63-92

———, "Exit Consents in Sovereign Bond Exchanges", *UCLA Law Review*, 2000, 48, pp. 59-84

BUCHHEIT Lee C., GULATI Mitu, THOMPSON Robert B., "The Dilemma of Odious Debts", *Duke Law Journal*, 2007, 56, pp. 1201-1262

BUE Charlotte, « La politique de développement de l'Union européenne : réformes et européanisation », *Critique internationale*, 2011, 53, pp. 83-99

BULOW Jeremy, ROGOFF Kenneth, "The Buyback Boondoggle", *Brookings Papers on Economic Activity*, 1988, 2, pp. 675-698

Bundesfinanzministerium, „Zur Auflösung der Bundeswertpapierverwaltung: Ein Rückblick auf die Schuldenverwaltung in Deutschland von 1820 bis 2006", Berlin, Bundesministrium der Finanzen, 2006

BURDA Michael C., "The European Debt Crisis: How Did We Get into this Mess? How Can We Get out of it?", in *A Debt Restructuring Mechanism for Sovereigns. Do we need a legal procedure?*, Christoph G. PAULUS, München, Verlag C.H. Beck, Hart Publishing, 2014, pp. 21-34

CALLAGHY Thomas M., "Innovation in the Sovereign debt regime: from the Paris club to enhanced HIPC and beyond", Washington, D.C., World Bank, 2002

CALMETTE Germain, *Recueil de documents sur l'histoire de la question des réparations (1919-1921)*, Paris, Alfred Costes, 1935

CALOMIRIS Charles W, "The Subprime Turmoil: What's Old, What's New, and What's Next », *The Journal of Structured Finance*, 2009, 15, pp. 6-52

CANTOR Richard, "Ratings and regulation", Basel, Bank for International Settlements, 2013

CARNELL Richard Scott, MACEY Jonathan R., MILLER Geoffrey P., *The Law of Banking and Financial Institutions*, Aspen, 2009

CARREAU Dominique, JULLIARD Patrick, *Droit international économique*, Paris, Dalloz, 2013

CARREAU Dominique, MARRELLA Fabrizio, *Droit international*, Paris, Pedone, 2012

CARREAU Dominique, SHAW Malcolm N., *La dette extérieure / The External Debt*, Dordrecht/Boston/London, Martinus Nijhoff Publishers, 1995

CARREAU Dominique, « La surveillance internationale des politiques budgétaires », in *Quelle souveraineté budgétaire pour les États ?*, Jean-Marc SOREL and Régis CHEMAIN, Paris, Pedone, 2013, pp. 81-86

———, « Dette d'État », *Dalloz – Répertoire de droit international*, 2009

———, « Le rééchelonnement de la dette extérieure des États », *Journal du Droit International*, 1985, 112, pp. 5-48

———, « Monnaie », *Dalloz – Répertoire de droit international*, 2009

CARUANA Jaime, "Debt: the view from Basel", Basel, Bank for International Settlements, 2015

CASSELLA Sarah, *La nécessité en droit international : de l'état de nécessité aux situations de nécessité*, Brill Academic Pub, 2011

CASTILLON Richard, *Les réparations allemandes : deux expériences – 1919-1932; 1945-1952*, Paris, PUF, 1953

CAZAL Julien, « L'arbitrage multipartite devant les tribunaux CIRDI », *Les Cahiers de l'Arbitrage*, 2013, 4, pp. 951-965

CHADHA Bankim, FOLKERTSLANDAU David, KING Mervyn A., MENDOZA Roberto G., "The Evolving Role of Banks in International Capital Flows", in *International Capital Flows*, Martin FELDSTEIN, University of Chicago Press, 1999, pp. 191-234

CHALTIEL Florence, « Le référendum en Grèce et le droit de l'Union », *Les Petites Affiches*, 2015, 149, pp. 8-14

CHARLESWORTH Hilary, « Le droit international, une discipline de la crise », in *Sexe, genre et droit international*, Hilary CHARLESWORTH, Paris, Pedone, 2013, pp. 221-243

CHEN Felicitas, "The Correlation between Human Rights and the Loan Policies of the World Bank and the EBRD", in *Ethics and human rights in a globalized world: an interdisciplinary and international approach*, Klaus HOFFMANN-HOLLAND, Mohr Siebeck, 2009, pp. 239-253

CHESTERMAN Simon, "The Turn to Ethics: Disinvestment From Multinational Corporations for Human Rights Violations – The Case of the Norway's Sovereign Wealth Fund", *American University International Law Review*, 2008, 23, pp. 577-615

CHEVALIER Pierre, « Dossier documentaire: immunités d'exécution des États. Cour de cassation (France), civ. 1, 28 mars 2013 », *Revue Générale de Droit International Public*, 2013, 117, pp. 203-232

CHIOTELLIS Aristides P., "Sovereign Debt Restructuring and the Internal Legal Framework: the Greek Experience", in *A Debt Restructuring Mechanism for Sovereigns. Do we need a legal procedure?*, Christoph G. PAULUS, München, Verlag C.H. Beck, Hart Publishing, 2014, pp. 99-117

CHORAFAS Dimitris N., *Sovereign Debt Crisis: The New Normal and the Newly Poor*, Palgrave Macmillan, 2011

CISSE Hassane, « Le fonds monétaire international et l'endettement extérieur des États », in *La dette extérieure / The external debt*, Martinus Nijhoff PUBLISHERS, 1995

COHEN Daniel, PORTES Richard, « Crises de la dette : prévention et résolution », Paris, La Documentation française, 2003

COLLY François, « Les emprunts de l'État et la loi organique du 1er août 2001 relative aux lois de finances », in *Études en l'honneur de Loïc Philip*, Paris, Economica, 2005, pp. 365-375

COMBACAU Jean, SUR Serge, *Droit international public*, Paris, Montchrétien, 2012

Comité de Bâle sur le contrôle bancaire, « Banques d'importance systémique mondiale : méthodologie révisée d'évaluation et exigence additionnelle de capacité d'absorption des pertes », Bâle, Banque des règlements internationaux, 2013

Commission du droit international, "ILC Report of the Commission to the General Assembly on the work of its thirty-third session", New York, United Nations, 1981

COMMITTERI Marco, SPADAFORA Francesco, "You Never Give Me Your Money? Sovereign Debt Crises, Collective Action Problems, and IMF Lending", IMF, 2013

De CONDORCET Marquis, *Oeuvres complètes de Condorcet*, Paris, 1804

COSIO-PASCAL Enrique, "Paris Club: Intergovernmental Relations in Debt Restructuring", in *Overcoming Developing Country Debt Crisis*, Barry HERMAN, José Antonio OCAMPO and Shari SPIEGEL, New York, Oxford University Press, 2010, pp. 231-276

———, "The Emerging Of A Multilateral Forum For Debt Restructuring: The Paris Club", UNCTAD, 2008

COTTARELLI Carlo, FORNI Lorenzo, GOTTSCHALK Jan, MAURO Paolo, "Default in Today's Advanced Economies: Unnecessary, Undesirable, and Unlikely", Washington D.C., International Monetary Fund, 2010

COUDERT Virginie, GEX Mathieu, « Pourquoi le règlement des CDS grecs n'a pas conduit à la débâcle redoutée », *Revue de la Stabilité Financière*, 2013, 17, pp. 153-170

COUILLAULT Bertrand, WEBER Pierre-François, « Vers un Code de bonne conduite volontaire pour restructurer la dette souveraine », Paris, Banque de France, 2003

Council of Economic Experts, "Annual report", Berlin, Bundesministerium der Finanzen, 2011

CROKE James, "Chuaigh Ar La – Debt of a Gaelsman: Ireland's Sovereign Debt Crisis, National and International Responses", *Northwestern Journal of International Law & Business*, 2012, 32, pp. 365-390

CROUZET François, *A history of the European Economy, 1000-2000*, Charlottesville, University of Virginia Press, 2001

CRUCES Juan J., TREBESCH Christoph, "Sovereign Defaults: The Price of Haircuts", *American Economic Journal: Macroeconomics*, 2013, 5, pp. 85-117

DAILLIER Patrick, FORTEAU Mathias, DINH Nguyen Quoc, PELLET Alain, *Droit international public*, Paris, L.G.D.J., 2009

DAS Udaibir S., PAPAIOANNOU Michael G., TREBESCH Christoph, "Sovereign Debt Restructurings 1950-2010: Literature Survey, Data, and Stylized Facts", International Monetary Fund, 2012

DEFOE Daniel, *An Essay Upon Public Credit: Being an Enquiry how the Public Credit Comes to Depend Upon the Change of the Ministry, Or the Dissolutions of Parliaments, and Whether it Does So Or No?*, W. Baynes, Paternoster-Row, J.S. Jordan, 1710

DELAUME Georges R., "Issues of Applicable Law in the Context of the World Bank's Operations", in *The Transnational Law of International Commercial Transactions*, Norbert HORN and Clive M. SCHMITTHOFF, Kluwer, 1982, pp. 317-328

DELMAS-MARTY Mireille, « Études juridiques comparatives et internationalisation du droit », in *Leçon inaugurale au Collège de France* (Paris: Librairie Fayard, 2003)

DENNIS Steven A., MULLINEAUX Donald J., "Syndicated loans", *Journal of Financial Intermediation*, 2000, 9, pp. 404-426

DERO-BUGNY Delphine, FRANCQ Stéphanie, PETIT Nicolas, LOUSBERG Charlotte, « Chronique – Cour de justice et Tribunal de l'Union européenne », *Journal du Droit International*, 2013, 2

DEUMIER Pascale, *Le droit spontané*, Économica, 2002

DIAZ-CASSOU Javier, ERCE Aitor, "IMF Interventions in Sovereign Debt Restructurings", in *Sovereign Debt: From Safety to Default*, Robert W. KOLB, John Wiley & Sons, 2011, pp. 179-188

DICKERSON A. Mechele, "Insolvency Principles: The Missing Link in the Odious Debt Debate", in *Sovereign Debt: From Safety to Default*, Robert W. KOLB, John Wiley & Sons, 2011, pp. 261-266

DOR Eric, « La Cour constitutionnelle de Karlsruhe suspecte les OMT d'être illégales », *Revue Banque*, 2014, 771, pp. 46-49

DRAGO Luis Maria, "The State Loans in Their Relation to International Policy", *American Journal of International Law*, 1907, 1, pp. 692-726

DRAKE Keegan S., "Disenfranchisement in Sovereign Bonds", in *A Debt Restructuring Mechanism for Sovereigns. Do we need a legal procedure?*, Christoph G. PAULUS, München, Verlag C.H. Beck, Hart Publishing, 2014, pp. 141-161

DRELICHMAN Mauricio, VOTH Hans-Joachim, "Lending to the borrower from Hell: Debt and Default in the Age of Philip II", *The Economic Journal*, 2011, 121, pp. 1205-1227

DUBET Anne, « Les rois d'Espagne et leurs créanciers. Une collaboration conflictuelle », in *La dette publique dans l'histoire*, Jean ANDREAU, Gérard BEAUR and Jean-Yves GRENIER, Paris, Comité pour l'histoire économique et financière de la France, 2006, pp. 243-267

DUPUY René-Jean, *La communauté internationale entre le mythe et l'histoire*, Paris, Economica, 1986

DUVALL Thomas A., "Debt Relief for Low-Income Countries", in *Sovereign Debt Management*, Lee BUCHHEIT and Rosa LASTRA, Oxford University Press, 2014, pp. 69-84

EATON Jonathan, FERNANDEZ Raquel, "Sovereign debt", in *Handbook of International Economics*, Ronald Winthrop JONES, Gene M. GROSSMAN, Peter B. KENEN and Kenneth ROGOFF, Elsevier, 1995, pp. 2031-2077

EATON Jonathan, GERSOVITZ Mark, "Debt with Potential Repudiation: Theoretical and Empirical Analysis", *The Review of Economic Studies*, 1981, 48, pp. 289-309

ECKERT Christian, « Le contrôle de la dette publique par le Parlement : un enjeu politique devenu majeur », *Revue française de Finances Publiques*, 2013, 123, pp. 3-20

EL-ERIAN Mohamed A., « Lorsque la dette souveraine des économies occidentales devient risquée », *Revue de la Stabilité Financière*, 2012, 16, pp. 31-38

ESPOSITO Carlos, LI Yuefen, BOHOSLAVSKY Juan Pablo, *Sovereign Financing and International Law. The UNCTAD Principles on Responsible Sovereign Lending and Borrowing*, New York, Oxford University Press, 2013

EULISS Richard, "The Feasibility of the IMF's Sovereign Debt Restructuring Mechanism: An Alternative Statutory Approach to Mollify American Reservations", *American University International Law Review*, 2003, 19, pp. 107-151

European Commission, « Livre vert sur la faisabilité de l'introduction d'obligations de stabilité », Bruxelles, Commission européenne, 2011

FAVERO Marc, « La standardisation contractuelle, enjeu de pouvoir entre les parties et de compétition entre systèmes juridiques », *Revue Trimestrielle de Droit Commercial*, 2003, n° 3, pp. 429-448

FEIBELMAN Adam, "Ecuador's sovereign default: a Pyrrhic victory for odious debt?", *Journal of International Banking Law and Regulation*, 2010, 25, pp. 357-362

Financial Stability Board, "Intensity and Effectiveness of SIFI Supervision", Washington D.C., IMF, 2010

FISCHER John Williams K.C, « Le droit international et les obligations financières internationales qui naissent d'un contrat », in *Recueil des cours de l'Académie de droit international de La Haye*, 1923

FISCHER Stanley, "On the Need for an International Lender of Last Resort", *Journal of Economic Perspectives*, 1999, 13, pp. 85-104

FLANDREAU Marc, GAILLARD Norbert, PACKER Frank, "To err is human: rating agencies and the interwar foreign government debt crisis", Bank of International Settlement, 2010

FLEURIET Michel, « La localisation des activités de banque d'investissement », *Revue d'économie financière*, 2000, 57, pp. 127-134

FONTANEL Jacques, COULOMB Fanny, « Spéculation internationale et régulation financière », *Annuaire Français de Relations Internationales*, 2006, Vol. VII

FORTEAU Mathias, «Le défaut souverain en droit international public : les instruments de droit international public pour remédier à l'insolvabilité des États», in *Insolvabilité des États et dettes souveraines*, Mathias AUDIT, Paris, LGDJ, 2011, pp. 209-232

FOSTER Sharon E., "Too Big to Fail – Too Small to Compete: Systemic Risk Should Be Addressed through Antitrust Law but Such a Solution Will Only Work if It is Applied on an International Basis", *Florida Journal of International Law*, 2010, 22, pp. 31-64

FOUCHARD Philippe, « Financement et endettement internationaux : aspects juridiques », *Journées de la Société de législation comparée*, 1986, Vol. 635, pp. 661-676

FRAGA Arminio, "Crisis Prevention and Management: Lessons from Mexico", in *From Halifax to Lyons : What Has Been Done About Crisis Management?*, Peter KENEN, Princeton University, 1996, pp. 46-55

FRISON-ROCHE Marie-Anne, *Responsabilité et régulations économiques*, Paris, Dalloz, 2007

FUENTES Miguel, SARAVIA Diego, "Sovereign Defaulters: Do International Capital Markets Punish Them?", ed. by Instituto de Economia, Santiago: Pontificia Universidad Católica de Chile, 2006

G10, "The resolution of sovereign liquidity crisis", 1996

GADANECZ Blaise, "The syndicated loan market: structure, development and implications", BIS, 2004

GAILLARD Norbert, *A century of sovereign ratings*, New York and London, Springer, 2011

GALLAIS-HAMONNO Georges, BERTHON Jean, *Les emprunts tontiniers de l'Ancien Régime. Un exemple d'ingénierie financière au XVIIIe siècle*, Paris, Publications de la Sorbonne, 2008

GBANDI Karlo Kondi, « La Cour suprême des États-Unis et la dette souveraine de l'Argentine : l'examen des rapports d'amicus curiae de la France et du Brésil », Sentinelle, 2014

GELOS Gaston R., SAHAY Ratna, SANDLERIS Guido, "Sovereign Borrowing by Developing Countries: What Determines Market Access?", Washington D.C., International Monetary Fund, 2004

GELPERN Anna, "A Skeptic's Case for Sovereign Bankruptcy", in *A Debt Restructuring Mechanism for Sovereigns: Do we need a legal procedure?*, Christoph G. PAULUS, Oxford, Nomos, C. H. Beck, Hart Publishing, 2014, pp. 261-278

———, "Hard, Soft, and Embedded. Implementing Principles on Promoting Responsible Sovereign Lending and Borrowing", in *Sovereign Financing and International Law. The UNCTAD Principles on Responsible Sovereign Lending and Borrowing*, Carlos ESPOSITO, Yuefen LI and Juan Pablo BOHOSLAVSKY, New York, Oxford University Press, 2013, pp. 347-382

———, "What Iraq and Argentina Might Learn from Each Other", *Chicago Journal of International Law*, 2005, 6, pp. 391-414

GELPERN Anna, SETSER Brad, "Domestic and External Debt: The Doomed Quest for Equal Treatment", *Georgetown Journal of International Law*, 2004, 35, pp. 795-814

Von GERBER Carl Friedrich Wilhelm, *Über öffentliche Rechte*, Tübingen, Laupp, 1852

GHERARI Habib, « Le développement de la coordination des politiques budgétaires en droit international », in *Quelle souveraineté budgétaire pour les États ?*, Jean-Marc SOREL and Régis CHEMAIN, Paris, Pedone, 2013, pp. 13-30

GIANSETTO Fanny, « Les fonds dits « vautours » et la dette souveraine. – Un nouvel enjeu de la régulation financière », *Cahiers de droit de l'entreprise*, 2012, 6

GIANVITI François, "The Design and Effectiveness of Collective Action Clauses", Washington D.C., International Monetary Fund, 2002

———, "The Reform of the International Monetary Fund (Conditionality and Surveillance)", *The International Lawyer*, 2000, 34, pp. 107-116

GIANVITI François, KRUEGER Anne O., PISANI-FERRY Jean, SAPIR André, HAGEN Jurgen Von, "A European Mechanism for Sovereign Debt Crisis Resolution: A Proposal", *Bruegel Blueprint Series*, 2010

GIDE Charles, *Cours d'économie politique*, 1923

GIDEONSE Harry, *War Debts*, Chicago, The University of Chicago Press, 1933

GIOVANOLI Mario, "The reform of the international financial architecture after the global crisis", *N.Y.U. International Law and Politics*, 2009, Vol. 42, pp. 81-123

GITLIN Richard, HOUSE Brett, "A blueprint for a Sovereign Debt Forum", 2014

GOLD Joseph, "Borrowing by the International Monetary Fund from Nonofficial Lenders", *The International Lawyer*, 1986, 20, pp. 455-483

GOLDMANN Mathias, "Responsible Sovereign Lending and Borrowing: The View from Domestic Jurisdictions", Heidelberg, United Nations Conference on Trade and Development, 2012

GRAEBER David, *Debt: The First 5000 Years*, Melville House, 2011

GRARD Loïc, « Le club de paris et les dettes publiques des États », in La dette extérieure / The external debt, Martinus Nijhoff PUBLISHERS, 1995, pp. 197-254

GRIZIOTTI Benvenuto, « La Banque des Règlements Internationaux », *Recueil des cours de l'Académie de droit international de La Haye*, 1932, IV, pp. 359-463

GUIER Edgar Nassar, « La position du Gouvernement américain en matière d'endettement des États : du plan Baker à l'initiative Brady », in *La dette extérieure / The external debt*, Martinus Nijhoff PUBLISHERS, 1995, pp. 111-137

GUDER Leonie F., *The Administration of Debt Relief by the International Financial Institutions: A Legal Reconstruction of the HIPC Initiative*, Berlin, Springer-Verlag Berlin and Heidelberg GmbH & Co. K, 2010

GULATI Mitu, GELPERN Anna, *A Modern Legal History of Sovereign Debt*, 2010

GYNTELBERG Jacob, HÖRDAHL Peter, TERS Kristyna, URBAN Jörg, "Intraday dynamics of euro area sovereign CDS and bonds", Basel, Bank for International Settlements, 2013

HAGAN Sean, "Debt Restructuring and Economic Recovery", in *Sovereign Debt Management*, Rosa M. LASTRA and Lee BUCHHEIT, Oxford, Oxford University Press, 2014, pp. 359-385

HAGAN Sean, VIÑALS José, "Resolution of Cross-Border Banks: A Proposed Framework for Enhanced Coordination", Washington D.C., International Monetary Fund, 2010

———, "Designing a Legal Framework to Restructure Sovereign Debt", *Georgetown Journal of International Law*, 2005, 36, pp. 299-402

HAHN Hugo J., "Public foreign debts and international law", *Law and state: a biannual coll. of recent German contributions to these fields*, 1986, 33, pp. 7-26

HALDANE Andy, "Private Sector Involvement in Financial Crises: Analytics and Public Policy Approaches", London, Bank of England, 1999

HALE Thomas, HELD David, *The Handbook of Transnational Governance: Institutions and Innovations*, Cambridge, Polity, 2011

HALLAK Issam, SCHURE Paul, "Loans versus Bonds: The Importance of Potential Liquidity Problems for Sovereign Borrowers", in *Sovereign Debt: From Safety to Default*, Robert W. KOLB, John Wiley & Sons, 2011, pp. 101-109

HAMON Philippe, « Les dettes du roi de France (fin du Moyen-Âge – XVIe siècle) : une dette "publique"? », in *La dette publique dans l'histoire*, Jean ANDREAU, Gérard BEAUR and Jean-Yves GRENIER, Paris, Comité pour l'histoire économique et financière de la France, 2006, pp. 85-97

HEAD John W., *Losing the global development war: a contemporary critique of the IMF, the World Bank, and the WTO*, Leiden, Martinus Nijhoff, 2008

———, "The Global Financial Crisis of 2008-2009 in Context – Reflections on International Legal and Institutional Failings, "Fixes", and Fundamentals", *Global Business & Development Law Journal*, 2010, 23, pp. 43-112

———, "Evolution of the governing law for loan agreements of the World Bank and other multilateral development banks", *American Journal of International Law*, 1996, Vol. 90, pp. 214-234

HELLEBRANDT Tomas, POSEN Adam S., TOLLE Marilyne, « La clé d'un assainissement budgétaire réussi : coopération ou confrontation avec la politique monétaire ? », *Revue de la Stabilité Financière*, 2012, 16, pp. 145-157

HELLEINER Eric, *States and the Reemergence of Global Finance: From Bretton Woods to the 1990s*, London / Ithaca, Cornell University Press, 1994

———, "A Bretton Woods moment? The 2007-2008 crisis and the future of global finance", *International Affairs*, 2010, 86, pp. 619-636

———, "Filling a Hole in Global Financial Governance? The Politics of Regulating Sovereign Debt Restructuring", in *The politics of global regulation*, Walter Mattli and Ngaire WOODS, Princeton University Press, 2009, pp. 89-120

———, "The Mystery of the Missing Sovereign Debt Restructuring Mechanism", *Contributions to Political Economy*, 2008, 27, pp. 91-113

HERMAN Barry, "Why the Code of Conduct for Resolving Sovereign Debt Crises Falls Short", in *Overcoming Developing Country Debt Crises*, Barry HERMAN, José Antonio OCAMPO and Shari SPIEGEL, New York, Oxford University Press, 2010

HERNDON Thomas, ASH Michael, POLLIN Robert, "Does High Public Debt Consistently Stifle Economic Growth? A Critique of Reinhart and Rogoff", Amherst: University of Massachusetts, 2013

HERRENSCHMIDT Jean-Luc, « Présentation des euro-crédits », in *Les euro-crédits. Un instrument du système bancaire pour le financement international*, Jean-Bernard BLAISE, Philippe FOUCHARD and Philippe KAHN, Paris, Libraires techniques de Paris, 1981

HERTZOG Robert, « À la recherche d'une théorie du système financier public complexe », in *Études en l'honneur de Loïc Philip*, Paris, Economica, 2005, pp. 401-421

HOFMANN Christian, "A Legal Analysis of the Eurozone Crisis", in *A Debt Restructuring Mechanism for Sovereigns. Do we need a legal procedure?*, Christoph G. PAULUS, München, Verlag C.H. Beck, Hart Publishing, 2014, pp. 43-73

HOLMGREN Christina, *La renégociation multilatérale des dettes : le Club de Paris au regard du droit international*, Bruxelles, Bruylant, 1998

HOWSE Robert, TEITEL Ruti, "Beyond Compliance: Rethinking Why International Law Really Matters", *Global Policy*, 2010, 1, pp. 127-136

HUMPHREY Thomas M, KELEHER Robert E, "The Lender of Last Resort: A Historical Perspective", *Cato Journal*, 1984, 4, pp. 275-321

ICMA, "ICMA Sovereign bond consultation paper supplement", Zurich, International Capital Market Association, 2014

———, "ICMA Sovereign bond consultation paper", Zurich, International Capital Market Association, 2013 and 2010

IIF, "Principles for Stable Capital Flows and Fair Debt Restructuring & Addendum", Institute of International Finance, 2012

IMF, "Greece: An Update of IMF Staff's Preliminary Public Debt Sustainability Analysis", Washington D.C., International Monetary Fund, 2015

———, "Greece: Preliminary Draft Debt Sustainability Analysis", Washington D.C., International Monetary Fund, 2015

———, "The Fund's Lending Framework and Sovereign Debt – Preliminary Considerations", Washington D.C., International Monetary Fund, 2014

———, "Sovereign Debt Restructuring – Recent Developments and Implications for the Fund's Legal and Policy Framework", Washington D.C., International Monetary Fund, 2013

———, "Staff Guidance Note for Public Debt Sustainability Analysis in Market-Access Countries", Washington D.C., International Monetary Fund, 2013

———, « Manuel sur la transparence des finances publiques », Washington D.C., International Monetary Fund, 2007

———, "Proposed Features of a Sovereign Debt Restructuring Mechanism", Washington D.C., International Monetary Fund, 2003

———, « Statistiques de la dette extérieure. Guide pour les statisticiens et les utilisateurs », Washington D.C., International Monetary Fund, 2003

———, "Guidelines on Conditionality", Washington D.C., International Monetary Fund, 2002

———, "Collective Action Clauses in Sovereign Bond Contracts – Encouraging Greater Use", Washington D.C., International Monetary Fund, 2002

———, "Fund Policy on Lending into Arrears to Private Creditors – Further Consideration of the Good Faith Criterion", Washington D.C., International Monetary Fund, 2002

———, "IMF Policy on Lending into Arrears to Private Creditors", Washington D.C., International Monetary Fund, 1999

IMF Survey, "IMF needs to do far more to help countries learn from each other's success and failures: interview with Mark Allen", Washington, D.C., International Monetary Fund, 2004

Independend Evaluation Group, "Debt Relief for the Poorest: An Evaluation Update of the HIPC Initiative", Washington D.C., World Bank, 2006

INOUE Jun, "Internationally Shared Goals and National Governments: a Case Study of France and Financing for Development", *Hitotsubashi Journal of Law and Politics*, 2010, 38, pp. 1-11

INTOSAI, « Numéro spécial sur le XXIe INCOSAI », *Revue internationale de la vérification des comptes publics*, 2014, 41, pp. 72-88

JACQUILLAT Bertrand, PERIGNON Christophe, SOLNIK Bruno, *Marchés financiers : Gestion de portefeuille et des risques*, Paris, Dunod, 2009

JAUFFRET-SPINOSI Camille, KELLY Claude, « La protection contractuelle », in *Les eurocrédits, un instrument du système bancaire pour le financement international*, Jean-Bernard BLAISE, Philippe FOUCHARD and Philippe KAHN, Paris, Librairies techniques, 1981, pp. 525-568

JEANNEAU Serge, « Objectifs et dispositifs de stabilité financière : dernières évolutions », Bâle, Banque des règlements internationaux, 2014

JEZE Gaston, « Les défaillances d'État », in *Recueil des cours de l'Académie de droit international de La Haye*, 1935

———, « La garantie des emprunts publics d'État », in *Recueil des cours de l'Académie de droit international de La Haye*, Martinus Nijhoff Publishers, 1925

JOSSELIN Daphné, "Regime Interplay in Public-Private Governance: Taking Stock of the Relationship Between the Paris Club and Private Creditors Between 1982 and 2005", *Global Governance*, 2009, 15, pp. 521-538

JOYCE Joseph P., *The IMF and global financial crises: Phoenix rising?*, New York, Cambridge University Press, 2013

JUGLAR Clément, *Des crises commerciales et de leur retour périodique en France, en Angleterre et aux États-Unis*, 1862

JULLIARD Patrick, STERN Brigitte, *Les emprunts russes : aspects juridiques*, Paris, Pedone, 2002

KAISER Jürgen, "Taking Stock of Proposals for More Ordered Workouts", in *Overcoming Developing Country Debt Crises*, Barry HERMAN, José Antonio OCAMPO and Shari SPIEGEL, New York, Oxford University Press, 2010, pp. 428-448

KALDEREN Lars, BLOMMESTEIN Hans, « Rôle et structure des offices de gestion de la dette », Paris, Organisation de co-opération et de développement économiques, 2002

KAMINSKY Raphaël, DALMASSO Joseph, « Une révolution en marche dans le droit des immunités – La fin des régimes spéciaux pour les immunités diplomatiques et l'arbitrage international ? », *La Semaine Juridique Entreprise et Affaires*, 2015, 38, pp. 22-25

KAPSTEIN Ethan B., “Resolving the Regulator's Dilemma: International Coordination of Banking Regulations”, *International Organization*, 1989, 43, pp. 323-347

KENEN Peter B., “The International Financial Architecture: Old Issues and New Initiatives”, *International Finance*, 2002, 5, pp. 23-45

KENNEDY David, “When Renewal Repeats: Thinking against the Box Millenium Issue: Shaping the Parameters of International Law in the New Millennium”, *New York University Journal of International Law and Politics*, 2000, 32, pp. 335-500

KENTIN Esther, “Economic Crisis and Investment Arbitration: The Argentine Cases”, in *Les aspects nouveaux du droit des investissements internationaux / New Aspects of International Investment Law*, Philippe KAHN and Thomas W. WÄLDE, Martinus Nijhoff Publishers, 2004, pp. 629-667

KINDLEBERGER Charles, ALIBER Z. Robert, *Manias, panics and crashes: a history of financial crises*, New York, Palgrave Macmillan, 2011

KLEINZ Angelika, *Individuum und Gemeinschaft in der juristischen Germanistik. Die Geschworenengerichte und das ‚gesunde Volksempfinden'*, Heidelberg, Universitätsverlag C. Winter, 2001

KREINER Signe, « Gestion de la dette publique et titres détenus : grandes orientations et caractéristiques », Paris, Organisation de co-opération et de développement économiques, 2002

KRUEGER Anne O., HAGAN Sean, “Sovereign Workouts: An IMF Perspective”, *Chicago Journal of International Law*, 2005, Vol. 6, pp. 203-218

KRUEGER Anne, “A New Approach to Sovereign Debt Restructuring”, Washington, D.C., International Monetary Fund, 2002

———, “International Financial Architecture for 2002: A New Approach to Sovereign Debt Restructuring”, in National Economists' Club Annual Members’ Dinner, American Enterprise Institute, ed. by International Monetary FUND (Washington, D.C., 2001)

KRUGMAN Paul, “Analytical Afterthoughts on the Asian Crisis”, in *Economic Theory, Dynamics and Markets: Essays in Honor of Ryuzo Sato*, Takashi NEGISHI, Rama VRAMACHANDRAN and Kazuo MINO, Kluwer, 2001, pp. 243-255

KUDRNA Zdenek, “Cross-Border Bank Resolution of Failed Banks in the European Union After the Crisis: Business as Usual”, *Journal of Common Market Studies*, 2012, Vol. 50, pp. pp. 283-299

LAAZOUZI Malik, « La neutralisation de la renonciation conventionnelle à l’immunité d’exécution de l’État étranger en France ; Note sous Cour de cassation, première Chambre civile, 28 mars 2013, Société NML Capital contre République argentine et Total Austral, pourvoi numéro 10-25.938 ; contre République argentine, pourvoi numéro 11-13.323 ; contre République argentine et BNP Paribas, pourvoi numéro 11-10.450 », *Revue des contrats*, 2013, 4, pp. 1485-1497

LACHAUME Jean-François, « Jurisprudence française concernant le droit international », *Annuaire Français de Droit International*, 1972, 18, pp. 939-940 et 979

LAGET-ANNAMAYER Aurore, SOREL Jean-Marc, « Le meccano de l’euro : les multiples contraintes d’une monnaie pas comme les autres », *Revue Générale de Droit International Public*, 2013, 117, pp. 833-870

LALIVE Jean-Flavien, « L'immunité de juridiction des États et des organisations internationales », in *Recueil des cours de l'Académie de droit international de La Haye*, Académie de Droit International de La Haye, The Hague, Nijhoff, 1953, pp. 205-396

LANDAU Jean-Pierre, « Quelle politique pour la dette souveraine ? », *Revue de la Stabilité Financière*, 2012, 16, pp. 213-223

De LAROSIERE Jacques, "The High-Level Group Report on Financial Supervision in the EU", Bruxelles, 2009

LASTRA Rosa María, "The Role of the International Monetary Fund", in Sovereign Debt Management, Rosa M. LASTRA and Lee BUCHHEIT, Oxford, Oxford University Press, 2014, pp. 49-68

———, "The role of the IMF as a global financial authority", *European Yearbook of International Economic Law*, 2011, 2, pp. 121-136

———, "Systemic risk, SIFIs and financial stability", *Capital Markets Law Journal*, 2011, 6, pp. 197-213

———, "International Financial Architecture", in *Legal Foundations of International Monetary Stability*, Rosa M. LASTRA, Oxford University Press, 2006, pp. 447-501

LEMAIRE Sophie, « L'arbitrage d'investissement et la restructuration de dettes souveraines (de l'expérience argentine au cas grec) », *Revue de l'Arbitrage*, 2014, 2014, pp. 53-73

———, « Sur la compétence et la recevabilité : l'acquisition de titres d'État constitue un investissement. Une action de masse peut être tranchée par un tribunal CIRDI ; Note sous Centre international de règlement des différends sur l'investissement, décision sur la compétence et la recevabilité, 4 août 2011, Abaclat et autres contre République d'Argentine », *Revue de l'Arbitrage*, 2013, 2, pp. 478-487

LEMOINE Benjamin, « Dette publique, débat confisqué. Pourquoi la France emprunte-t-elle sur les marchés? », *La Vie des idées*, 2013

———, « Les « dealers » de la dette souveraine », *Sociétés contemporaines*, 2013, 4, pp. 59-88

LEVY Denis, « L'arrêt de la Cour Internationale de Justice dans l'affaire relative à certains emprunts norvégiens (France c. Norvège) », *Annuaire Français de Droit International*, 1957, 3, pp. 152-163

LIENAU Odette, *Rethinking Sovereign Debt: Debt and Reputation in the Twentieth Century*, Harvard University Press, 2014

———, "The longer-term consequences of sovereign debt restructuring", in *Sovereign Debt Management*, Lee BUCHHEIT and Rosa LASTRA, Oxford University Press, 2014, pp. 85-100

LINDERT Peter H., MORTON Peter J., "How Sovereign Debt Has Worked", in *Developing Country Debt and Economic Performance*, Jeffrey D. SACHS, Chicago, University of Chicago Press, 1989, pp. 39-106

LIPP Ernst-Moritz, "Why the Debt Crisis Led to a Systemic Crisis and How to Escape from it", in *A Debt Restructuring Mechanism for Sovereigns. Do we need a legal procedure?*, Christoph G. PAULUS, München, Verlag C.H. Beck, Hart Publishing, 2014, pp. 35-39

de MALBERG Raymond Carré, *Contribution à la théorie générale de l'État*, Paris, Sirey, 1920

MALLARME André, « L'arbitrage vénézuélien devant la Cour de la Haye (1903-1904) », *Revue Générale de Droit International Public*, 1906, pp. 423-500

MANCIAUX Sébastien, « Note sous CIRDI, Abaclat et autre contre Argentine (ARB/07/5), décision sur la compétence et la recevabilité, 4 août 2011 », *Journal du Droit International*, 2012, 1, pp. 286-314

de MARGERIE Gilles, de VAUPLANE Hubert, « Les défauts du défaut : Quelques clefs pour comprendre la crise de la dette souveraine », *En Temps Réel*, 2011, 48

MARICHAL Carlos, *Bankruptcy of Empire: Mexican Silver and the Wars between Spain, Britain and France, 1760-1810*, Cambridge Cambridge University Press, 2007

MARMOZ Franck, « Les emprunts "toxiques" souscrits par les collectivités territoriales : quelle réponse juridique ? », *Revue française de Finances Publiques*, 2012, n° 120, pp. 89-103

MARTHA Rutsel Silvestre J., "International Organizations as Sovereign Bondholders: An Unexplored Dimension of the Sovereign Debt Crisis", *Manchester Journal of International Economic Law*, 2013, 10, pp. 2-18

———, "Preferred Creditor Status under International Law: The Case of the International Monetary Fund", *The International and Comparative Law Quarterly*, 1990, 39, pp. 801-826

MARTUCCI Francesco, « La Grèce et la crise de dette souveraine. – En attendant Godot, allons voir Godeau », *La Semaine Juridique Edition Générale*, 2015, 29, pp. 851-852

———, « Traité sur la stabilité, la coordination et la gouvernance, traité instituant le mécanisme européen de stabilité. Le droit international public au secours de l'UEM », *Revue des affaires européennes*, 2012, pp. 717-732

MARTY Richard, « Les clauses d'événements défavorables et de déchéance du terme dans les contrats de financement. Material adverse change and Cross default clauses », *La Semaine Juridique Entreprise et Affaires*, 2011, n° 12, pp. 29-37

MASSOT Pascale, « Globalisation économique et fragmentation de la décision politique : le cas des fonds souverains chinois », *Revue internationale de politique comparée*, 2011, Vol. 18, pp. 201-230

MCGOVERN Daniel, "Different Market Windows on Sovereign Debt: Private-sector Credit from the 1980s to the present", in *Sovereign Debt: Origins, Crisis and Restructuring*, Vinod K. AGGARWAL and Brigitte GRANVILLE, Royal Institute of International Affairs, 2003

MEDEIROS Carlos, POLAN Magdalena, RAMLOGAN Parmeshwar, "A Primer on Sovereign Debt Buybacks and Swaps", Washington D.C., International Monetary Fund, 2007

MEETARBHAN Milan J. N., « Vers un droit international de la dette exterieure? », in *La dette extérieure / The external debt*, Martinus Nijhoff PUBLISHERS, 1995, pp. 485-534

MENETREY Séverine, *L'amicus curiae, vers un principe commun de droit procédural ?*, Paris, Dalloz-Sirey, 2010

MERINO Alberto de Gregorio, "Legal developments in the Economic and Monetary Union during the debt crisis: The mechanisms of financial assistance", *Common Market Law Review*, 2012, 49, pp. 1613-1645

MERLER Silvia, PISANI-FERRY Jean, « Une relation risquée : l'interdépendance entre dette bancaire et dette souveraine et la stabilité financière dans la zone euro », *Revue de la Stabilité Financière*, 2012, 16, pp. 225-235

MICHALET Charles-Albert, « La dimension monétaire et financière du capitalisme mondial », in *Les euro-crédits, un instrument du système bancaire pour le financement international*, Jean-Bernard BLAISE, Philippe FOUCHARD and Philippe KAHN, Paris, Librairies techniques, 1981, pp. 653-677

MICHALOWSKI Sabine, *Unconstitutional Regimes and the Validity of Sovereign Debt: A Legal Perspective*, Ashgate, 2007

MIGAUD Didier, LEVIONNOIS Alain, « La gestion de la dette publique locale », Paris, Cour des comptes, 2011

MILLER Marcus H., THOMAS Dania, "Sovereign Debt Restructuring: The Judge, the Vultures, and Creditor Rights", in *Sovereign Debt: From Safety to Default*, Robert W. KOLB, John Wiley & Sons, 2011, pp. 211-226

MITCHENER Kris James, WEIDENMIER Marc D., "Supersanctions and sovereign debt repayment", *Journal of International Money and Finance*, 2010, 29, pp. 19-36

MÖLLER Ralf, *Generationengerechtigkeit im Steuerrecht : die generationengerechte Fortentwicklung des Steuerrechts unter besonderer Berücksichtigung der prognostizierten demographischen Entwicklung*, Hamburg, Kova, 2005

MONTEAGUDO Manuel, "The Debt Problem: The Baker Plan (1985) And The Brady Initiative (1989) – History, Experience, Practice And Prospects", in *La dette extérieure / The external debt*, Martinus Nijhoff PUBLISHERS, 1995, pp. 139-164

De MONTESQUIOU Aymeri, « Agences de notation: pour une profession règlementée », Paris, Sénat, 2012

MORALES Rafael A., "Equality Of Treatment Of Creditors In The Restructuring Of Foreign Debt", in *La dette extérieure / The external debt*, Martinus Nijhoff PUBLISHERS, 1995

MORIN Edgar, LE MOIGNE Jean-Louis, *L'intelligence de la complexité*, Paris, L'Harmatan, 2000

NERSISYAN Yeva S., RANDALL Wray L., « Un excès de dette publique handicape-t-il réellement la croissance ? », *Revue de l'OFCE*, 2011, 116, pp. 173-190

NORTON Ellie, "International Investment Arbitration and the European Debt Crisis", *Chicago Journal of International Law*, 2012, Vol. 13, pp. pp. 291-316

NURICK Lester, "Certain Aspects of the Law and Practice of the International Bank for Reconstruction and Development", in *The Effectiveness of International Decisions*, Stephen Myron SCHWEBEL, Leyden, Sijthoff, 1971, pp. 100-128

OECD, « Coopération pour le développement 2013 : Mettre fin à la pauvreté », Paris, Organisation de co-opération et de développement économiques, 2013

———, « Améliorer la viabilité des finances publiques », in *Études économiques de l'OCDE : Grèce 2009*, Paris, Éditions OCDE, 2010,

———, « La gestion de la dette publique et les marchés des valeurs d'État au XXIe siècle », Paris, Organisation de co-opération et de développement économiques, 2002

———, « Transparence budgétaire : les meilleurs pratiques de l'OCDE », Paris, OCDE, 2002

OECHSLI Christopher G., "Procedural Guidelines for Renegotiating LDC Debt: An Analogy to Chapter 11 of the U.S. Bankruptcy Reform Act", *Virginia journal of international law*, 1981, 21, pp. 305-342

OLIVARES-CAMINAL Rodrigo, "Statutory Sovereign Debt Resolution Mechanisms", in *Sovereign Debt Management*, Rosa M. LASTRA and Lee BUCHHEIT, Oxford, Oxford University Press, 2014, pp. 333-358

———, "Is there a need for an international insolvency regime in the context of sovereign debt? A case for the use of corporate debt restructuring techniques", *Journal of International Banking Law and Regulation*, 2009, 24, pp. 21-34

OPPETIT Bruno, « L'adaptation des contrats internationaux aux changements de circonstances : la clause de hardship », *Journal de Droit International*, 1974.794-814

ORLEAN André, *De l'euphorie à la panique : penser la crise financière*, Paris Éditions Rue d'Ulm, 2009

OST Francois, van de KERCHOVE Michel, *De la pyramide au réseau ? Pour une théorie dialectique du droit*, Bruxelles, Facultés universitaires Saint-Louis, 2002

ÖZLER Sule, "Have Commercial Banks Ignored History?", *American Economic Review*, 1993, 83, pp. 608-620

PANETTA Fabia, FAEH Thomas, GRANDE Giuseppe, HO Corrinne, KING Michael, LEVY Aviram, SIGNORETTI Federico M., TABOGA Marco, ZAGHINI Andrea, "An Assessment of Financial Sector Rescue Programmes", Bank for International Settlements, 2009

PANIZZA Ugo, STURZENEGGER Federico, ZETTELMEYER Jeromin, "The Economics and Law of Sovereign Debt and Default", *Journal of Economic Literature*, 2009, 47, pp. 651-698

De PAOLI Bianca, HOGGARTH Glenn, SAPORTA Victoria, "Costs of sovereign default", Bank of England, 2006

Paris Club, « Rapport annuel d'activité », Paris, Club de Paris, 2013

PARK Susan, VETTERLEIN Antje, *Owning Development. Creating Policy Norms in the IMF and the World Bank*, New York, Cambridge University Press, 2010

PARRA Sebastián Nieto, "Who saw Sovereign Debt Crises coming?", Paris, OECD, 2008

PAULUS Christoph G., *A Debt Restructuring Mechanism for Sovereigns: Do we need a legal procedure?*, Baden-Baden, C. H. Beck, Hart Publishing, Oxford, Nomos, 2014

———, "Should Politics be Replaced by a Legal Proceeding?", in *A Debt Restructuring Mechanism for Sovereigns: Do we need a legal procedure?*, Christoph G. PAULUS, Oxford, Nomos, C. H. Beck, Hart Publishing, 2014, pp. 191-212

———, "The Interrelationship of Sovereign Debt and Distressed Banks: A European Perspective", *Texas International Law Journal*, 2014, 49, pp. 201-219

———, „Staatspleite, Anleihenprozess, UN-Vollversammlung", *Zeitschrift für das gesamte Insolvenzrecht*, 2014, 47, pp. 2315-2317

———, „Jüngste Entwicklungen im Resolvenzrecht", *Zeitschrift für Wirtschafts- und Bankrecht*, 2013, 67, pp. 489-536

———, "A Resolvency Proceeding for Defaulting Sovereigns", *International Insolvency Law Review*, 2012

———, "Sovereign Defaults to be Solved by Politicians or by a Legal Proceeding?", *Law and Economics Yearly Review*, 2012, 1, pp. 203-233

———, "A Standing Arbitral Tribunal as a Procedural Solution for Sovereign Debt Restructurings", in *Sovereign Debt and the Financial Crisis: Will This Time Be Different?*, Gallina A. VINCELETTE and Carlos A. Primo BRAGA, Washington D.C., World Bank, 2010

PAULUS Christoph G., KARGMAN Steven T., "Reforming the Process of Sovereign Debt Restructuring: A proposal for a Sovereign Debt Tribunal", New York, United Nations, 2008

PEBEREAU Michel, « Rompre avec la facilité de la dette publique », Paris, Commission sur la dette publique, 2006

PETCH Tolek, *Legal Implications of the Euro Zone Crisis. Debt Restructuring, Sovereign Default and Euro Zone Exit*, Kluwer Law International, 2014

PETTIFOR Ann, *The coming First World debt crisis*, New York, Palgrave, 2006

PHILIPPON Thomas, HELLWIG Christian, "Eurobills, not Eurobonds", 2011

PICARD Roger, HUGON Paul, *Le problème des dettes inter-alliées – nécessité d'une révision*, Paris, Librairie Plon, 1934

POULIN Bruno, « Restructuration des dettes souveraines et traités bilatéraux de promotion et de protection des investissements; Note sous Abaclat and Others v. The Argentine Republic, affaire CIRDI number ARB/07/05, décision sur la compétence et la recevabilité en date du 4 août 2011 », *Les Cahiers de l'Arbitrage*, 2011, pp. 1059-1068

POWER Philip J., "Sovereign Debt: The Rise of the Secondary Market and Its Implications for Future Restructurings", *Fordham Law Review*, 1996, 64, pp. 2701–2772

PUHR Christian, « L'organisation bancaire des euro-crédits : la pratique de la syndication, la constitution du syndicat », in *Les euro-crédits. Un instrument du système bancaire pour le financement international*, Jean-Bernard BLAISE, Philippe FOUCHARD and Philippe KAHN, Paris, Libraires techniques de Paris, 1981

RADELET Steven, SACHS Jeffrey, "The East Asian Financial Crisis: Diagnosis, Remedies, Prospects", *Brookings Papers on Economic Activity*, 1998, 29, pp. 1-90

RAFFER Kunifert, *Debt Management for Development. Protection of the Poor and the Millennium Development Goals*, Cheltenham, Edward Elgar, 2010

———, "Improving Debt Management on the Basis of UNCTAD's Principles", in *Sovereign Financing and International Law. The UNCTAD Principles on Responsible Sovereign Lending and Borrowing*, Carlos ESPOSITO, Yuefen LI and Juan Pablo BOHOSLAVSKY, New York, Oxford University Press, 2013, pp. 163-187

REINHART Carmen M., ROGOFF Kenneth S., *This Time is Different. Eight Centuries of Financial Folly*, Princeton/Oxford, Princeton University Press, 2009

———, "Financial and sovereign debt crises: Some lessons learned and those forgotten", Washington D.C., International Monetary Fund, 2013

———, "Errata: "Growth in A Time of Debt"", Harvard University, 2013

———, "From Financial Crash to Debt Crisis", *The American Economic Review*, 2011, 101, pp. 1676-1706

———, "Growth in a Time of Debt", *American Economic Review: Papers & Proceedings*, 2010, 100, pp. 573-578

REISMAN Michael, WILLARD Andrew, *International Incidents: The Law that Counts in World Politics*, Princeton, Princeton University Press, 2014

RIALS Stéphane, *Le juge administratif français et la technique du standard. Essai sur le traitement juridictionnel de l'idée de normalité*, Paris, LGDJ, 1980

RICHMOND Christine, DIAS Daniel A., "Duration of Capital Market Exclusion: Stylized Facts and Determining Factors", 2008

RIEFFEL Lex, *Restructuring Sovereign Debt: The Case for Ad Hoc Machinery*, Washington D.C., Brookings Institution Press, 2003

RIVIER Raphaële, *Droit international public*, Paris, PUF, 2012

ROBERT Eric, « Rééchelonnement de la dette ou règlement judiciaire? Analyse de la jurisprudence interne et internationale au regard des enjeux de la renégociation de la dette », in *La dette extérieure / The external debt*, Martinus Nijhoff PUBLISHERS, 1995, pp. 607-670

ROBICHEK E. Walter, "International Monetary Fund: An Arbiter in the Debt Restructuring Process", *Columbia Journal of Transnational Law*, 1984, 23, pp. 143-154

David Rockefeller Center for Latin American Studies, "Living with debt. How to Limit the Risks of Sovereign Finance", Washington D.C., Inter-American Development Bank, 2006

ROGOFF Kenneth, ZETTELMEYER Jeromin, "Bankruptcy Procedures for Sovereigns: A History of Ideas, 1976–2001", Washington D.C., International Monetary Fund, 2002

ROGOFF Kenneth, "International Institutions for Reducing Global Financial Instability", *Journal of Economic Perspectives*, 1999, 13, pp. 21-42

RONDE Hans, *Von Versailles bis Lausanne : der Verlauf der Reparationsverhandlungen nach dem ersten Weltkrieg*, Stuttgart, Kohlhammer, 1950

de ROOVER Raymond, *The Rise and Decline of the Medici Bank, 1397-1494*, Cambridge, Harvard University Press, 1963

ROSE Andrew K., "One Reason Countries Pay their Debts: Renegotiation and International Trade", *Journal of Development Economics*, 2005, 77, pp. 189-206

ROSENBERG Emily S., *Financial Missionaries to the World: The Politics and Culture of Dollar Diplomacy, 1900–1930*, 2004

ROUBINI Nouriel, SETSER Brad, *Bailouts or Bail-ins? Responding to Financial Crises in Emerging Economies*, Peterson Institute for International Economics, 2004

SACHS Jeffrey, TORNELL Aaron, VELASCO Andrés, "The Mexican Peso Crisis: Sudden Death or Death Foretold?", *Journal of International Economics*, 1996, 41, pp. 265-283

SACHS Jeffrey, "Do We Need an International Lender of Last Resort?", in *Frank D. Graham Lecture* (Princeton University: 1995)

SACK Alexander Nahum, « Les effets des transformations des États sur leurs dettes publiques et autres obligations financières », in *Recueil Sirey*, Paris, 1927, pp. 46-157

De SAINT-MAUR Jean du Pré, « Perspectives du marché des euro-crédits », in *Les eurocrédits, un instrument du système bancaire pour le financement international*, Jean-Bernard BLAISE, Philippe FOUCHARD and Philippe KAHN, Paris, Librairies techniques, 1981, pp. 633-652

SALAMANCA Luis Jorge Garay, "The 1980s Crisis in Syndicated Bank Lending to Sovereigns and the Sequence of Mechanisms to Fix it", in *Overcoming Developing Country Debt Crises*, Barry HERMAN, José Antonio OCAMPO and Shari SPIEGEL, New York, Oxford University Press, 2010, pp. 111-139

SANDROCK Otto, "Is international arbitration inept to solve disputes arising out of international loan agreements?", *Journal of International Arbitration*, 1994, 11, pp. 33-60

SANTULLI Carlo, « L'Euro : analyse juridique de la "crise de la dette" », *Revue Générale de Droit International Public*, 2011, 115, p. 19

SAULNIER-CASSIA Emmanuelle, « Le Traité instituant le mécanisme européen de stabilité et le Traité sur la stabilité, la coordination et la gouvernance au sein de l'Europe, sous contrôles constitutionnels », *Revue trimestrielle de droit européen*, 2013, 1, pp. 160-163

SCELLE Georges, « Règles générales du droit de la paix », in *Recueil des cours de l'Académie de droit international de La Haye*, Hague Academy of International Law, Martinus Nijhoff Publishers, 1933, pp. 327-703

SCHIER Holger, *Towards A Reorganisation System For Sovereign Debt: An International Law Perspective*, Leiden, Martinus Nijhoff Publishers, 2007

SCHILL Stephan W., "International Investment Law and the Host State's Power to Handle Economic Crises", *Journal of International Arbitration*, 2007, 24, pp. 265-286

SCHLEMMER Engela C, "The enforcement of sovereign debt", in *International monetary and financial law: the global crisis*, Mario GIOVANOLI and Diego DEVOS, Oxford, Oxford University Press, 2010, pp. 418-446

SCHNEIDER Friedrich Benjamin, *Odious Debts. Status quo und Regelungsmodell unter besonderer Berücksichtigung internationaler Menschenrechts*, Berlin, Duncker & Humblot, 2015

SCHWARCZ Steven L., "Looking Forward: 2005-2010 – A Sovereign Debt Restructuring Reverie", *Chicago Journal of International Law*, 2005, 6, pp. 381-390

———, "Sovereign Debt Restructuring: A Bankruptcy Reorganization Approach", *Cornell Law Review*, 2000, 85, pp. 956-1034

SCIALOM Laurence, *Économie bancaire*, Paris, La découverte, 2013

SCOTT James Brown, "The Venezuelan Preferential Case between Germany, Great Britain, Italy and Venezuela et al.", New York, Carnegie Endowment for International Peace, 1916

SEE Arnaud, « Une nouvelle "discipline" budgétaire ? Les sanctions des politiques budgétaires "indisciplinées" dans l'Union européenne », in *Quelle souveraineté budgétaire pour les États ?*, Jean-Marc SOREL and Régis CHEMAIN, Paris, Pedone, 2013, pp. 143-159

SEIBER Marilyn J., *International Borrowing by Developing Countries*, New York, Pergamon Press, 1982

SERBINI Bénédicte, « Les enjeux de la restructuration de la dette souveraine grecque pour le mécanisme européen de stabilité », *Cahiers du Laboratoire d'économie appliquée au développement*, 2011

SETSER Brad, "The Political Economy of the SDRM", in *Overcoming Developing Country Debt Crises*, Barry HERMAN, José Antonio OCAMPO and Shari SPIEGEL, New York, Oxford University Press, 2010

SGARD Jérôme, « Restructurer les dettes souveraines : la méthode efficace du FMI », *L'Économie politique*, 2012, 3, pp. 79-92

———, "The IMF meets commercial banks: sovereign debt restructurings between 1970 and 1989", *mimeo*, 2012

———, « La faillite souveraine en économie : l'économie politique des défauts souverains », in *Insolvabilité des États et dettes souveraines*, Mathias AUDIT, Paris, LGDJ, 2011, pp. 25-40

SHIRAKAWA Masaaki, « Soutenabilité de la dette publique : condition préalable à la stabilité du système financier et des prix », in Dette publique, politique monétaire et stabilité financière, *Revue de la stabilité financière*, Paris, Banque de France, 2012, pp. 189-202

SIEKMANN Helmut, VIG Vikrant, WIELAND Volker, "The ECB's Outright Monetary Transactions in the Courts", Frankfurt, Institute for Monetary and Financial Stability, 2015

SIMON Denys, « L'Europe monétaire et financière devant ses juges : la réponse de la Cour de justice à la Cour constitutionnelle allemande », *Europe*, 2015, 8-9, pp. 5-8

———, « La réponse du berger à la bergère : suite du dialogue Luxembourg/Karlsruhe », *Europe*, 2015, 7, pp. 1-2

———, « Sur quelques aspects juridiques de la conditionnalité du FMI et leurs conséquences », *European Journal of International Law*, 1996, 7, pp. 42-66

SINGH Dalvinder, "The Role of the IMF and World Bank in Financial Sector Reform and Compliance", in *Redefining sovereignty in international economic law*, Wenhua SHAN and Penelope SIMONS, Oxford, Hart, 2008, pp. 331-362

SMITH Adam, « Du revenu du souverain ou de la république », in *Recherches sur la nature et les causes de la richesse des nations*, 1776

Société des Nations, « Rapport du Comité pour l'étude des contrats d'emprunts internationaux », Genève, Publications de la SDN, 1939

SOREL Jean-Marc, *Le droit international économique à l'aube du XXIème siècle. En hommage aux Professeurs Dominique Carreau et Patrick Juillard.*, Paris, Pedone, 2009

SOREL Jean-Marc, CHEMAIN Régis, *Quelle souveraineté budgétaire pour les États ?*, Actes du colloque du 5 décembre 2012 au Palais Brongniart, Paris, Pedone, 2013

———, « Conclusions. Une fable moderne : l'État, l'Union européenne, les marchés financiers et l'aléa moral », in *Quelle souveraineté budgétaire pour les États ?*, Jean-Marc SOREL and Régis CHEMAIN, Paris, Pedone, 2013, pp. 193-200

———, « L'institutionnalisation des relations internationales », in *Droit des organisations internationales*, Evelyne LAGRANGE and Jean-Marc SOREL, Paris, LGDJ, Lextenso éditions, 2013, pp. 11-34

———, « Le droit international au début du XXIe siècle : un salutaire chaos permanent mêlant humanisme et réalisme », in *Regards d'une génération sur le Droit International*, Emmanuelle JOUANNET, Hélène Ruiz FABRI and Jean-Marc SOREL, Paris, Pedone, 2008, pp. 395-411

———, « L'évolution des institutions financières internationales : entre redéploiement et fragilité, une restructuration systémique en chantier », *Annuaire Français de Droit International*, 2006, pp. 481-504

SPINK Christopher, GEDDIE John, "IMF Set to be Dragged into Greek Official Sector Involvement", *International Financing Review*, 2013

STIGLITZ Joseph, "Principles for a New Financial Architecture", in *General Assembly on Reforms of the International Monetary and Financial System*, The Commission of Experts of the President of the UN, 2009

STRIK Daniella, "Investment Protection of Sovereign Debt and Its Implications on the Future of Investment Law in the EU", *Journal of International Arbitration*, 2012, Volume 29, pp. 183-204

STRUPP Karl, « L'intervention en matière financière », in *Recueil des cours de l'Académie de droit international de La Haye*, 1925, pp. 1-124

STURZENEGGER Federico, ZETTELMEYER Jeromin, *Debt Defaults and Lessons from a Decade of Crises*, Cambridge, London, The MIT Press, 2007

———, "Creditors' Losses versus Debt Relief: Results from a Decade of Sovereign Debt Crisis", *Journal of the European Economic Association*, 2007, 5, pp. 343-351

———, "Haircuts: Estimating Investor Losses in Sovereign Debt Restructurings, 1998-2005", Washington D.C., International Monetary Fund, 2005

SUTER Christian, *Debt Cycles in the World-Economy: Foreign Loans, Financial. Crises, and Debt Settlements, 1820-1990*, Col.: Westview Press, 1992

TARNOFF Curt, TIERSKY Alex, "State, Foreign Operations Appropriations: A Guide to Component Accounts", Washington D.C., Congress, 2014

TARULLO Daniel K., "The Role of the IMF in Sovereign Debt Restructuring", *Chicago Journal of International Law*, 2005, Vol. 6, pp. 287-309

TAVERNIER Yves, « Rapport d'information sur les activités et le contrôle du Fonds monétaire international et de la Banque mondiale », Assemblée nationale, 2000

TEUNISSEN Jan Joost, AKKERMAN Age, *The crisis that was not prevented: lessons for Argentina, the IMF, and globalisation*, The Hague, Fondad, 2003

THIVEAUD Jean-Marie, « Crises et cycles, visions de l'histoire, du temps et de l'argent : Essai de généalogie d'un modèle épistémologique », *Revue d'économie financière*, 1993, 26, pp. 391-416

TIROLE Jean, « La crise de l'euro : quelques éléments de réflexion sur la réforme institutionnelle », *Revue de la Stabilité Financière*, 2012, 16, pp. 253-272

———, "Lessons from the Crisis", in *Balancing the Banks. Global Lessons from the Financial Crisis*, Mathias DEWATRIPONT, Jean-Charles ROCHET and Jean TIROLE, Princeton, Oxford, Princeton University Press, 2010, pp. 10-77

TOMZ Michael, *Reputation and International Cooperation: Sovereign Debt Across Three Centuries*, Princeton University Press, 2007

TOUZE Sébastien, « L'affaire des emprunts russes devant la Cour européenne des droits de l'homme », *Revue trimestrielle des droits de l'homme*, 2003, 15, pp. 283-316

TRANCHANT Baptiste, « Jurisprudence française en matière de droit international public », *Revue Générale de Droit International Public*, 2015, 1, pp. 302-308

TREBESCH Christoph, "The Cost of Aggressive Sovereign Debt Policies: How Much is the Private Sector Affected?", Washington D.C., International Monetary Fund, 2009

TROPER Michel, « L'Europe politique et le concept de souveraineté », in *L'Europe en voie de Constitution. Pour un bilan critique des travaux de la Convention*, Olivier BEAUD, Arnaud LECHEVALIER, Ingolf PERNICE and Sylvie STRUDEL, Bruxelles, Bruylant, 2004, pp. 117-137

TROTABAS Louis, *Précis de science et législation financières*, Paris, Dalloz, 1953

TURGOT Anne-Robert-Jacques, *Réflexions sur la formation et la distribution des richesses*, Paris, 1766

TVERSKY Amos, KAHNEMAN Daniel, "The Framing of Decisions and the Psychology of Choice", *Science*, 1981, 211, pp. 453-458

ULBRICH Holley H., *Public Finance in Theory and Practice*, Routledge, 2011

UNCITRAL, *Legislative Guide on Insolvency Law*, New York, United Nations, 2005

UNCTAD, "Sovereign Debt Workouts: Going Forward. Roadmap and Guide", Vienna, United Nations, 2015

———, "Trade and Development Report. Global Governance and Policy Space for Development", Geneva, United Nations Conference on Trade and Development, 2014

———, “Sovereign debt crises and restructurings: Lessons learnt and proposals for debt resolution mechanisms”, in 25 October 2012, The ECOSOC Chamber, UN Headquarters, ed. by United Nations (New York: Special event of the Second Committee of the General Assembly 2012)

———, “Trade and Development Report. Responding to the Global Crisis. Climate Change Mitigation”, Geneva, United Nations Conference on Trade and Development, 2009

———, “Trade and Development Report. Global Trends and Prospects, Financial Architecture”, Geneva, United Nations Conference on Trade and Development, 2001

———, “Trade and Development Report. Financial Instability. Growth in Africa”, Geneva, United Nations Conference on Trade and Development, 1998

———, “Trade and Development Report”, New York, United Nations Conference on Trade and Development, 1986

———, *The History of UNCTAD: 1964-1984*, New York, United Nations, 1985

———, “Selected Issues Relating to the Establishment of Common Norms in Future Debt Reorganizations”, Geneva, UN Conference on Trade and Development, 1977

United Nations, “Recommendations of the Commission of Experts of the President of the United Nations General Assembly on Reforms of the International Monetary and Financial System”, New York, United Nations, 2009

UN Secretary General, “External debt sustainability and development”, 2014

USUNIER Laurence, « La coutume internationale invoquée pour anticiper l’entrée en vigueur d’une convention internationale ; Note sous Cour de cassation, première Chambre civile, 28 mars 2013, pourvoi numéro 10-25.938, Cour de cassation, première Chambre civile, 28 mars 2013, pourvoi numéro 11-10.450 et Cour de cassation, première Chambre civile, 28 mars 2013, pourvoi numéro 11-13.323 », *Revue Trimestrielle de Droit Civil*, 2014, 2, pp. 319-323

VAROUFAKIS Yánis, *Le Minotaure planétaire : l’ogre américain, la désunion européenne et le chaos mondial*, Paris, Éditions du Cercle, 2015

De VAUPLANE Hubert, « Le rôle du juge pendant la crise : entre ombre et lumière », *Revue des affaires européennes*, 2012.773-778

———, « Pourquoi la Grèce n’est-elle pas juridiquement en défaut ? », *Revue Banque*, 2011, 742-743, pp. 116-119

De VICUÑA Antonio Sáinz, “Restructuring in a Monetary Union: Legal Aspects”, in *Sovereign Debt Management*, Rosa M. LASTRA and Lee BUCHHEIT, Oxford, Oxford University Press, 2014, pp. 177-193

VICUÑA Francisco Orrego, “Of Contracts and Treaties in the Global Market”, *Max Planck Yearbook of United Nations Law*, 2004, 8, pp. 341-357

VILLAROMAN Noel G., “Debt Servicing and its Adverse Impact on Economic, Social and Cultural Rights in Developing Countries”, *Journal of Human Rights*, 2010, 9, pp. 487-501

WAIBEL Michael, *Sovereign Defaults Before International Courts and Tribunals*, New York, Cambridge University Press, 2011

———, "Echoes of History: The International Financial Commission in Greece", in *A Debt Restructuring Mechanism for Sovereigns. Do we need a legal procedure?*, Christoph G. PAULUS, München, Verlag C.H. Beck, Hart Publishing, 2014, pp. 3-19

———, « La faillite souveraine en droit – Un État peut-il faire faillite ? », in *Insolvabilité des États et dettes souveraines*, Mathias AUDIT, Paris, L.G.D.J., 2011, pp. 41-63

———, "Opening Pandora's Box: Sovereign Bonds in International Arbitration", *American Journal of International Law*, 2007, 101, pp. 711-759

———, "Two Worlds of Necessity in ICSID Arbitration: CMS and LG&E", *Leiden Journal of International Law*, 2007, 20, pp. 637-648

WATT Horatia Muir, « Immunité d'exécution ; Note sous Cour de cassation, première Chambre civile, 28 mars 2013, société NML Capital contre République argentine, pourvoi numéro 10-25.938 », *Revue critique de droit international privé*, 2013, 3, pp. 671-677

WAUTELET Patrick, « Les fonds vautours. Vulture Funds, Creditors and Sovereign Debtors: how to find a Balance? », in *Insolvabilité des états et dettes souveraines*, Mathias AUDIT, Paris, L.G.D.J. Lextenso Éditions, 2011, pp. 103-164

WEBER Pierre-François, « (Re)structuration des dettes souveraines – Où en est-on ? », *Revue de la Stabilité Financière*, 2005, 7, pp. 115-135

WECKEL Philippe, METOU Miranda, COUMA Tidiani, « Chronique de jurisprudence internationale », *Revue Générale de Droit International Public*, 2012, 3, pp. 711-736

WEIDEMAIE W. Mark C., "Sovereign debt after NML v Argentina", *Capital Markets Law Journal*, 2013, 8, pp. 123-131

———, "Contracting for State Intervention: The Origins of Sovereign Debt Arbitration", *Law and Contemporary Problems*, 2010, 73, pp. 335-355

WEIL Prosper, « Problèmes relatifs aux contrats passés entre un État et un particulier », in *Recueil des cours de l'Académie de droit international de La Haye*, Martinus Nijhoff Publishers, 1969

WEILLER Laura, « Revirement : abandon de l'exigence du caractère spécial de la renonciation à l'immunité d'exécution », *Procédures*, 2015, 7, pp. 22-23

Von WEIZSÄCKER Jakob, DELPLA Jacques, "The Blue Bond Proposal", Bruxelles, Bruegel, 2010

WILLIAMS John Fischer, *International Law and International Financial Obligations Arising from Contracts*, Leyden, Bibliotheca Visseriana, 1924

Working Group on Financial Stability, "Financial Reform: A Framework for Financial Stability", G30, 2009

World Bank, « Manuel du service de la dette », Washington D.C., World Bank, 2009

WOOD Duncan, *Governing global banking. The Basel Committee and the Politics of Financial Globalization*, Ashgate, 2005

WOOD Philip R., "Essay: Sovereign Syndicated Bank Credits in the 1970s", *Law and Contemporary Problems*, 2010, 73, pp. 7-28

———, *The Law and Practice of International Finance*, Sweet & Maxwell, 2008

———, *International Loans, Bonds, Guarantees, Legal Opinions*, London, Sweet & Maxwell, 2007

ZAPATA Roberto Dañino, "Why Treaties Matter?", London, 2006

ZETTELMEYER Jeromin, TREBESCH Christoph, GULATI Mitu, "The Greek Debt Restructuring: An Autopsy", *Economic Policy*, 2013, 28, pp. 513-563